Practical Guide to
Software Quality Management

The Artech House Computer Science Library

ISBN: 0-89006-682-5   *ATM Switching Systems,* Thomas M. Chen and Stephen S. Liu

ISBN: 0-89006-510-1   *Authentication Systems for Secure Networks,* Rolf Oppliger

ISBN: 0-89006-691-4   *Client/Server Computing: Architecture, Applications, and Distributed Sytems Management,* Bruce Elbert and Bobby Martyna

ISBN: 0-89006-757-0   *Computer-Mediated Communications: Multimedia Applications,* Rob Walters

ISBN: 0-89006-660-4   *Computer Telephone Integration,* Rob Walters

ISBN: 0-89006-614-0   *Distributed and Multi-Database Systems,* Angelo R. Bobak

ISBN: 0-89006-812-7   *A Guide to Programming Languages: Overview and Comparison,* Ruknet Cezzar

ISBN: 0-89006-552-7   *Heterogeneous Computing,* Mary M. Eshagian, editor

ISBN: 0-89006-492-X   *Introduction to Document Image Processing Techniques,* Ronald G. Matteson

ISBN: 089006-799-6   *Managing Computer Networks: A Case-Based Reasoning Approach,* Lundy Lewis

ISBN: 0-89006-654-X   *Networks and Imaging Systems in a Windowed Environment,* Marc R. D'Alleyrand

ISBN:0-89006-865-8   *Practical Guide to Software Quality Management,* John W. Horch

ISBN: 0-89006-831-3   *Survival in the Software Jungle,* Mark Norris

ISBN: 0-89006-778-3   *UNIX Internetworking,* Second Edition, Uday O. Pabrai

ISBN: 0-89006-609-4   *Wireless LAN Systems,* A. Santamaría and F. J. López-Hernández

ISBN: 0-89006-717-1   *Wireless: The Revolution in Personal Telecommunications,* Ira Brodsky

ISBN: 0-89006-740-6   *X Window System User's Guide,* Uday O. Pabrai

For further information on these and other Artech House titles, contact:

Artech House	Artech House
685 Canton Street	Portland House, Stag Place
Norwood, MA 02062	London SW1E 5XA England
617-769-9750	+44 (0) 171-973-8077
Fax: 617-769-6334	Fax: +44 (0)171-630-0166
Telex: 951-659	Telex: 951-659
email: artech@artech-house.com	email: artech-uk@artech-house.com

Practical Guide to Software Quality Management

John W. Horch

Artech House
Boston • London

Library of Congress Cataloging-in-Publication Data
Horch, John W.
   Practical guide to software quality management / John W. Horch.
     p.   cm.
   Includes bibliographical references and index.
   ISBN 0-89006-865-8
   1. Computer software—Quality control.   I. Title.
QA76.76.Q35H67   1996
005.1'068'5—dc20   96-19493
                                   CIP

British Library Cataloguing in Publication Data
Horch, John W.
   Practical guide to software quality managment
   1. Software engineering—Quality control
   I. Title
   005.1'0685

   ISBN 0-89006-865-8

Cover and text design by Darrell Judd

© 1996 ARTECH HOUSE, INC.
685 Canton Street
Norwood, MA 02062

International Standard Book Number: 0-89006-865-8
Library of Congress Catalog Card Number: 96-19493

10 9 8 7 6 5 4 3 2 1

Contents

Preface   *xi*

Introduction   *xiii*

Chapter 1

The elements of a complete software quality system   **1**

1.1 Definitions   2

1.2 The elements of a software
   quality system   6

  1.2.1   Standards   7

  1.2.2   Reviewing   9

  1.2.3   Testing   11

  1.2.4   Defect analysis   13

  1.2.5   Configuration management   15

  1.2.6   Security   17

  1.2.7   Education   18

  1.2.8   Vendor management   18

1.3 Additional Issues   19

  1.3.1   Maintenance   20

  1.3.2   Documentation   21

  1.3.3   Organizational considerations   22

  1.3.4   Implementation of the total SQS   23

1.4 Summary   24

1.5 The next step   25

Chapter 2

Standards   **27**

2.1 Areas of standardization   28

  2.1.1   The software life cycle   29

2.1.2 Documentation 31
2.1.3 Coding 32
2.1.4 Naming 32
2.1.5 Operating procedures and protocols 34
2.1.6 User development 34
2.1.7 Emerging technologies 36

2.2 Sources of standards 36
2.2.1 External standards developers 37
2.2.2 Purchased standards 39
2.2.3 Inhouse development 40

2.3 Selection of standards 42

2.4 Promulgation of standards 43
2.4.1 Availability 43
2.4.2 Compliance 44
2.4.3 Maintenance 45

2.5 Summary 45

2.6 The next step 46

Chapter 3

Reviews 47

3.1 Types of reviews 49
3.1.1 Inprocess reviews 49
3.1.2 Phase-end reviews 52

3.2 Review subjects 54

3.3 Documentation reviews 54
3.3.1 Requirements reviews 56
3.3.2 Design reviews 58
3.3.3 Test documentation reviews 60
3.3.4 User documentation reviews 61
3.3.5 Other documentation reviews 62

3.4 Summary 63

3.5 The next step 64

Chapter 4

Testing 65

4.1 Types of testing 67
4.1.1 Unit testing 67
4.1.2 Module testing 68
4.1.3 Integration testing 69
4.1.4 User or acceptance testing 70
4.1.5 Special types of tests 71

4.2 Test planning and conduct 74
4.2.1 Test plans 74
4.2.2 Test cases 76
4.2.3 Test procedures 78
4.2.4 Test data input 78
4.2.5 Expected results 80
4.2.6 Test analysis 80
4.2.7 Test tools 81
4.2.8 Reviewing the test program 82

4.3 Who does the testing 83

4.4 Summary 85

4.5 The next step 86

Chapter 5

Defect analysis 87

5.1 Analysis concepts 88
5.1.1 Measures 88
5.1.2 Metrics 89
5.1.3 Product analysis 89
5.1.4 Process analysis 89

5.2 Locating data 90
5.2.1 Defect reporting 90
5.2.2 Other data 92

5.3 Defect repair and closure 93

5.4 Selecting metrics 96
5.4.1 Available metrics 96

5.4.2 *Applicable metrics 96*

5.4.3 *SQS goal-oriented metrics 98*

5.5 Collecting measurements 100

5.5.1 *Classification of defects 100*

5.5.2 *Other defect measures 102*

5.5.3 *Nondefect measures 103*

5.6 Quality Tools 104

5.6.1 *Tally sheet 104*

5.6.2 *Scatter diagram 105*

5.6.3 *Graph 105*

5.6.4 *Histogram 106*

5.6.5 *Pareto diagram 107*

5.6.6 *Flowchart 107*

5.6.7 *Cause and effect diagram 108*

5.6.8 *Process control charts 109*

5.7 Implementing defect analysis 112

5.7.1 *Rules 112*

5.7.2 *Designing the program 114*

5.7.3 *Metric characteristics 115*

5.8 Summary 116

5.9 The next step 116

Chapter 6

Configuration management 119

6.1 Configuration management
components 121

6.1.1 *Configuration identification 121*

6.1.2 *Configuration control 122*

6.1.3 *Configuration accounting 123*

6.2 Configuration identification 126

6.2.1 *Configuration item 126*

6.2.2 *Release 128*

6.2.3 *Version 128*

6.2.4 *Edition 129*

6.3 Configuration control 129

6.3.1 *Change processing 129*

6.3.2 *Change control boards 131*

6.3.3 *Software libraries 132*

6.4 Configuration accounting 133

6.4.1 *Baselines 133*

6.4.2 *Accounting 135*

6.5 Summary 136

6.6 The next step 137

Chapter 7

Associated quality concerns 139

7.1 Security 140

7.1.1 *Database security 140*

7.1.2 *Teleprocessing security 142*

7.1.3 *Viruses 144*

7.1.4 *Risk analysis 145*

7.1.5 *Disaster recovery 146*

7.2 Education 147

7.2.1 *Developer education 148*

7.2.2 *Support training 149*

7.2.3 *User education 151*

7.2.4 *Operations training 152*

7.2.5 *Education delivery 153*

7.3 Vendor management 155

7.3.1 *Off-the-shelf software 156*

7.3.2 *Tailored shells 158*

7.3.3 *Contracted new development 159*

7.4 Maintenance 160

7.4.1 *Types of maintenance 160*

7.4.2 *Documentation 165*

7.4.3 *Regression testing 165*

7.5 Summary 166

7.6 The next step 167

Chapter 8

Software documentation   169

8.1 Management documents   171

   8.1.1 Software development plan   172

   8.1.2 SQS plan   173

   8.1.3 Configuration management plan   174

   8.1.4 Additional plans   174

8.2 Development documents   175

   8.2.1 Requirements specification   176

   8.2.2 Design specifications   178

   8.2.3 Other development documents   179

8.3 Test documentation   180

   8.3.1 Test plan   181

   8.3.2 Test cases   182

   8.3.3 Test data   182

   8.3.4 Test procedures   182

   8.3.5 Test reports   183

8.4 User documentation   183

   8.4.1 Input requirements   183

   8.4.2 Output description   184

   8.4.3 Operation instructions   184

   8.4.4 Maintenance   185

8.5 Training documentation   185

8.6 Documentation standards   186

8.7 Summary   187

8.8 The next step   188

Chapter 9

Quality system implementation   189

9.1 Planning the implementation   190

9.2 The quality charter   191

9.3 Changing the organizational culture   192

   9.3.1 Culture change   192

   9.3.2 Management commitment   193

   9.3.3 Organizational commitment   193

9.4 Organizational considerations   194

   9.4.1 SQS task performance   195

   9.4.2 Reporting level   196

9.5 Development organization
participation   199

9.6 Implementation strategies   200

   9.6.1 Single-project implementation   200

   9.6.2 Single-element implementation   201

   9.6.3 Combined implementation   202

   9.6.4 Adapting the SQS   202

9.7 SQS improvement   203

   9.7.1 Assessment   203

   9.7.2 Certification   204

   9.7.3 Awards   204

9.8 Summary   204

9.9 The next step   205

Appendixes   207

Appendix A

Sample outline of software development plan   209

Appendix B

Sample outline of SQS plan   213

Appendix C

Sample outline of configuration management plan   217

Appendix D

Sample outline of software requirements specification   219

Appendix E

Sample outline of software preliminary design specification   221

Appendix F

Sample outline of software detailed design specification   223

Appendix G

Sample outline of test plan (system)   227

Appendix H

Sample outline of test case   231

Appendix I

Sample outline of test report   233

Appendix J

Sample quality management charter   235

Acronyms   243

About the author   247

Index   249

Preface

THIS BOOK EXPLORES the various aspects of a total software quality system. It identifies the eight basic elements of the software quality systems and shows how each element fits into the total picture of software quality management.

The subject matter, which is presented at a high level, is suitable for managers and engineers as a introduction to a software quality program. The audience for this book includes those who have been charged with the responsibility of creating and implementing a total software quality system in their organizations. It also will be of use to those who need an overview of a total software quality framework. Individuals who have some parts of a system in place, such as a configuration management system or a standards program, and want to go forth with a full software quality effort also will find this text of interest.

The book delineates the elements of a total software quality system, explains briefly what each element comprises, and discusses the role of the software quality practitioner with respect to each element. It shows how the full set of elements interacts and how to integrate the elements to form a whole software quality system.

Introduction

THIS BOOK IS a primer for those who need to understand the concepts as well as the value of software quality management. It describes the eight major software quality elements and how they combine to form a solid software quality program. It is not intended to be a reference for the experienced software quality practitioner or the definitive text on how to accomplish all the software quality tasks available today.

The implementation of a software quality system depends heavily on the organization and its software work. The sample software quality system plan provided in Appendix B covers all eight basic elements and should prove sufficient for most organizations. Companies that are being audited for compliance with an ISO 9000 standard or one of the several process maturity or process improvement models may need to augment the sample plan to address organization-specific issues.

The basic elements of the quality system apply to any software development or maintenance. Small organizations will use the elements commensurate with their needs, whereas large organizations will find their application more sophisticated and elaborate. Organizations, large or small, that are involved in the most current techniques and applications, such as client-server, graphical user interfaces, distributed processing, and the like, will need to extend these elements beyond the basics given here. Similarly, organizations using advanced development methodologies such as information engineering, object-oriented techniques, mathematical proofs of correctness, and so on, will implement these quality system elements in more sophisticated ways than more traditionally oriented organizations.

So, then, why should *you* read this book? Perhaps your situation parallels one of the following scenarios:

- You have done a good job testing the last few projects, and your boss promotes you to software quality manager.

- Corporate headquarters decides that all software projects will be subject to quality management, and, as the director of information services, you are to implement a software quality program.

- The chair of the ISO 9000 certification project informs you that you are to bring the software area into line with the quality management precepts of ISO 9001.

- An assessment of the software development organization, against the SEI's CMM, shows your organization to be at level 1. As vice president of management information systems, you are to take action to raise that level.

- You are senior systems analyst, and the head of software quality wants you to learn more about software quality and how you affect it.

Any one of those situations would be a good reason to start your understanding of quality systems with this book. After you have gained insight into software quality systems, other books are available to assist you in the application of each specific element described in this text. If you are a tester, there are excellent texts on all sorts of testing concerns and applications. As a disaster recovery manager, you can find much material that will help you prepare for and recover from disasters.

Each chapter concludes with the sections "The Next Step" and "Additional Reading." The first section includes one or two texts that I believe can answer the question, "Where do we go from here?" Additional Reading includes texts generally applicable to the software quality elements discussed in the chapter. Inclusion in the list should not be inferred as an endorsement of a particular book or a negative endorsement of a text not included. Anyone who has browsed through the computer section of a bookstore or library knows there are far too many books to list in an introductory volume such as this one. (You will note that a few of the Additional Reading texts are from outside the United States, which may constitute an endorsement of sorts, as I believe those titles to be of sufficient value to warrant the extra effort it may take to acquire them.)

The order of the chapters in this volume is, perhaps, an indication of the relative importance I attach to the eight elements of a software quality program. I recognize that this is almost certainly not the order in which you will implement (or may have implemented) whatever software quality activities you are undertaking. I suspect that most, if not all, organizations do some sort of testing, conduct a few reviews, and follow standards already in place to determine the implementation sequence. The order of the chapters in this book should serve, rather, as an agenda for the evaluation of a software quality program and its improvement.

Chapter 1 introduces my view of what constitutes a beneficial—and intentional—software quality system. Chapters 2 through 7 present discussions of the elements of a quality system, their areas of interest or application, and why they are important in a software quality system.

Chapter 8 just as well could have been the first chapter. No project is complete without the documentation that defines its purpose and direction and describes its approach and progress. The documentation itself may be considered to be outside the purview of a quality system. It is, however, the basis for the vast majority of the quality system. A popular misconception is that the product of software development is the code, the whole code, and nothing but the code. Code is merely one of the documents that are the ongoing and sequential set of software development products. As anyone involved in a dispute over the terms of an agreement will tell you, "If it isn't written, it isn't!" The importance of documentation cannot be overemphasized. Its inclusion in a book on quality is part of that emphasis.

Chapter 9 considers the implications and concerns surrounding the actual implementation of the software quality system. Although this text is not a step-by-step "cookbook" on how to implement quality management, Chapter 9 discusses things you should remember when planning the introduction or improvement of a quality system.

To emphasize the importance of documentation, the appendixes contain examples or starting-point outlines for some of the documentation discussed in the rest of the text. Many of the outlines are taken from or are based on Institute of Electrical and Electronics Engineers (IEEE) standards that address the specific topic. Appendix J, "Sample Software Quality Charter," was contributed by an organization that requested anonymity. The charter is, though, the charter in place in that organization.

Chapter 1

The elements of a complete software quality system

S TARTING A SOFTWARE quality program from scratch is a time-consuming task that is often doomed to failure before it is begun. In-adequate preparation, misused terms, lack of planning, and failure to recognize the individual roles of all members of the organization are only a few of the pitfalls that await the overanxious practitioner.

As stated in the Introduction, this is a "what-to book." It is intended to introduce you to the concepts involved in a *software quality system* (SQS) and to suggest how to implement the parts of such a system. This chapter defines some software quality terms, describes the basic elements of a SQS, and addresses some important concerns. The balance of the book elaborates on each element and discusses implementation of an overall SQS.

1.1 Definitions

Several terms are granted many meanings throughout the computing industry, particularly in the software sector. This text uses certain of these variably defined terms as defined here.

Activity. A task or body of effort directed at the accomplishment of an objective or the production of all or part of a product.

Arithmetic defect. A software flaw in a mathematical computation.

Audit. According to ANSI N45.2.10-1973, "an activity to determine through investigation the adequacy of, and adherence to, established procedures, instructions, specifications, codes, and standards or other applicable contractual and licensing requirements, and the effectiveness of implementation."

Client. The person or organization that causes a product to be developed or maintained. The client is often also the customer.

Component. A general term for a portion of a product, for example, a chapter of a document or a unit or module of software. A component may include the entire product.

Consumer. The person or organization that acquires a software product. The consumer may be either the customer or the user.

Control defect. A software flaw in a decision process.

Customer. The person or organization that pays for the product.

Element. See *unit*.

Entity. Part of the overall company organization, for example, the software quality group, a development group.

Guideline. A preferred practice or procedure that is encouraged, but not enforced, throughout the organization.

Input/output defect. A software flaw in the process of passing information into or out of the software element.

Inspection.   According to IEEE Standard 100-1992, "a formal evaluation technique in which software requirements, design, or code is examined in detail by a person or group other than the author to detect faults, violations of development standards, and other problems."

ISO 9000, 9001, …   International standards for quality systems published by the International Organization for Standardization (ISO) and intended to be used as the international definition of quality systems to be applied by producers or suppliers. Certification of an organization to ISO 9001, 9002, or 9003 attests that the organization has a documented quality system and evidence of its application.

Item.   See *component*.

Module.   A group of units that together perform some convenient individual function or subfunction within a software system.

Peer review.   An informal examination by a coworker of the producer, usually of a small portion of a product. In some literature, the term peer review means any of the informal reviews.

Phase.   Any of several convenient divisions of the software life cycle, typically including concept development, requirements, design, coding, test, installation and acceptance, operation and maintenance, and retirement. Phases may or may not be sequential.

Process.   The group of activities and procedures by which a producer develops or maintains a product.

Producer.   The person or organization that, following a process, develops or maintains a product.

Product.   The intermediate or final output from any given phase of the software life cycle, for example, specifications, code, or test results.

Program.   According to IEEE Standard 100-1992, "a schedule or plan that specifies actions to be taken."

Quality.   Compliance of a product with the expectations of the user, based on the product's requirements.

Quality assurance.   The set of activities intended to detect, document, analyze, and correct process defects and to manage process changes.

Quality control.   The set of activities intended to detect, document, analyze, and correct product defects and to manage product changes.

Quality group.   The organizational entity responsible for monitoring and reporting the performance of the product development functions and activities.

Quality management.   The empowering and encouraging of the producer to identify and submit improvements to the product development process.

Quality practitioner.   A person whose task is to perform one or more of the functions or activities that make up the quality system. The quality practitioner may or may not be assigned to a quality group.

Quality system.   The total set of quality control, quality assurance, and quality management activities dedicated to the provision of quality products.

Requirement.   According to IEEE Standard 100-1992, "a condition of capability that must be met or possessed by a system or system component to satisfy a contract, standard, specification, or other formally imposed documents."

Review.   A formal or informal meeting at which an output (product or component) of the software development life cycle is presented to the customer, user, or other interested parties for examination, evaluation, and approval.

SEI CMM.   A five-level model of an organization's software process maturity, called the *capability maturity model* (CMM), developed by the Software Engineering Institute (SEI).

Software.   Computer programs, procedures, and possibly associated documentation and data pertaining to the operation of a computer system.

Software development life cycle.   The portion of the software life cycle devoted to the actual creation of the software system, generally beginning with requirements generation and ending with installation of the software system into active production.

Software life cycle.   The entire period during which a software system is active, beginning with its initial conceptual development and ending with its removal from active use and its archiving.

Software system.   A total, integrated aggregation of software components that performs the set of specific functions as defined by its approved requirements.

Standard.   A practice or procedure that is imposed and enforced throughout the organization.

Subsystem.   A group of modules that together perform one of the major functions of a software system.

Total quality.   The culture that maximizes the likelihood that a product conforms with its requirements on an ongoing basis.

Total quality system.   The set of activities required to provide decision-making, action-capable management with the information necessary to beneficially affect the product development process.

Unit.   According to IEEE Standard 610.12-1990, "a software component that is not subdivided into other components." Sometimes called an element, a unit is also known as the "smallest replaceable component."

Unit development folder.   The "diary" of the development of a software component. The unit development folder usually contains the portion of the approved requirements being addressed by the component, the design and test information that applies, and any additional information applicable to an understanding of the development approach used for the component.

User.   The person who actually performs a job function with the assistance of the product.

Walkthrough.   A review method in which a producer leads other members of the development team through a product or a portion thereof that the producer has developed. During a walkthrough, the other members of the team ask questions and comment on technique, style, possible errors, violations of development standards, and other issues.

1.2 The elements of a software quality system

An SQS has two goals. The first goal is to build quality into the software from the beginning. That means ensuring that the problem or the need is clearly and accurately stated and that the requirements for the solution are properly defined, expressed, and understood. Nearly all the elements of an SQS are oriented toward requirement validity and satisfaction.

For quality to be built into a software system from its inception, the software requirements must be clearly understood and documented. Unless the actual requirements and the needs of the user are known and understood, there is little likelihood that the user will be satisfied with any software system that is delivered. Further discussion of requirements is provided in Chapters 6 and 8.

The second goal of the SQS is to keep quality in the software throughout the *software life cycle* (SLC). This chapter describes the eight elements of the SQS and discusses their contributions to these two goals.

The eight elements of an SQS are as follows:

- Standards;
- Reviewing;
- Testing;
- Defect analysis;
- Configuration management;
- Security;
- Education;
- Vendor management.

While each element can be shown to contribute to both goals, there are heavier relationships between some elements and one or the other of the two goals. Those particular relationships will become obvious as each element is discussed in the chapters that follow.

Every SLC model has divisions, or periods of effort, into which the work of developing and using the software is divided. These divisions or periods are given various names, depending on the particular life cycle paradigm being applied. For this discussion, the periods of effort, together with their common names, are defined as follows:

- Recognition of a need or problem (i.e., concept definition);
- Definition of the software solution to be applied (i.e., requirements definition);

- Development of the software that solves the problem or satisfies the need (i.e., design and coding);
- Proving that the solution is correct (i.e., testing);
- Implementing the solution (i.e., installation and acceptance);
- Using the solution (i.e., operation);
- Improving the solution (i.e., maintenance).

Regardless of their names, each division represents a period of effort directed at a particular part of the overall life cycle. The divisions may be of various lengths and applied in various sequences.

There are also associations between certain elements and the various divisions of the SLC. Again, most of the elements support most of the SLC, but certain elements are more closely associated with particular periods than with others.

Figure 1.1 displays the eight elements as a cube supporting the goals of software quality and the periods of the SLC with which each element is most closely associated.

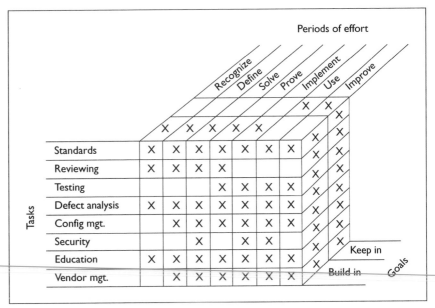

Figure 1.1
Quality tasks, life cycle periods, and goals.

1.2.1 **Standards**

Software development is becoming a science. The old days of free-form creativity in the development of software are gradually giving way to more controlled and scientific approaches. As some observers have noted, software is moving from an arcane art to a visible science.

As Figure 1.2 illustrates, a standards manual can have input from many sources. Standards are intended to provide consistent, rigorous, uniform, and enforceable methods for software development and operation activities. The development of standards, whether by professional societies such as the IEEE, international groups such as the International Organization for Standardization/International Electrotechnical Commission Joint Technical Committee One (ISO/IEC JTC1), industry groups, or software development organizations themselves, is recognizing and furthering that movement.

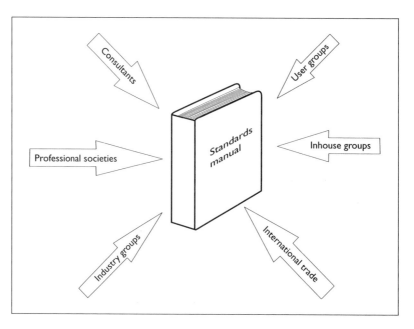

Figure 1.2
Standards sources.

Standards cover all aspects of the SLC, including the very definition of the SLC itself. Probably more than any of the other elements, standards can govern every phase of the life cycle. Standards can describe considerations to be covered during the concept exploration phase, as well as specify the format of the final report describing the retirement of a software system that is no longer in use.

Standards come into being for many reasons. They might document experience gained in the day-to-day running of a computer center and the most efficient methods to be used. Laws and government regulations often impose standard procedures on business and industry. Industries can band together to standardize interfaces between their products, as is done in the communications field. Contracts often specify standard methods of performance. And, in many cases, standards arise out of common sense.

Whether a standard comes from within a company, is imposed by government, or is adopted from an industry source, it must have several characteristics. First of all, the standard must be necessary. No standard will be observed for long if there is no real reason for its existence. Second, it must be feasible. Again, common sense tells us that if it is not possible to comply with the tenets of a standard, then that standard will be ignored. Finally, the standard or, more precisely, adherence to it must be measurable; that is, it must be possible to demonstrate that the standard is being followed. Each of these characteristics supports the total enforceability of the standard. An unenforceable standard is of no use to anyone.

Software standards should be imposed so that the producer of a software product or component can pay attention to the technical aspects of the task rather than to the routine aspects that may be the same for every task. Standards, such as those for document formats, permit the producer to concentrate on technical issues and content rather than on format or layout details.

Standards, while worthwhile, are less than fully effective if they are not supported by policies that clearly indicate their imposition and the intent of responsible management to see that the standards are followed and enforced. Often, specific practices are useful, so that implementation of the standard is uniform.

Not everything must be standardized. Guidelines that call out the preferred methods or approaches to many things are fully adequate. A set of standards that covers every minute aspect of an organization's activity can lose respect simply from its own magnitude. Competent and comprehensive guidelines give each person some degree of freedom in those areas where specific methods or approaches are not absolutely necessary. That leaves the standards to govern those areas where a single particular way of doing business is required.

1.2.2 Reviewing

Reviews permit ongoing visibility into the activities of software development and installation. Product reviews, also called technical reviews, are formal or informal examinations of products and components throughout the development phases of the life cycle. They are conducted throughout the software development life cycle (SDLC). Informal reviews generally occur during SDLC phases, while formal reviews usually mark the ends of the phases. Figure 1.3 illustrates this point.

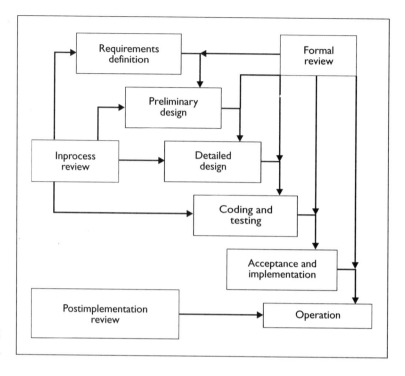

Figure 1.3
SDLC reviews.

Informal reviews include walkthroughs and inspections. Walkthroughs are informal but scheduled reviews, usually conducted in and by peer groups. The author of the subject component (design specification, test procedure, coded unit, or the like) "walks through" the component, explaining it to a small group of peers. The role of the peers is to look for defects in or problems with the component. Those problems then are corrected before the component becomes the basis for further development.

Inspections are a newer, more structured type of walkthrough. Although the basic goal of an inspection—removal of defects—is the same as that of the walkthrough, the format of the meeting and the roles of the participants are more strictly defined, and more formal records of the proceedings are prepared.

Process reviews may be held at any time. The purpose of a process review is to examine the success of the software process in effect. Data for the review are collected in the technical reviews and usually are based on defects identified by the technical reviews. Opportunities for improvements to the current process are sought. Management reviews are specialized process reviews, performed on behalf of senior management, to examine project status and effective use of resources based on the current process.

Also included in the quality control review activity are audits. Audits are examinations of components for compliance with a content and format specification or for consistency with or comparison to a predecessor. An inprocess audit of the *unit development folder* (UDF) (also called the software development file in some organizations) is usually informal. It compares the content and status of the UDF against standards governing the preparation and maintenance of the UDF. Its goal is to ascertain that UDFs are being used as required.

The *physical audit* (PA), often included as a part of the configuration management process, is an example of a formal audit. It compares the final form of a code against the final documentation for that code. The goal of the PA is to ensure that the two products, documentation and code, are in agreement before being released to the user or customer. Another formal audit is the *functional audit* (FA). The functional audit, again often a configuration management responsibility, compares the test results with the currently approved requirements to ensure that all requirements have been satisfied.

1.2.3 Testing

Testing provides increasing confidence and, ultimately, a demonstration that the software requirements are being satisfied. Test activities include planning, design, execution, and reporting. Figure 1.4 is a simple conceptual view of the testing process. The basic test process is the same, whether it is applied to system testing or to the earliest module testing.

Test planning begins during the requirements phase and parallels the requirements development. As each requirement is generated, the corresponding method of testing for that requirement should be a consideration. A requirement is faulty if it is not testable. By starting test planning with the requirements, nontestability often is avoided. In the same manner that requirements evolve and change throughout the software development, so, too, do the test plans evolve and change. This emphasizes the need for early and continuing configuration management of the requirements and the test plans.

Test design begins when the software design begins. Here, as before, a parallel effort with software development is appropriate. As the design of the software takes form, test cases, scenarios, and data are developed that will exercise the designed software. Each test case also will include specific expected results so that a pass-fail criterion is established. Just as each requirement must be measurable and testable, so must each test be measurable. A test whose completion is not definitive tells little about the subject of the test. Expected results give the basis against which the success or failure of the test is measured.

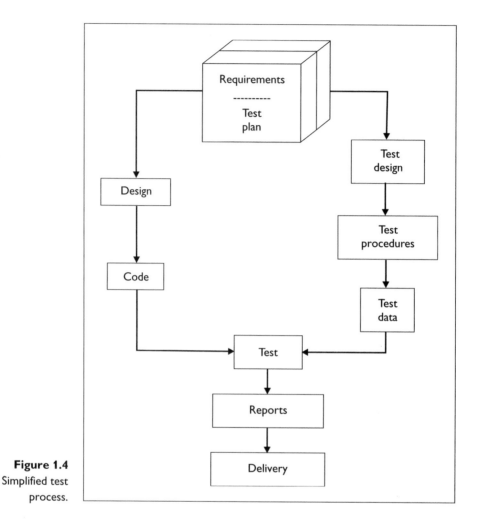

Figure 1.4
Simplified test
process.

Actual testing begins with debugging and early unit and module tests conducted by the programmer. These tests usually are informally documented (perhaps by notations in the UDF). They are not closely monitored by the software quality practitioner, since they frequently are experimental and meant to help the programmer in day-to-day software generation. Formal test execution generally begins with integration tests in which modules are combined into subsystems for function testing. In larger systems, it is frequently advisable to begin formal testing at the module level after the programmer is satisfied that the module is ready for formal testing.

Test execution requires the use of detailed test procedures, which are step-by-step directions that tell the test conductor exactly what to do as the test is run. Every action, input, expected output, and response should be documented, so the test conductor does not have to make test design decisions while the test is being run. Preparation of the test procedures is begun during the design phase and completed during the coding and debugging activities. By the time the coding phase is complete, all preparations for the formal testing activities also should be in place. Test cases, scenarios, data, and procedures, together with expected results and completion criteria, should be ready to be applied from module testing (if included on the particular project) through qualification and acceptance tests.

Test reports document the actual results of the testing effort as it progresses. For each test that is run, a report of the expected results, the actual results, and the conclusions of the test conductor concerning success of the test should be prepared. Included in the report are the anomalies that were found and recommended corrective actions. Errors, defects, faults, questionable or unexpected results, and any other nonpredicted outcomes are recorded and assigned for action. Once the anomaly has been addressed, the test, or an appropriate portion thereof, is rerun to show that the defect has been corrected. As the tests progress, so do the levels of detail of the test reports, until the final acceptance test report is prepared documenting the fitness of the software system for use in its intended environment.

1.2.4 Defect analysis

Defect analysis is the combination of defect detection and correction and defect trend analysis. Defect detection and correction, together with change control, are a record of all discrepancies found in each software component and the disposition of each discrepancy, perhaps in the form of a software problem report or software change request.

As shown in Figure 1.5, each needed modification to a software component, whether found through a walkthrough, review, test, audit, operation, or other means, is reported, corrected, and formally closed. A problem or requested change may be submitted by anyone with an interest in the software. The situation will be verified by the developers, and the configuration management activity will agree to the change. Verification of the situation is to ensure that the problem or a need for the change actually exists. Configuration management may wish to withhold permission for the change or delay it until a later time; perhaps because of concerns such as interference with other software, schedule and budget considerations, or the customer's desires. Once the change has been completed and tested, it will be reported by configuration management to all concerned parties, installed into the operational software by the developers or operations staff, and tested for functionality and compatibility in the full environment.

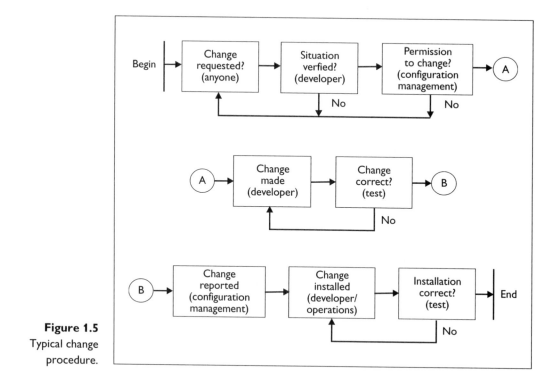

Figure 1.5
Typical change
procedure.

This procedure is required throughout a project to make sure that all defects found are properly fixed and closed. It also serves future projects by providing a means for feeding defect information back into the development life cycle and modifying the software development process so that future occurrences of certain defects are reduced. Figure 1.6 places the change procedure into the larger picture of development process analysis and improvement.

A running record of defects, their solutions, and their status is provided by the defect trend analysis effort. (The actual changes are made according to the configuration control process.) As mentioned above, the record of defects and their solutions can serve to:

- Prevent defects from remaining unsolved for inappropriate lengths of time;

- Prevent unwarranted changes;

- Point out inherently weak areas in the software;

- Provide analysis data for development process evaluation and correction;

- Provide warnings of potential defects through analysis of defect trends.

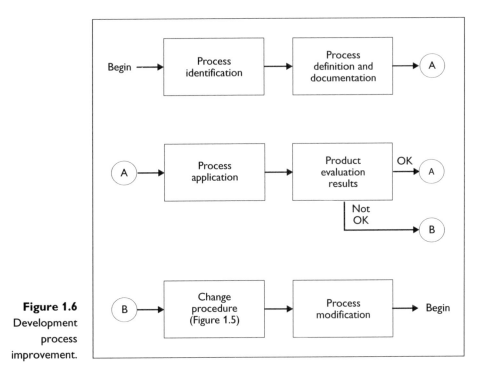

Figure 1.6
Development
process
improvement.

Formal recording and closure procedures applied to defects are insufficient if corresponding reports are not generated so that project management has visibility into the progress and status of the project. Regular reports of defect detection and correction activity keep management apprised of current defect areas and can warn of potential future trouble spots. Further, analysis of ongoing defect and change reports and activities provide valuable insight into the software development process and enhance the software quality practitioner's ability to suggest error avoidance and software development process modification.

1.2.5 Configuration management

Configuration management is a threefold discipline. Its intent is to maintain control of the software, both during development and after it is put into use and changes begin.

As shown in Figure 1.7, configuration management is, in fact, three related activities: identification, control, and accounting. If the physical and functional audits are included as configuration management responsibilities, there are four activities. Each activity has a distinct role to play. As system size grows, so do the scope and importance of each activities. In very small or one-time-use systems, configuration management may be minimal. As systems grow and become more complex, or as changes to the system become more important, each activity takes on a more definite role in the overall management of the software and its integrity. Further, some configuration management may be informal for the organization itself, to keep track of how the development is proceeding and to maintain control of changes, while other will be more formal and be reported to the customer or the user.

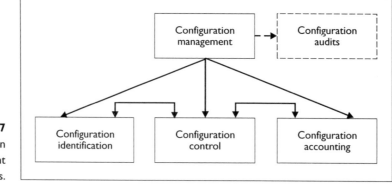

Figure 1.7
Configuration
management
activities.

Configuration identification is, as its name implies, the naming of each component (document, unit, module, subsystem, and system) so that at any given time, the particular component of interest can be uniquely identified. That is important when software is being documented, tested, changed, or delivered to the customer, in other words, throughout the entire SLC. Unless it is known which specific version or component of the software is being affected (i.e., coded, changed, tested), the software is out of control. Tests may be run on the wrong version of the code, changes may be made to an obsolete version of a document, or a system composed of the wrong versions of the various components may be delivered to the user or customer.

Configuration control prevents unauthorized changes to any software product. Early in the SLC, documentation is the primary product. Configuration control takes on an increasingly formal role as the documents move from draft to final form. Once published, any changes to the documents are formally processed so that capricious, unnecessary, or unapproved changes are not made. As the life cycle moves into the coding, testing, and operation and maintenance phases, changes to either documents or code are closely controlled. Each change is verified for necessity and correctness before being approved for insertion, so that control of the software can be maintained.

Configuration accounting keeps track of the status of each component. The latest version or update of each software component is recorded. Thus, when changes or other activities are necessary with respect to the component, the correct version of the component can be located and used. Each new edition of a document, each new assembly or compilation of the code, each new build of the software system is given a new specific identifier (through configuration identification) and recorded. All changes to that version or edition of a component are also referenced to it so that, if necessary, the history of activity with respect to any component can be recreated. This might be necessary in the loss of the current version or to return to a previous version for analysis or other purposes.

1.2.6 Security

Security activities apply both to data and to the physical data center itself. These activities are intended to protect the usefulness of the software and its environment.

The highest quality software system is of no use if the data center in which it is to be used is damaged or destroyed. Events such as broken water pipes, fire, malicious damage by a disgruntled employee, and storm damage are among the most common causes of data center inoperability. Even more ominous is the rising incidence of terrorist attacks on certain industries and in various countries around the world.

Another frequent damager of the quality of output of an otherwise high-quality software system is data that have been unknowingly modified. If the data on which the system is operating have been made inaccurate, whether intentionally or by accident, the results of the software will not be correct. To the user or the customer, such software appears to be inadequate.

Additionally, though not really a software quality issue per se, is the question of theft of data. The security of stored or transmitted data is of paramount concern in most organizations. From the theft of millions of dollars by interception of electronic funds transfers to an employee who just changes personnel or payroll records, data security is a major concern.

Finally, the recent onslaught of hackers and viruses must be considered. These threats to software quality must also be recognized and countered.

The role of the software quality practitioner is, again, not to police the data or to provide security for the data or the data center. The software quality practitioner is responsible for alerting management to the absence or apparent inadequacy of security provisions in the software. In addition, the software quality practitioner must bring the issue of data center security and disaster recovery to management's attention.

1.2.7 Education

Education ensures that the people involved with software development and those people using the software once it has been developed are able to do their jobs correctly.

It is important to the quality of the software that the producers be educated in the use of the various development tools at their disposal. Programmers charged with writing object-oriented software in C++ cannot perform well if the only language they know is Visual Basic. It is necessary that the programmers be taught to use C++ before beginning the programming assignment. Likewise, the producers also must be taught the operating systems, data modeling techniques, debugging tools, special work stations, test tools, and so on.

The proper use of the software once it has been developed and put into operation is another area requiring education. In that case, the actual user of the software must be taught proper operating procedures, data entry, report generation, and whatever else is involved in the effective use of the capabilities of the software system.

The personnel in the data center must be taught the proper operating procedures before the system is put into full operation. Loading and initializing a large system may not be a trivial task. Procedures for recovering from abnormal situations may be the responsibility of the data center personnel. Each of the many facets of the operation of a software system must be clear so that the quality software system that has been developed may continue to provide quality results.

The software quality practitioner is not usually the trainer or educator. Those functions are normally provided by some other group or means. The role of the software quality practitioner is, as always, to keep management attention focused on the needs surrounding the development and use of a quality software system. The software quality practitioner is expected to monitor the requirements for and the provision of the education of the personnel involved in the SLC.

Last, the support personnel surrounding software development must know their jobs. The educators, configuration management and software quality practitioners, security and database administrators, and others must be competent in fostering an environment in which quality software can be built, used, and maintained.

1.2.8 Vendor management

When software is to be purchased, the buyer must be aware of and take action to gain confidence in the quality of the software being purchased. Not all purchased software can be treated in the same way, as will be seen below. Each type of purchased software will have its own SQS approach, and each type must be handled in a manner appropriate to the degree of control the purchaser has over the development process used by the producer. There are three basic types of purchased software:

- Off-the-shelf software;
- *Tailored-shell* software;
- Contracted software.

Off-the-shelf software is the package carried at retail outlets, for example, spreadsheets, word processors, and graphics programs. These packages come as they are with no warranty that they will do what you need to have done. They are also almost totally outside the buyer's influence with respect to quality.

The second category may be called the *tailored shell*. The customer purchases a basic, existing framework, and the vendor then adds specific capabilities as required by contract. This is somewhat like buying a stripped version of a new car and then having the dealer add a stereo, a sun roof, and other extras. The only real influence the customer has over quality is on the custom-tailored portions.

The third category is contracted software, which is contractually specified and provided by a third-party developer. In this case, the contract can also specify the software quality activities that the vendor must perform and which the buyer will audit. The software quality practitioner has the responsibility in each case to determine the optimum level of influence and how that influence can be most effectively applied. The purchaser's quality practitioners must work closely with the vendor's quality practitioners to ensure that all required steps are taken.

1.3 Additional Issues

Several other issues can and will affect the scope and the authority of the SQS. These issues include maintenance of the software once it is in operation, documentation of the development and configuration of the software, placement of the software quality practitioners within the overall organization, and the concerns of implementing the quality system.

1.3.1 **Maintenance**

Software maintenance can best be viewed and treated as an extension or a repetition of the development process.

Software maintenance includes two primary activities: correction of defects not found during development and testing and enhancement of the software to meet new or changed requirements after installation. As suggested in Figure 1.8, each maintenance action or project is treated in much the same way as original development, and the parallels with the SDLC can be seen. The maintenance process begins with identification of the need for a change. The occurrence of an error due to a previously unencountered defect will trigger a change. New requirements may come from requests from the users, the need for increased throughput in the data center, a change in processing technology such as from mainframes to a client-server approach, or just the desire to reengineer old legacy code.

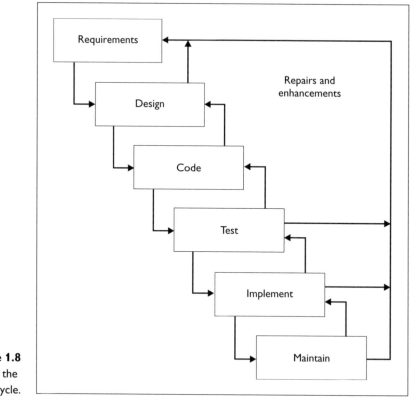

Figure 1.8
Recycling the
life cycle.

Whatever the reason for the change, effort is expended in determining exactly what will be needed (concept definition and requirements specification); how the change will be effected (design); the actual creation of the new or modified software (code and unit test); and the testing, approval, and installation of the change (integration, testing, and installation). Thus, in almost all cases (there are exceptions to most rules), maintenance can be seen primarily as a return to the regular SDLC activities, though usually on a smaller scale.

It is important to note the need for rigorous configuration management during the maintenance phase. Especially in periods of rapid change, such as might be found during the modification of software to address new government regulations or the introduction of a new weapon system in a combat vehicle, there is significant danger of making changes to the wrong version of a module or subsystem. If multiple changes are made simultaneously, as is often the case, one change may unknowingly affect another. The software quality practitioner must take an aggressive role in confirming that all configuration management procedures are followed. That is in addition to the software quality practitioner's regular monitoring role in all software development activities, whether original development or maintenance.

1.3.2 Documentation

The purpose of documentation is to record what is required of the software, how that goal is to be accomplished, proof that the software was provided, and how to use and maintain the software. The role of the software quality practitioner is to monitor the documentation activities and keep management apprised of their status and quality.

It's like the old adage, "If you don't know where you're going, any road will take you there—but it doesn't matter, because you won't realize that you've arrived." Without adequate documentation, the task at hand is never accurately specified. What is really wanted is not made clear. The starting and ending points are poorly specified, and no one is sure when the project is complete. Inadequate documentation is like not knowing where you are going. The system designers are not sure what the customer or user really wants, the programmer is not sure what the designer intends, and the tester is not sure what to look for. Finally, the customers or users are not sure that they got what they wanted in the first place.

The depth of the documentation depends on the scope of the specific project. Small projects can be successful with reduced documentation requirements. But as the size of the project increases, the need for more complete documentation also increases. In the case of small or uncomplicated projects, the information contained in some documents can be provided in higher level documents. As system size increases, additional documents may be needed to adequately cover such topics as interfaces and data design. More comprehensive test documentation will also be required such as specific test plans, cases, and reports.

Too much documentation can be as bad as too little. The time spent documenting a project is wasted if the documentation does not add to the required body of knowledge about the project. Overdocumentation can introduce inconsistencies, conflicting information, and other kinds of defects that, in the long run, detract from performance.

Documentation should be sufficient to accurately and completely tell what to do (concept and requirements), how to do it (plan and design), how to show that it was done (test), and how to use the system (user). The software quality practitioner monitors and reviews the documentation to see that it satisfies those needs.

1.3.3 Organizational considerations

The placement of the software quality practitioner or group within the organization is a critical factor in its effectiveness. While there are several acceptable structures, each dependent on the specific total business organization, certain conditions must be observed to enable the SQS to be effective. Figure 1.9 depicts several possible organizational reporting arrangements. Each has its merits and faults, which will be explored in Chapter 9.

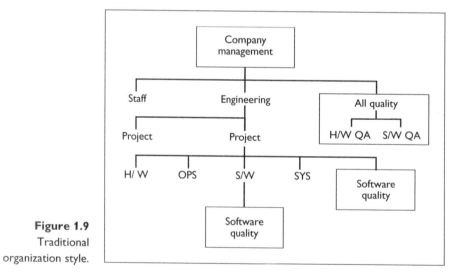

Figure 1.9
Traditional organization style.

It is important to note that in some companies the SQS functions and activities may not be under the auspices of a formal software quality group at all. Because the SQS functions should be carried out by those parts of the organization best qualified to perform them, some companies stop at that point and have various managers responsible for individual SQS functions. That approach would seem to have some economies connected with it, since there is not the cost of a dedicated staff just for software quality. However, the coordination among the various responsible managers may in fact be time consuming enough to actually cost more than a software quality group. In addition, when a manager has an assignment such as the development of a new software system and some ancillary tasks such as documentation coordination, configuration management, training, security, or software quality, the development task usually gets the bulk of the manager's attention and other tasks less attention or effort.

Software quality is everyone's individual responsibility. All participants in the SLC are expected to perform their jobs correctly. Unfortunately, that goal often is unachieved. Software quality tasks, then, must be assigned to the group or individual who can and will be accountable for assessing and reporting on the quality of the software throughout its life cycle.

1.3.4 Implementation of the total SQS

Implementation of an SQS requires delegation of authority (a charter to perform the activities), cooperation of the organization (which is usually gained through demonstration of usefulness over time), and order (a logical progression of steps leading to the actual application and performance of the SQS activities).

No activity should be started until management has created a formal charter of responsibilities, accountabilities, and authority vested in the SQS and assigned that charter to the software quality practitioner or group. That, however, only creates the SQS; it does not establish the set of functions and activities that must be performed or the order in which they will be inaugurated. The software quality practitioners themselves must plan, design, and implement the overall SQS.

The four major elements in a successful SQS are the quality culture of "do it right the first time," a quality charter that specifies the responsibilities and authorities of each person with respect to quality, a software quality manual that details the various components of the organization's SQS, and the SQS standards and procedures themselves. Table 1.1 shows how the various affected parts of an organization must contribute to the elements for the institution of an effective and acceptable SQS.

Senior management	SQS program element	Technical personnel
Insist on	Culture	Input to
Commit to	Charter	Input to
Input to	Manual	Input to
Fully support	Total SQS	Cooperate with

Table 1.1
Key software
quality roles

An important aspect of the whole process is the continued involvement of the development group from the very beginning. As each part of the SQS is conceived and planned, the quality charter established, the quality manual prepared, and the SQS implemented, the involvement of the producers will help ensure their acceptance and cooperation. Their participation, from the beginning, reduces the elements of surprise and, sometimes, distrust on the part of those whose work is the subject of the software quality activities.

Management, too, must be kept fully apprised of the activities and progress of the implementation of the SQS. Management provides the initial impetus for the SQS with its insistence on the concept of an organizational culture based on quality. Next, it starts the process through its demonstrated commitment to the quality charter. Continued support for the effort depends on management's continued belief that an SQS will be beneficial in the long run. By maintaining close contact with management during the startup period, potential future pitfalls can be recognized and avoided.

Finally, management and all the groups involved must work out and accept a logical implementation plan. The needs of the various groups and their priorities must be reflected in the actual implementation schedule.

In the final analysis, the startup of a SQS closely resembles the creation of a software system. Each part of the SDLC is paralleled in the SQS, and each must be carefully addressed. Most of all, however, every affected organization should be a party to the planning, design, and implementation of the SQS.

1.4 Summary

A total SQS is more than reviews or testing or standards. It is the comprehensive application of an eight-element discipline. The role of the software quality function is to review the state of the software development process and its products and to report that state to decision-making, action-capable management. It is not the role of the software quality function to manage, direct, or control the software development process.

The ultimate objective of a SQS is to provide, based on the results of the eight elements, information that will permit decision-making, action-capable management to beneficially affect the software development process.

While it is not an absolute necessity that the SQS functions be under the cognizance of a software quality organization, the accountability for the SQS functions becomes more visible and addressable if a software quality group actually exists. That group is not necessarily responsible for the actual performance of the SQS functions, but it should alert management to the need for and the efficacy of those functions. The functions themselves are to be performed by the organizational entities most qualified to perform them, for example, training by the training department and configuration management by the configuration management department.

The software quality practitioners must be administratively and financially independent of the parts of the organization that they will monitor, that is, at least on the same organizational level within a project or in a matrix management situation in which the SQS is administered by an organizational element completely outside the project organization.

So that the software quality practitioners have the authority commensurate with their responsibilities and accountabilities, there should be a written charter from senior management that specifies the roles, objectives, and authority of the SQS and the software quality practitioners. The preparation and approval of the charter will serve to get the commitment of senior management to whatever SQS is finally implemented. This commitment of senior management is key to the success, both near and long term, of an SQS. Without the formal commitment of senior management, an SQS and the software quality practitioners who execute it are at high risk from political and financial variations within the organization.

1.5　The next step

To delve into the topic of software quality management, the reader might find the following two texts of interest:

- *Improving Software Quality: An Insider's Guide to TQM* by Lowell J. Arthur (New York: John Wiley & Sons, 1993).
- *Software Quality: Concepts and Plans* by Robert H. Dunn (Englewood Cliffs, NJ: Prentice-Hall, 1990).

ADDITIONAL READING

Barret, Derm, *Fast Focus on TQM: A Concise Guide to Companywide Learning*, Portland, OR: Productivity Press, 1994.

Boehm, B. W., *Software Engineering Economics*, Englewood Cliffs, NJ: Prentice-Hall, 1981.

Crosby, P. B., *Quality Is Free*, New York: McGraw-Hill, 1979.

Dunn, Robert, and Richard Ullman, *Quality Assurance for Computer Software*, New York: McGraw-Hill, 1982.

Evans, Michael W., and John J. Marciniak, *Software Quality Assurance and Management*, New York: John Wiley & Sons, 1987.

Humphrey, Watts S., *Managing the Software Development Process*, Reading, MA: Addison-Wesley, 1989.

Schulmeyer, G. Gordon, *Zero Defect Software*, New York: McGraw-Hill, 1990.

Walton, Mary, *The Deming Management Method*, New York: Putnam, 1986.

Chapter 2

Standards

STANDARDS ARE THE keystone of an SQS. They provide the basis against which activities can be measured and evaluated. Further, they provide common methods and practices so that a task can be accomplished the same way each time it is performed.

Standards applied to software development provide uniform direction on how the development is to be conducted. Standards also apply to the balance of the SLC. They can prescribe everything from the form on which an original system concept is submitted for consideration to the storage location in the computer center for four-ply printer paper. The degree of standardization is, of course, a company decision. It is important, however, that the development portion of the SLC be standardized as much as is practical. Intelligent standards can increase productivity since many mundane decisions need not be made every time a software system is undertaken.

Standards arise from many sources. They may come from the day-to-day activities within the organization as the "best way to do it" surfaces in some area. An example might be the method by which access to the interactive software development facility is allocated. The companies in a given industry often band together to set standards so that their products can be used together or so that information passing between them means the same thing to everyone (e.g., the telephone industry standards for interconnection). Computer user groups and computer-industry associations often work on standards dealing with software development.

A subgroup of the IEEE, the Software Engineering Standards Committee, develops standards for software development. These standards deal with topics ranging from the SLC as a whole down through individual activities in the life cycle, such as testing and documentation. Still another source of standards is outside consulting firms that can be retained to study an individual company's specific situation and develop a set of standards especially tailored to that company's needs.

More and more organizations are recognizing the importance of stable, identified processes and their relationship to the overall direction of the organization. Standards play an important role in the development, maintenance, and execution of organizational mission statements, policies, and process procedures. External standards often define or limit the breadth of an organization's freedom in the conduct of its business. Internal standards define the organization's own performance expectations and requirements. Definition of processes is often in the context of standards, which are all subject to evaluation during process reviews.

Standards are one of the yardsticks against which the processes of software development and usage can be evaluated. Deviation from various applicable standards is an indication that the software development process is veering away from the production of quality software.

2.1 Areas of standardization

Standardization can be applied to any or all of the areas of software development and maintenance. Such broad use of standards is rarely the case and usually is not appropriate. Areas that are usually involved in the standardization effort include, but are by no means limited to, the following:

- SLC;
- Documentation;
- Coding;
- Naming;

- Operating procedures and protocols;
- User development.

2.1.1 **The software life cycle**

The SLC describes the whole software process from conception through retirement of a given system. Two life cycles are used in discussing software. The overall SLC for a system, an example of which is shown in Figure 2.1, begins with the original idea for the software system, or its conception, and the evaluation of that concept for necessity and feasibility. The life cycle ends when the software system is retired from use and set aside. Figure 2.1 also shows that, in the full life cycle, there is the SDLC, the portion of the overall SLC that deals expressly with the development of the software system. It begins with the formation of the formal requirements documentation, which states specifically what the system will do, and ends with the implementation of the system into full use. Clearly, there are other software development paradigms; the example shown is one that is commonly used.

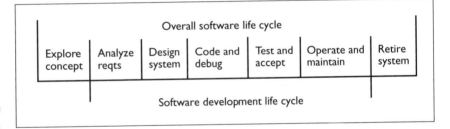

Figure 2.1
Two software
life cycles.

The SLC, and thus the SDLC, is usually divided into portions of work or effort called *phases*. Because of the number of functions and activities performed in the life of a software system, the activities are grouped into phases so they can be conveniently referenced, monitored, and managed. In Figure 2.1, the SLC is divided into six major phases, plus the effort required to retire a system at the end of its useful life. The SDLC comprises the middle five major phases. In any particular organization, the various activities may be grouped differently, or the phases may be combined, further divided, or given different names.

It is appropriate at this point to recognize the methodology called *prototyping*. Prototyping, a simplified overview of which is presented in Figure 2.2, in an increasingly popular adjunct to the SDLC as we present it in this text. Prototyping has as its goal the quick analysis of the problem to be solved and experimentation with potential solutions. Used properly, prototyping is a powerful requirements analysis and design tool. Used improperly, it can lead to undocumented and unmaintainable software.

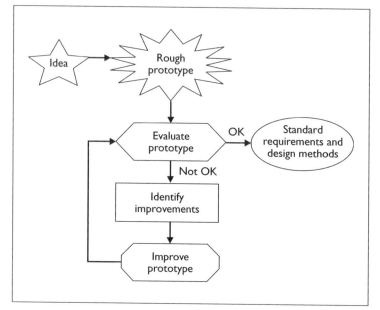

Figure 2.2
General
prototyping
approach.

A detailed discussion of prototyping is beyond the intent and scope of this text. It is the subject of much current literature, and the interested reader is encouraged to pursue the topic. It is sufficient to observe that, while the development of a prototype system can support activities in the SDLC, the prototyping development itself is expected to follow a standard SDLC.

The SLC is the basis for many of the standards that are applicable to the development and use of quality software. One of the first standards that should be prepared is a description of the life cycle, sometimes called the *software development methodology*. Which phases comprise the SLC and the SDLC and which activities comprise each of the phases must be clearly delineated. Once the life cycle phases are defined, the process of determining proper subjects for standardization within the life cycle activities can begin.

Most standards will be applicable to activities during the SDLC, since that is where the heaviest concentration of tasks is found. That in no way means that standards for the other phases should be ignored or not prepared. As the SQS matures, it will determine, together with the rest of the software organization, new areas to which standards can be usefully applied.

The arrival of computer-aided software engineering tools has opened another opportunity and necessity for SLC standardization. Which tools to use; how to specify, acquire, and apply them; and the interfaces among them may need to be addressed by standards.

2.1.2 Documentation

Comprehensive documentation standards are a basic necessity for thorough design, test, operation, and maintenance.

A major complaint against most software systems is that they are poorly documented. A generality is that documentation is done, if at all, after the software system is delivered. Thus, while in the best of worlds, the documentation describes the delivered system, it often fails to describe what was originally requested by the customer. Further, there is often little documentation of the test program applied to the software system. That makes the software's ability to perform as desired suspect. Also, user documentation—how to use the software system—frequently is accused of being unusable.

Standards for documentation should address two fronts: the required documentation for each software system and the format and content requirements for that documentation.

A comprehensive set of documentation standards can help ensure that the documentation of a software system is capable of the tasks for which it is intended. Without standards to govern what to document and how to document it, the system may well go into production and fail for one of the following reasons:

- It is not what the customer really wanted.
- The users and operators don't know how it works.

The most important document and, frequently, the least standardized and least well done is the requirements document. The requirements document is intended to spell out specifically the problem or need that the software is to address. It must describe the intended software system from an external, operational point of view. Once the requirements have been determined and expressed, they must be managed. Every system being developed will undergo requirements changes. Some will be necessary, some just "nice to have"; others actually may be harmful or detrimental to the system as a whole. Without rigorous standards for the analysis, definition, expression, and control of the requirements, a software development project is in danger of failing to satisfy its users.

2.1.3 **Coding**

Coding standards can help reduce "artistry" and enhance clarity and maintainability. Some coding standards take effect earlier than others, sometimes reaching back into the design phases. A standard that calls for structured coding techniques usually will imply the imposition of a standard that calls for structured design techniques. Conversely, standards requiring object-oriented development techniques often will lead to standards for coding in one or another of the newer languages that support object development.

Standards such as these are intended to permit greater understanding throughout the balance of the SLC. Peers who are involved in walkthroughs and inspections are better able to understand the code as they prepare for the review. Maintainers have a much easier time correcting and enhancing code that is well structured and follows adequate standards.

Some coding standards deal with which specific language is to be used. Many shops that rely on large mainframe-based systems still use Cobol or PL/I as their standard application language. Another, differently oriented development organization may standardize on Pascal, C, or C++. Defense contractors are required by Department of Defense (DoD) regulations to use Ada as their standard language. Some organizations have several standard languages, depending on which type of application is being developed, or even specific characteristics of a given application.

Beyond standards that specify a given language, an organization may prepare standards for subroutine calls, reentrant or recursive coding techniques, reuse of existing code, or restrictions on verbs or coding constructs.

Most organizations have specific approaches that are preferred or, perhaps, prohibited. The coding standards will reflect the needs and the personality of the organization. A set of standards is useful in creating an environment where all the programmers know the rules that govern their work. If a coding convention is beneficial to the performance of the coding staff, it should be made a standard so that all coding can benefit from it. On the other hand, if a particular coding technique is found to be detrimental, a standard prohibiting its use is appropriate so that all programmers know to avoid it.

2.1.4 **Naming**

Standard naming conventions assist in readability and configuration management. The standardization of naming conventions for system components (units, modules, etc.), data, and even entry points in the code is both easy and beneficial. There is usually little resistance to a consistent naming or labeling scheme, and its benefits are the ease of identifying the object being named or labeled. Beyond that, configuration management, especially configuration identification, is much more difficult if there are no consistent rules or standards for component identification.

Naming standards are based on consistent identifiers in specific locations in the name. As Figure 2.3 shows, identifiers may be assigned to decreasing hierarchical levels in a system, the first characters specifying the system itself and subsequent characters defining lower levels in the system. Data can be similarly named, as can subroutines and even external interfaces.

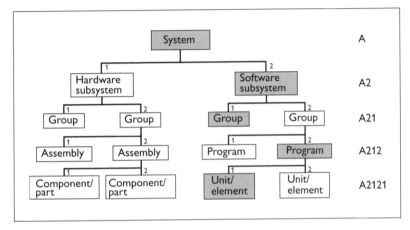

Figure 2.3
Identification based on hierarchy.

The important point in naming conventions is that all components of a given software system can be identified as belonging to that system. That in turn can simplify the bookkeeping for testing, integration, and delivery of the system, since each component is uniquely identified. As will be discussed later, that also is important for the management of the overall configuration. To have the user or customer accept one version of the system and then mistakenly deliver a different version obviously is undesirable.

Configuration identification, while going beyond the basic naming standards and conventions, depends on unique identifiers for all components of a particular software system. It can perform its function with whatever naming standards, conventions, schemes, or methods are used. However, a standard naming convention greatly eases the configuration identification task.

The tasks of the software developer and tester are also simplified if standard naming conventions are used. Confusion and doubt as to exactly which interface is to be exercised or which module is to be tested are minimized. The developer can easily determine the subroutine to call or entry point to use if there are standard rules and formats for the names of those items.

2.1.5 Operating procedures and protocols

Operating procedures are standardized so that everyone does the same thing the same way with a given software system. Standardizing the operational environment is important to software system results. Correct data entered in different ways can give different, yet seemingly correct, results. The sequencing of subsystem operations in nonstandard ways may lead to varied results, all of which might be taken as correct. To be sure, much of the opportunity for variation in the use or operation of a software system can be eliminated by the software itself. On the other hand, software cannot easily control *all* procedures, so standards are used to govern the remaining variables.

Standard user procedures tend to reduce errors and defects, maximize system response time, simplify user education, and increase understanding of system outputs.

Standards applied to users may address time of day or cycle considerations with respect to the running of the system. A payroll system may be run on Friday as a standard to permit proper interface with the timecard reporting system. A corresponding standard may call for running on Thursday in holiday situations. By having standards for use, the user is not put in the position of making decisions that could conflict with those made by someone else. Further, it reduces the likelihood that a person making the same decision will make it differently from time to time.

The standardization of operating procedures and protocols applies to both large centralized data centers, client-server installations, standalone and networked workstations, and specific application systems. Specific application systems standards can regulate when the system is run, how to recover from system crashes, and the like. Equally important, though, the overall operation of the data center or network should have governing standards. Such things as scheduled maintenance time, job entry rules, mass storage allocation, remote job entry procedures, log-on and log-off procedures, password use, data access, and distributed computing are all subjects for appropriate standardization. Such standards have high payback in smoother operation, reduced errors and defects, and easier education of personnel.

2.1.6 User development

User development of software needs strict standards so that the actions of one user do not affect other users or the data center itself.

The rapidly growing capability for user-developed software provides a fast, easy method of providing quick service for small tasks. An associated area is the availability of off-the-shelf software from both regular commercial suppliers and online bulletin boards. Software can be purchased, downloaded, and made into an integral part of larger systems being developed. Users have the ability to buy a package, merge it with another package, write some special code for their own needs, and run the amalgam of software without the intervention of the regular software organization. While convenient and often productive, this has opened the door for uncontrolled software development, potentially damaging access to the organizational database, excessive loading of the data processing facilities, and wasteful duplication of effort and resources. Standards for user development of software are needed to address those potential conditions.

User understanding and observation of standards are required to avoid a negative impact on the overall data processing facility. Uncontrolled purchase of small, local (departmental) computational facilities can be an unnecessary drain on a company's resources and can lead to incompatibilities between local facilities and the main data center or network. Further, as software is developed, it can, if unregulated, lead to problems with data interface, integrity, and security. Acquisition of software from nonstandard sources or suppliers also increases the likelihood of virus infections and other security concerns.

User development of software can be a beneficial addition to the computational capabilities of an organization. Standards are easier to develop and enforce in the traditional mainframe environments, since all processing is done under a central operating system. As control and processing are moved toward the decentralized environment, enforcement becomes more difficult. Not only are user development standards more necessary, but increased surveillance of storage and files is appropriate, to reduce the chances of misuse of unauthorized or nonlicensed commercial software. Standards for user development, ranging from equipment and language selection to data security and networking, will permit maximum user flexibility and still maintain central control for efficient overall data processing.

Changes to standards affecting user work flow and tasks may also be affected by new standards governing user development of software. Users should have the opportunity to participate in the standardization activities. They might even have a trial-use period. The quality practitioner will want to ensure that addressing the dangers inherent in uncontrolled user development are not creating unnecessary restrictions.

2.1.7 **Emerging technologies**

The software development and maintenance world is in a period of great expansion and change. While most of the "new" technologies can be traced back to "old" methods and look more like changes than innovations, the applications of the technologies are often new or at least different. Some of us see object-oriented design and development as little more than a refinement of subroutines and independent modules. Client-server technology probably really began when IBM introduced its CICS operating system; the "clients" were terminals, and the "server" was a big mainframe. Graphical user interfaces are more of a new development than the others.

In any event, developers are having a hard time finding standards to govern these technologies. That is not to say that no standards are available. It is to say that few of the standards have gained wide industrial acceptance and are more de facto standards than formal standards. That places the burden on the users of these technologies to develop their own approaches and standards. The alternative is to gamble on adopting one or another of the de facto standards and to hope that the industry as a whole goes in the same direction. The same is true for the burgeoning field of multimedia software.

2.2 **Sources of standards**

It was stated in Section 2.1 that standards should cover as much of the overall SLC as is practical and appropriate for a given organization. That is clearly a large and important task. Certainly, in an organization of more than minimum size, it will involve more than just one or two persons. Even then, to create all the standards needed can be an overwhelming task and one that cannot be accomplished in a timely manner. The goal should be to identify the minimum set of standards that will serve the organization's actual needs and the sources for those standards.

Software standards can come from many sources. The standards coordinator (or whoever has the responsibility for standards) can make use of all or any of the standards-acquisition means and sources. The three main standards-acquisition methods are to:

- Develop them inhouse;
- Buy them from consultants or other similar organizations;
- Adapt industry-prepared and consensus-approved standards.

The three main standards sources are:

- External standards developers;
- Purchased standards;
- Inhouse development.

2.2.1 External standards developers

Standards are available from several sources. Some externally available standards are useful as starting points for an inhouse standards program. Some are likely to be imposed as a condition of commerce with a particular business field or with other countries. One advantage to the standards developed by various industry and other groups is that they reflect the consensus of the groups involved. Several industry-segment points of view usually are represented, so that a wide range of applications is available. Table 2.1 presents some typical standards subjects and representative external standards and sources applicable to them. The list is certainly not all inclusive, but it does indicate the breadth of standards available.

International standards

Of increasing interest is the activity in the international sector with respect to software standards. The ISO has published what is called the 9000 series of standards (ISO 9000, 9001, 9002, 9003, 9004) dealing with quality. Standard 9001, "Quality Systems—Model for Quality Assurance in Design, Development, Production, Installation and Servicing," is the one most often applied to software development because it includes all aspects of product development from requirements control through measurements and metrics applied to the quality program and the control of the products.

Written from a primarily manufacturing point of view, ISO 9001 is difficult to relate to the software realm. Therefore, the ISO added an annex to ISO 9000, called Part 3. This annex explains how the requirements of ISO 9001 can be applied to software. A working group of Standards Australia has prepared AS 3563, which is a better interpretation of ISO 9001 for software.

Also active is the international group ISO/IEC JTC1, formed through the cooperation of ISO and the IEC. This group is dedicated to information technology standards and includes several subcommittees that affect the development of software. Organizations that do, or expect to do, business with countries other than their own, are well advised to seek out and comply with the tenets of the international standards. At the time of this writing, ISO/IEC had published IS 12207, "Information Technology—

Software life cycle processes," and was working on several standards that will support 12207.

Major subject	Specific area	Standard developer	Standard number
Software life cycle	Life cycle processes	IEEE ISO/IEC	1074, 1074.1 12207
	Project management	IEEE	1058
	Development	DoD IEEE ISO	498 1074 12207
	Reviews	IEEE NIST	1028, 1059 500-165
	Testing	IEEE NIST ISO/IEC	829, 1008, 1012, 1059 500-75, 500-165 9126
	Quality program	IEEE AS ISO NRC	1298 3563.1, 3563.2 9000 et al. NUREG/CR-4640
	Metrics	IEEE	982.1, 982.2, 1044, 1044.1, 1045, 1061
	Case tools	IEEE	1175, 1209, 1343
Documentation	Quality plans	IEEE IEEE/EIA	730, 730.1 1498/IS 640
	Requirements specifications	IEEE ISO/IEC	830 12207
	Design specifications	IEEE ISO/IEC	1016, 1016.1 12207
	User documentation	IEEE	1063
Naming	Configuration management	IEEE EIA	1042, 828 649
User development	Software packages	ISO/IEC	12119

Table 2.1

Representative standards sources

Industrial and professional groups

Several industry and professional societies are developing generic standards that can be used as is or tailored as appropriate.

A number of professional and technical societies are increasingly active in the preparation of software standards. The IEEE and the Electronic Industries Association (EIA) have ongoing working groups addressing standards and guidelines in the software engineering area. The American National Standards Institute (ANSI) is the coordinating body for standards of all types in the United States. Another group becoming active in the software area is the American Society for Quality Control.

These, and other, groups are preparing generic software engineering standards that can be adopted as they are written or adapted by an individual organization. Many of them are also suitable for inclusion in software acquisition contracts as well as inhouse use.

Government agencies

In addition to the previously mentioned groups, many software standards are available from various government agencies, in particular the DoD and the National Institute of Standards and Technology (NIST). As a large buyer of software, as well as a developer, the federal government has prepared and is still generating standards meant primarily for software acquisition contracts. These are frequently applicable, in whole or in part, to a specific organization's internal standards needs. The DoD has recently declared its intention to cease active writing of its own standards and to adopt existing software standards.

Manufacturers' user groups

Another source of software standards can be found in computer user groups. GUIDE International (IBM), SHARE (IBM), DECUS (DEC), and other major user groups often address the question of software standards as a part of their activities. The standards generated by these user groups usually are generic in nature. They are sometimes standalone but frequently benefit from tailoring.

2.2.2 Purchased standards

Standards can be purchased and then tailored to the needs of a specific organization. Companies sometimes will provide their standards manuals to other, similar companies for a fee. That is especially true in industries in which there is a great deal of interaction or interfacing, such as between telephone companies. Although there may be strong resistance to this practice in industries in which competition is strong, in general, most organizations are willing to share, even on an informal basis, their software standards. It must be remembered, though, that standards received from another company, no matter how similar, are tailored to that company's specific situation and needs. Standards obtained in this way should be only a starting point for the standards effort in the receiving company.

Another avenue for purchased standards is through a consultant or consulting company. Many consultants will prepare a full set of software standards tailored to a specific client company. This can be an easy way to get an initial set of the most critical standards in place quickly. The consultant can then continue the standards development effort or turn the rest of the task over to the client company. The advantage of this approach is rapid standards development, usually utilizing the consultant's prior experience in the particular industry and software area. The main disadvantage is the perception of the consultant as an outsider who "doesn't really understand the situation." Involvement of the affected departments, as "consultants" to or joint participants with the real consultant can usually diminish this perception.

2.2.3 Inhouse development

Standards, from whatever source, may have to be tailored or adapted to the individual needs and environment of the specific organization or project. Inhouse development is the only way to ensure that each standard reflects those needs and the environment. There are at least three major approaches to inhouse standards development, in addition to an enormous number of variations and combinations. The three major approaches are:

- Ad hoc standardization;
- Standards groups;
- Standards committees.

Ad hoc standardization

Members of the SLC staff may be assigned, as an additional but temporary part of their job, the responsibility and authority to create and institute software standards. Since the affected staff are involved with the various parts of the entire life cycle of all projects, they have a high degree of insight into the SLC and its standardization needs. They can become aware of areas and tasks that need standardization, observe the various methods in use, and propose the most appropriate methods as candidates to be standards. As the monitor of the SLC activities, the software quality practitioner is in the proper position to determine the appropriateness of a standard once it is in use.

An advantage of ad hoc standardization is that the "experts" in the area being standardized can be called on to write—and to follow—the standard. A disadvantage is that the writers may not be aware of side issues or potential conflicts with other standards. The corporate memory of the continuity and consistency of the standards program may be lost.

In general, it is not recommended that the software quality practitioner write standards. That role could place the practitioners in the position of imposing standards on tasks and activities that they themselves do not perform. For example, the software quality practitioner does little coding, rarely operates the data center, and usually does not perform data entry.

Standards groups

A second method of inhouse development is through a separately chartered standards group (SG). Since the SG has, as its whole task, the generation of standards, it often can spend more time researching a standard or looking to outside sources for a particular standard. The advantage of having an SG is maintaining the continuity and corporate memory of the standards program.

An SG, however, suffers the same disadvantage as the software quality practitioner: standardizing from outside a task or activity. That is, the SG members usually are not in a position to follow the standards they create. In addition, an SG usually does not have the insight available to the software quality practitioner as to needed standards or standards appropriateness.

Standards committees

The third major approach to standards development is the chartering of a standards committee (SC). Usually, the SC comprises the managers of each of the departments in the data processing organization: applications development, operations, systems programming, and so on, as shown in Figure 2.4. The SC is responsible for identifying needed standards and those requiring modification or replacement. The specific generation of a standard is assigned to the manager of the department that will be most affected by the standard—language standard to applications development, database definition standard to database administration, and so on. The advantage of this approach is that the most knowledgeable and affected department prepares the standard with inputs from all other interested departments. The disadvantage is the usually difficult task of involving the actual department managers so that full departmental visibility is ensured.

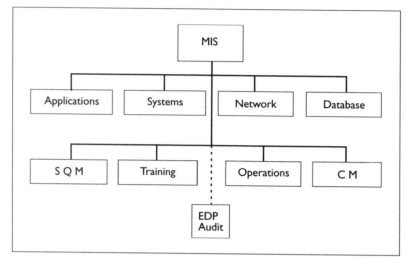

Figure 2.4
Standards
committee.

Standards coordinator

In any of the above approaches or combinations thereof, a specific person should have the job of ensuring that needed standards are identified, created, and followed. That person, the standards coordinator, may be a software quality practitioner, the manager of the SG, or the chairperson of the SC. The important matter is that he or she have the ear of the software quality practitioner or upper management to ensure that standards receive the attention they merit and require.

It is the role of the standards coordinator to ascertain the standards requirements for each installation and situation and then arrange for those needed standards to be available, invoked, and followed. As is the case with the software quality practitioner, the standards coordinator usually should not prepare the standards.

It is the responsibility of the standards coordinator to provide standards as needed and to monitor compliance with them. It is the role and responsibility of everyone in the organization to identify potential standards needs and to adhere to those standards that have been applied. It is the role of management to enforce the application of and compliance with the implemented standards.

2.3 Selection of standards

Standards must be selected that apply to the company's specific needs, environment, and resources. Standards for almost everything are available, often from several different sources. As described in Section 2.2, standards can be obtained from industry and professional groups, other companies, private consultants, or the government. They also can be prepared in-house. The major concern, then, is not where to find standards but to be sure that the ones being obtained are necessary and proper for the given organization. Even in a particular company, all the standards in use in one data center may not apply to a second data center. For example, the company's scientific data processing needs may call for standards that are different from those for its financial data processing center.

Many things can affect the need for standards and the standards needed. As stated, different data processing orientations may call for specific standards. Such things as run times, terminal response times, language selection, operating systems, and telecommunications protocols are all subject to standardization on different terms in different processing environments. Even such things as programmer workstation size and arrangement, data-input and results-output locations, training and educational needs, and data access rights often are determined on a basis that includes the type of processing as a consideration.

Not all standards available for a given subject or topic may apply in every situation. Language standards, particularly selection of the languages to be used, may have exceptions or not be applied at all. A particular standard life cycle model may be inappropriate in a given instance or for a specific project. Data access or telecommunications standards may be modified or waived to fit a particular project or installation.

2.4 Promulgation of standards

Standards must be available to the intended users. They also must be followed and kept up to date with user environment.

2.4.1 Availability

Two common methods of providing standards to the standards user are currently popular. The foremost method of publishing standards is by way of a standards manual. The standards manual is usually a large loose-leaf binder with the organization's standards filed in some logical order. It can also be a set of binders, each covering some subset of the total standards set. The loose-leaf binder approach is a convenient and generally inexpensive way of keeping the standards filed, up to date, and accessible.

This approach has some drawbacks, however. Unless some official updating method is used, holders of the manuals may be careless about making changes to their copies as new, revised, or obsolete standards are added, replaced, or removed. Using an incorrect standard is sometimes worse then using none at all. Loose-leaf pages, especially in a heavily used book or section, frequently become torn out of the book and lost. A common excuse for not following a standard is that the offender's standards book was misplaced, borrowed, or never issued.

In a large organization, the cost of providing and maintaining a set of standards books may become a significantly costly item. One way to cut that cost is to restrict the distribution of manuals to some subset of the using population. However, that solution has the usual effect of diminishing the use of the standards because of the increased difficulty of access.

One way to counter some of the more severe drawbacks of the book-style manual is to make the standards available online. In organizations that have widespread usage of terminals, there is an increasing trend to having the full set of standards available for access through the terminal network. In that way, someone who wants to look up a standard need only call up the standard on the screen for review. In addition, the problems associated with correcting and updating the standards are eliminated—the only copy of the standards is the one in the database. Once that is changed, everyone has access to the new version without having to manually update individual books.

Like all methods, though, the online one has its drawbacks, not the least of which is cost. In a large organization that already has widespread terminal usage and a large database capability, automation of a standards manual will be a relatively inexpensive situation. In those organizations that do not have the facilities already in place, however, putting the standards online probably is not cost-justifiable, since there will be limited automated access and the book method will probably have to be used as well.

2.4.2 Compliance

Standards that are not followed are frequently worse than no standards at all. Standards are intended to improve the overall quality of software as it progresses through the life cycle. When a standard has been established and implemented for a particular subject, the organization as a whole expects the standard to be followed. If it is not followed, some things may be done incorrectly or lead to errors on the part of those who work in other portions of the life cycle.

The role of the software quality practitioner—specifically, the standards coordinator—is to monitor and report to management on the adherence of the entire computational organization to the standards that have been implemented. It is not the role of the software quality practitioner or the SC to enforce the standards. Enforcement is the responsibility of management.

Not every case of noncompliance with a standard represents disregard for or lack of knowledge about the standard. In some cases, lack of compliance may be a signal that the standard is no longer appropriate or applicable. While it is not practical to investigate every case of noncompliance, it is necessary to look for trends in noncompliance that may indicate missing, faulty, or even incorrect standards. Observation of noncompliance trends can give clues that may indicate the need for companion standards to those that already exist, additional standards that complement those in place, or modification or replacement of existing standards. The software quality practitioner or the standards coordinator is responsible for identifying such cases through an ongoing review of the standards and their continuing applicability.

2.4.3 Maintenance

Standards must be kept current with the changing computational environment. No matter from where the standards have come, nor how they are made available, they will quickly fall into disuse if they do not continue to reflect the needs of the organization. Standards become obsolete as mainframes, operating systems, federal regulations, business emphases, and the like change and evolve. Probably no installation is the same today as it was as little as a year ago. Further, some of the subjects of standards also have changed. Thus, some method of keeping standards up to date must be provided. Clues that it is time to review a standard include increasing instances of noncompliance, the installation of new equipment or support software, expansion into a new area of business emphasis, the advent of new government regulations, and so on.

The standards coordinator is the person primarily responsible for standard maintenance, but anyone in the organization can point out the potential need for change. Just as in the sequence for requesting changes to software, there should be a formal standards change request and a standard method for processing that change request. Once the request is received, the standards coordinator can verify the need for the change, present it to the standards generating group, and get the change made and distributed.

2.5 Summary

Standards are the keystone of the SQS. They provide the basis against which reviewing and monitoring are conducted. Areas of standardization cover the entire SLC from the definition of the SLC itself through the methods by which software is withdrawn from use. All aspects of the SLC are open to standardization, even the process by which the standards themselves are created. Standards may be purchased, obtained from professional and user groups, and specifically developed for or by the organization.

No matter how standards come into being, they must be relevant to the organization and the software development process, that is, they must reflect the needs of the organization. Standards must be appropriate to the environment in which the software is to be developed and used.

Finally, the application of standards must be uniform and enforced across the full organization, at least at the project level. While it is desirable from a consistency point of view to impose the same standards on all software development groups in an organization, it is not always feasible from a business standpoint. Within a single project, however, there must be uniformity of standards.

2.6 The next step

Two texts that can help the reader's standards development activities are:

- *The ISO 9000 Book: A Global Competitor's Guide to Compliance and Certification* by John T. Rabbitt and Peter A. Bergh (New York: Quality Resources, 1993).

- *Software Engineering Standards & Specifications—An Annotated Index & Directory* by Stan Magee and Leonard L. Tripp (Englewood, CO: Global Professional Publications, 1994).

ADDITIONAL READING

Deming, W. Edwards, *Out of the Crisis*, MIT Center for Advanced Engineering Study, Cambridge, MA, 1986.

Dunn, Robert, *Software Quality: Concepts and Plans*, Englewood Cliffs, NJ: Prentice-Hall, 1990.

ISO/IEC JTC1/SC7, *Information Technology—Software life cycle processes—ISO/IEC 12207*, ISO/IEC Copyright Office, Geneva, Switzerland, 1995.

Software Engineering Standards Committee, *IEEE Standards Collection—Software Engineering*, IEEE, New York, 1994 (or current edition).

Standards Australia, *Software Quality Management System—AS 3563-1991—Parts 1 & 2*, North Sydney, Australia, 1991.

Chapter 3

Reviews

REVIEWS ARE THE first and primary form of quality control activity. Quality control is concerned with the search for faults in the various products of software development. While testing, as will be discussed in Chapter 4, also is concerned with the search for faults, reviews are more effective because they look for faults sooner than testing. Reviews are conducted during the process of the development, not at the end, as is the case with testing. Quality control has as its mission the detection and elimination of errors in the product, and reviews are the front line in that mission.

Reviews take place throughout the SLC and verify that the products of each phase are correct with respect to the phase inputs and outputs. Reviews take on many forms. They may be informal peer reviews, walk-throughs, inspections, formal verification reviews, or audits. Regardless of its form, the primary purpose of a review is the identification of defects in the product being considered. Boehm and others have developed graphs, similar to that in Figure 3.1, that show that the costs of defects rise steeply the longer they remain in the products. Reviews are aimed at finding the errors as they are made, rather than depending on the test and operation phases to uncover them.

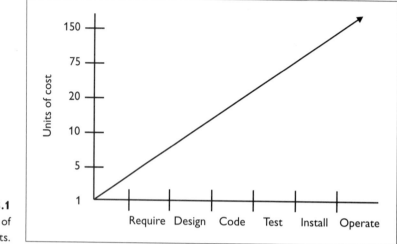

Figure 3.1
Costs of
identified defects.

Each review has a specific purpose, objective, audience, and cast of participants. Some reviews may be held multiple times during the development, such as design walkthroughs. Others, such as the functional audit, are of such magnitude that they normally are one-time events that form the basis for major decisions about the product. In each case, however, a format and a procedure for the review should be reflected in the organization's standards.

The chief role of the software quality practitioner is to confirm that the reviews are scheduled appropriately throughout the SLC and that they are held as scheduled. In some organizations, a software quality practitioner is tasked to be the chair of the review. Whatever his or her official role, it is imperative that in all reviews, except perhaps very informal walkthroughs, the software quality practitioner is an active participant. The practitioner should also make sure that minutes and action items are recorded as necessary, and that any action items are suitably addressed and closed before approving and recording the review as complete.

It must be noted that the entire goal of an SQS is to increase the quality of the delivered product. That, of course, entails the intentional seeking of errors and defects. It also entails an opportunity for the unskilled manager to make personnel decisions based on the defects found. Some managers are tempted to use the number of errors made by a developer as the basis for performance evaluations. That is a self-defeating approach for two reasons. First, employees may begin to react to the stress of reviews and try to minimize their defect-finding effectiveness so as to not "look bad." Second, as the effectiveness of the reviews goes down, the defects being delivered to the customer will increase, which undermines the customer's confidence.

3.1 Types of reviews

Reviews take on various aspects depending on their type. The two broad types of reviews are the *inprocess review* and the *phase-end review*.

3.1.1 Inprocess reviews

Inprocess reviews are informal reviews that are intended to be held during the conduct of each SDLC phase. The term *informal* implies that there is little reporting to the customer on the results of the review. Scheduling of the reviews, while intentional and a part of the overall project plan, is rather flexible. That allows reviews to be conducted as necessary: earlier if the product is ready, later if the product is late. One scheduling rule of thumb is to review no more than the producer is willing to throw away. Another rule of thumb is to have an inprocess review every two weeks. Figure 3.2 offers suggestions on the application of these two rules. Each project will determine the appropriate rules for its own inprocess reviews.

There is a "spectrum of rigor" across the range of inprocess reviews. The least rigorous review is the peer review, followed, in increasing rigor, by walkthroughs of the inprocess product, such as a requirements document or a design specification. The most rigorous review is the inspection. These are discussed more completely next. Table 3.1 summarizes some of the characteristics of inprocess reviews.

Peer reviews

The peer review is the least rigorous of the reviews and, thus, usually the least stressful. In a peer review, the producer asks a coworker to check the product to make sure that it is basically correct. Questions like "Did I get the right information in the right place?" and "Did I use the right formula?" are the main concerns of the peer review. The results of the review are often verbal or, at the most, a red mark or two on the draft of the product.

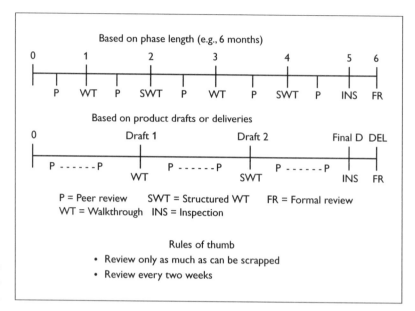

Figure 3.2
Scheduling rules
of thumb.

Review type	Records	Configuration management	Participants	Stress level
Peer	None	None	Coworker	Very low
Walkthrough	Marked-up copy	Probably none	Interested project members	Low to medium
Structured walkthrough	Defect reports	Informal	Selected project members	Medium
Inspection	Defect report database	Formal	Specific role players	High

Table 3.1
Characteristics of
inprocess reviews

Peer reviews are mostly used during the drafting of the product and cover small parts at a time. Since there is virtually no distribution of the errors found or corrections suggested, the producer feels little stress or threat that he or she will be seen as having done a poor job.

Walkthroughs

As the producer of a particular product gets to convenient points in his or her work, a group of peers should be requested to review the work as the producer describes, or walks through, the product with them. In that way defects can be found and corrected immediately, before the product is used as the basis for the next-phase activities. Since it is usually informal and conducted by the producer's peers, there is less tendency on the part of the producer to be defensive and protective, leading to a more open exchange and correspondingly better results.

Results of the walkthrough should be recorded on software defect reports such as those discussed in Chapter 6. This makes the defects found a bit more "public," which can increase the stress on the producer.

Inspections

Another, more rigorous inprocess review is the inspection. While its similarities with the walkthrough are great, the inspection requires a more specific cast of participants and more elaborate minutes and action item reporting. Unlike the walkthrough, which may be documented only within the UDF, the inspection requires a written report of its results and strict recording of trouble reports. Being more rigorous, the inspection tends to be more costly in time and resources than the walkthrough and is generally used on projects with higher risk or complexity. However, the inspection is usually more successful at finding defects than the walkthrough, and some companies use only the inspection as their inprocess review.

It is fairly obvious that the inspection, with its regularized recording of defects, will be the most stressful and threatening of the inprocess reviews. Skilled managers will remove defect histories from their bases of performance evaluations. Doing so and treating each discovered defect as "one that didn't get to the customer," the manager can reduce the stress associated with the reviews and increase their effectiveness.

The software quality role with respect to inspections is also more well defined. The software quality practitioner is a recommended member of the inspection team and may serve as the recorder. The resolution of action items is carefully monitored by the software quality practitioner, and the results are formally reported to project management.

Inprocess audits

Audits, too, can be informal as the SDLC progresses. One common informal audit is that applied to the UDF or software development notebook. The notebook or folder is the repository of the notes and other material that the producer has collected during the SDLC. Its required contents should be spelled out by a standard, along with its format or arrangement. Throughout the SDLC, the software quality practitioner should audit the UDFs to make sure they are being maintained according to the standard.

3.1.2 **Phase-end reviews**

Phase-end reviews are formal reviews that usually occur at the end of each SDLC phase and establish the baselines for work in the succeeding phases. For example, the software requirements review (SRR) is a formal examination of the requirements document and sets the baseline for the activities in the design phase to follow. The participants include not only the producer and the software quality practitioner but the user or customer as well. The phase-end reviews are a primary means of keeping the user or customer aware of the progress and the direction of the project. A phase-end review is not considered finished until the action items have been closed, software quality has approved the results, and the user or customer has approved going ahead with the next phase. Phase-end reviews permit the user or customer to verify that the project is proceeding as intended or to give redirection as needed. They are also major reporting points for software quality to indicate to management how the project is adhering to its standards, requirements, and resource budgets.

Figure 3.3 shows various phase-end reviews throughout the SDLC. The formal reviews, such as the SRR, the preliminary design review (PDR), and the critical design review (CDR), are held at major milestone points in the SDLC and create the baselines for subsequent SDLC phases. The test readiness review (TRR) is completed prior to the onset of acceptance or user testing.

Table 3.2 presents the typical subjects of each of the four major development phase-end reviews. Those documents listed as required are considered the minimum acceptable set of documents required for successful software development and maintenance.

The postimplementation review (PIR) is held once the software system is in production. The PIR usually is conducted six to nine months after implementation. Its purpose is to determine whether the software has, in fact, met the user's expectations for it in actual operation. The software quality practitioner can use data from the PIR to help improve the software development process. Table 3.3 lists some of the characteristics of the PIR.

Usually included in the category of phase-end reviews are the formal audits: the FA and the PA (see Figure 3.3). These two audits, held at the end of the SDLC, are the final analyses of the software product to be delivered against its approved requirements (FA) and its current documentation (PA).

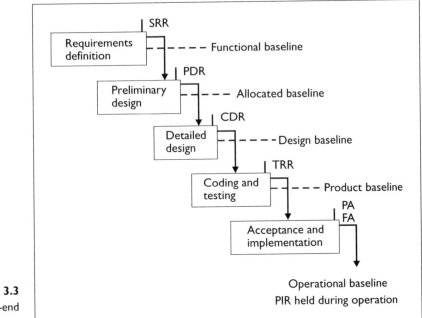

Figure 3.3
Typical phase-end
reviews.

Review	Required documents	Optional documents
SRR	Software requirements specification, software test plan, software development plan, quality system plan, configuration management plan, standards and procedures, cost/schedule status report	Interface requirements specification
PDR	Software top-level design, software test description, cost/schedule status report	Interface design, database design
CDR	Software detailed design, cost/schedule status report	Interface design, database design
TRR	Software product specification, software test procedures, cost/schedule status report	User's manual, operator's manual

Table 3.2
Phase-end
review subject
documents

The FA compares the software system being delivered against the currently approved requirements for the system. That comparison usually is accomplished through an audit of the test records. The PA is intended to ensure that the full set of deliverables is an internally consistent set, for example, the user manual is the correct one for a particular version of the software. The PA relies on the configuration management records for the delivered products.

Timing	3–6 months after software system implementation
Software system goals versus experience	Return on investment, schedule results, user response, defect history
Usage of results	Input to process analysis and improvement too often ignored

Table 3.3
Characteristics of
the PIR

The software quality practitioner frequently is charged with the responsibility of conducting both audits. In any case, the practitioner must be sure that the audits are conducted and report the findings to management.

3.2 Review subjects

Reviews continue throughout the SDLC with development reviews that focus on code and its related products.

Design and code reviews held during the course of the various phases are usually in the form of walkthroughs and inspections. These reviews are held to get an early start on the elimination of defects in the products being examined. They are generally informal, which makes them more productive and less threatening to the egos and feelings of the producers.

Test reviews are much the same as the code reviews, covering the test program products rather than the software products. They include the same types of formal and informal reviews and are held throughout the SDLC. Their function is to examine the test program as it is being developed and to make sure that the tests will exercise the software in such a manner as to find defects and to demonstrate that the software complies with the requirements.

3.3 Documentation reviews

A number of types of documentation reviews, both formal and informal, are applicable to each of the software documents.

The most basic of the reviews is the peer walkthrough, in which a group of the author's peers look for defects and weaknesses in the document as it is being prepared. Finding defects as they are introduced avoids more expensive corrective action later in the SDLC, and the document is more correct when it is released.

Another basic document review is the format review, which can be either formal or informal. When it is a part of a larger set of document reviews, the format review usually is an informal examination of the overall format of the document to be sure that it adheres to the minimum standards for layout and content. In its informal style, little attention is paid to the actual technical content of the document. The major concern is that all required paragraphs are present and addressed. In some cases, the format review is before or in conjunction with the document's peer walkthrough.

A more formalized approach to the format review is taken when no content review is scheduled. In that case, the review will also take the technical content into consideration. A formal format review usually takes place after the peer walkthroughs and is scheduled for shortly before delivery of the document. In that way, it serves as a quality-oriented audit and may lead to formal approval for publication.

When the format review is informal in nature, a companion content review should evaluate the actual technical content of the document. There are a number of ways in which the content review can be conducted. First is a review by the author's supervisor, which generally is used when formal customer-oriented reviews, such as the PDR and CDR, are scheduled. This type of content review serves to give the producer confidence that the document is a quality product prior to review by the customer.

A second type of content review is one conducted by a person or group outside the producer's group but still familiar enough with the subject matter to be able to critically evaluate the technical content. Also, there are the customer-conducted reviews of the document. Often these are performed by the customer or an outside agency (such as an independent verification and validation contractor) in preparation for an upcoming SRR, PDR, or CDR.

Still another type of review is the algorithm analysis. The algorithm analysis examines the specific approaches called out in the document that will be used in the actual solutions of the problems being addressed by the software system. Because of their cost in time and resources, algorithm analyses usually are restricted to very large or critical systems. Such things as missile guidance, electronic funds transfer, and security systems are candidates for this type of review. Payroll and inventory systems rarely warrant such indepth study.

Software quality practitioners extensively involved with documentation reviews. They must make sure that the proper reviews are scheduled throughout the development life cycle. That includes a determination of the appropriate levels of formality as well as the actual reviews to be conducted. The software quality practitioner also monitors the reviews to see that they are conducted and that defects in the documents are corrected before the next steps in publication or development are taken. In some cases, the software quality department itself is the reviewing agency, especially where there is not a requirement for in-depth technical analysis. In all cases, the software quality practitioner will report to management on the results of the reviews.

3.3.1 Requirements reviews

Requirements reviews are intended to show that the problem to be solved is completely spelled out. Informal reviews are held during the preparation of the document. A formal review is appropriate prior to delivery of the document.

The requirements specification is the keystone of the entire software system. Without firm, clear requirements, there will no way to determine if the software successfully performs its intended functions. For that reason, the informal requirements review looks not only at the problem to be solved but at the way in which the problem is stated. A requirement that says "compute the sine of x in real time" certainly states the problem to be solved—the computation of the sine of x—but it leaves a great deal to the designer to determine, for instance, the range of x, the accuracy to which the value of sine x is to be computed, the dimension of x (radians or degrees), and the definition of "real time."

Requirements statements must meet a series of criteria if they are to be considered adequate as the basis of the design of the system. Included in these criteria are:

- Necessity;
- Feasibility;
- Correctness;
- Completeness;
- Clarity;
- Measurability;
- Testability.

A requirement is sometimes included simply because it seems like a good idea; it may add nothing useful to the overall system. The requirements review assesses the necessity of each requirement. In conjunction with the necessity of the requirement is the feasibility of that requirement.

A requirement may be thought to be necessary, but if it is not achievable, some other approach will have to be taken or some other method found to address the requirement.

Completeness, correctness, and clarity are all criteria that address the way a given requirement is stated. A good requirement statement will present the requirement completely, that is, present all aspects of the requirement. The sine of x example was shown to be lacking several necessary parts of the requirement. The statement also must be correct. If, in fact, the requirement should call for the cosine of x, a perfectly stated requirement for the sine of x is not useful. And, finally, the requirement must be stated without ambiguity. A statement that correctly and completely states the requirement but cannot be understood by the designer is as useless as no statement at all. The language of the requirements should be simple and straightforward and not use jargon. That also means that somewhere in the requirements document terms and acronyms are clearly defined.

Measurability and testability go together. Every requirement will ultimately have to be demonstrated before the software can be considered complete. Requirements that have no definite measure or attribute that can be shown as present or absent cannot be specifically tested. The sine of x example uses the term "real time," hardly a measurable or testable quality. A more acceptable statement would be "every 30 milliseconds, starting at the receipt of the start pulse from the radar." In that way, the time interval for "real time" is defined, as is the starting point for that interval. When the test procedures are written, the interval can be measured, and the compliance or noncompliance of the software with this requirement can be shown exactly.

The formal SRR is held at the end of the requirements phase. It is a demonstration that the requirements document is complete and meets the criteria stated above. It also creates the first baseline for the software system, which is the approved basis for commencement of the design efforts. All design components will be tracked back to this baseline for assurance that all requirements are addressed and that nothing not in the requirements appears in the design.

The purpose of the requirements review, then, is to examine the statements of the requirements and determine if they adhere to the criteria for requirements. For the software quality practitioner, it may not be possible to determine the technical accuracy or correctness of the requirements. That task will be delegated to those who have the specific technical expertise. The software quality department or its agent (perhaps an outside contractor or another group within the organization) will review the documents for the balance of the criteria.

Each nonconformance will be recorded, along with suggested corrections. The records are returned to the authors of the documents, and the correction of the nonconformances tracked. The software quality practitioner also reports the results of the review and the status of the corrective actions to management.

3.3.2 Design reviews

Design reviews verify that the evolving design is both correct and traceable back to the approved requirements.

Informal design reviews follow closely the style and execution of the informal requirements reviews. Like the requirements, all aspects of the design must adhere to the criteria for good requirements statements. The design reviews go further, though, since there is more detail to be considered, since the requirements are broken down into smaller and smaller pieces in preparation for coding.

Walkthroughs and inspections are inprocess reviews that occur during the preparation of the design. They look at design components as they are completed.

Design documents describe how the requirements are apportioned to each subsystem and module of the software. As the apportionment proceeds, the elements of the design are traced back to the requirements. The reviews that are held determine if the design documentation describes each module according to the same criteria used for requirements.

There are at least two major design reviews, the PDR and the CDR. In addition, for larger or more complex systems, the organization standards may call for reviews that concentrate on interfaces or database concerns. Finally, there may be multiple occurrences of these reviews if the system is large, critical, or complex.

The number and the degree of each review are governed by the standards and needs of the specific organization.

The first formal design review is the PDR, which takes place at the end of the initial design phase and presents the functional breakdown of the requirements into executable modules. The PDR presents the design philosophy and approach to the solution of the problem as stated in the requirements. It is important that the customer or user take an active role in the PDR. Defects in the requirements, misunderstandings of the problem to be solved, and needed redirections of effort can be resolved in the course of a properly conducted PDR.

Defects found in the PDR are assigned for solution to the appropriate people or groups; upon closure of the action items, the second baseline of the software is established. Changes made to the preliminary design are also reflected as appropriate in the requirements document, so that the requirements are kept up to date as the basis for acceptance of the software later on. The new baseline is used as the foundation for the detailed design efforts that follow.

At the end of the detailed design, the CDR is held. This, too, is a time for significant customer or user involvement. The result of the CDR is the "code-to" design that is the blueprint for the coding of the software. Much attention is given in the CDR to the adherence of the detailed design to the baseline established at PDR. The customer or user, too, must approve the final design as being acceptable for the solution of the problem presented in the requirements. As before, the criteria for requirements statements must be met in the statements of the detailed design.

So that there is assurance that nothing has been left out, each element of the detailed design is mapped back to the approved preliminary design and the requirements. The requirements are traced forward to the detailed design, as well, to show that no additions have been made along the way that do not address the requirements as stated. As before, all defects found during CDR are assigned for solution and closure. Once the detailed design is approved, it becomes the baseline for the coding effort.

Another review that is sometimes held is the interface design review. The purpose of this review is to assess the interface specification that will have been prepared if there are significant interface concerns on a particular project. The format and conduct of this review are similar to the PDR and CDR, but there is no formal baseline established as a result of the review. The interface design review will contribute to the design baseline.

A database design review may be conducted on large or complex projects. Its intent is to ascertain that all data considerations have been made as the database for the software system has been prepared. This review will establish a baseline for the database, but it is an informal baseline, subordinate to the baseline from the CDR.

The role of the software quality practitioner in these reviews is significant. In many cases, the practitioner is the chair of the review. The practitioner will have provided formal assessments of the documents being reviewed and will report on the defects found in them together with corrective actions that have been taken to date. It is also the task of the software quality practitioner to monitor and report on the progress and status of any outstanding corrective actions or action items that result from each review.

One of the two goals of the SQS is to facilitate the building of quality into the software products as they are produced. Design reviews provide a great opportunity for the realization of that goal. By maintaining a high standard for the conduct and completion of the reviews and the establishment of the respective baselines, the software quality practitioner can make significant contributions to the attainment of a quality software product.

3.3.3 **Test documentation reviews**

Test documentation is reviewed to ensure that the test program will find defects and will test the software against its requirements.

The objective of the test program as a whole is to find defects in the software products as they are developed and to demonstrate that the software complies with its requirements. Test documentation is begun during the requirements phase with the preparation of the initial test plans. Test documentation reviews, then, also begin at this time as the test plans are examined for their comprehensiveness in addressing the requirements.

The initial test plans are prepared with the final acceptance test in mind, as well as the intermediate tests that will examine the software during development. It is important, therefore, that each requirement be addressed in the overall test plan. By the same token, each portion of the test plan must specifically address some portion of the requirements. It is understood that the requirements, as they exist in the requirements phase, will probably undergo some evolution as the software development process progresses. This does not negate the necessity for the test plans to track the requirements as the basis for the testing program. At each step further through the SDLC, the growing set of test documentation must be traceable back to the requirements. The test program documentation also must reflect the evolutionary changes in the requirements as they occur.

As the SDLC progresses, more of the test documentation is prepared. During each phase of the SDLC, additional parts of the test program are developed. Test cases with their accompanying test data are prepared, followed by the test scenarios and specific test procedures to be executed. For each test, pass/fail criteria are determined, based on the expected results from each test case or scenario. In each instance, the test documentation is reviewed to ascertain that the test plans, cases, scenarios, data, procedures, and so on, are complete, necessary, correct, measurable, consistent, and unambiguous. In all, the most important criterion for the test documentation is that it specifies a test program that will find defects and demonstrate that the software requirements have been satisfied.

Test documentation reviews take the same forms as the reviews of the software documentation itself. Walkthroughs of the test plans are conducted during their preparation, and they are formally reviewed as part of the SRR. Test cases, scenarios, and test data specifications are also subject to walkthroughs and sometimes inspections. During the PDR and the CDR, these documents are formally reviewed.

During the development of test procedures, there is a heavy emphasis on walkthroughs, inspections, and even dry runs, to show that the procedures are comprehensive and actually executable. By the end of the coding phase, the acceptance test should be ready to be performed, with all documentation in readiness.

The acceptance test is not the only test with which the test documentation is concerned, of course. All through the coding and testing phases, there have been unit, module, integration, and subsystem tests. Each of these tests has also been planned and documented, and that documentation has been reviewed. These tests have been a part of the overall test planning and development process, and the plans, cases, scenarios, data, and so on, have been reviewed right along with the acceptance test documentation. Again, the objective of all these tests is to find the defects that prevent the software from complying with its requirements.

3.3.4 User documentation reviews

User documentation not only must present information about the system, it must be meaningful to the reader.

The reviews of the user documentation are meant to determine that the documentation meets the criteria already discussed. Just as important, however, is the requirement that the documentation be meaningful to the user. The initial reviews will concentrate on completeness, correctness, and readability. The primary concern will be the needs of the user to understand how to make the system perform its function. Attention must be paid to starting the system, inputting and outputting data, and the meaning of error messages and what the user can do about them.

The layout of the user document and the comprehensiveness of the table of contents and the index can enhance or impede the user in the use of the document. Clarity of terminology and avoidance of system-peculiar jargon are important to an understanding of the document content. Reviews of the document during its preparation help to uncover and eliminate errors and defects of this type before they are firmly imbedded in the text.

A critical step in the review of the user documentation is the actual trial use of the documentation by one or more typical users before the document is released. In that way, omissions, confusing terminology, inadequate index entries, unclear error messages, and so on, can be found. Most of those defects are the result of the authors' close association with the system rather than outright mistakes. By having representatives of the actual using community try out the documentation, such defects are more easily identified and recommended corrections obtained.

Changes to user work flow and tasks may also be affected by the new software system. To the extent that they are minor changes to input, control, or output actions using the system, they may be summarized in the user documentation. Major changes to behavior or responsibilities may require training or retraining. Hands-on trial use of the user documentation can point out the differences between old and new processes and highlight those that require more complete coverage than will be available in the documentation itself.

3.3.5 **Other documentation reviews**

In addition to the normally required documentation, other documents are produced during the software system development that must be reviewed as they are prepared. These documents include the software development plan, the software quality system plan, the configuration management plan, and various others that may be contractually invoked or called for by the organization's standards. Many of these other documents are of an administrative nature and are prepared prior to the start of software development.

The software development plan, which also goes by many other names, lays out the plan for the overall software development effort. It will discuss schedules, resources, perhaps work breakdown and task assignment rules, and other details of the development process as they are to be followed for the particular system development.

The software quality system plan and the configuration management plan address the specifics of the implementation of those two disciplines for the project at hand. They, too, should include schedule and resource requirements as well as the actual procedures and practices to be applied to the project. Additional documents may be called out by the contract or the organization's standards, as well.

Since these are the project management documents, it is important that they be reviewed at each of the formal reviews during the SLC and that modifications to the documents or the overall development process be made as necessary to keep the project within its schedule and resource limitations.

Reviews of all these documents concentrate on the basic criteria and on the completeness of the discussions of the specific areas covered. Attention must be paid to compliance with the format and content standards imposed for each document.

Finally, the software quality practitioner must ascertain that all documents required by standards or the contract are prepared on the required schedule and are kept up to date as the SLC progresses. Too often, documentation that was appropriate at the time of delivery is not maintained as the software is maintained in operation. That leads to increased difficulty and cost of later modification. It is important to include resources for continued maintenance of the software documentation, especially the maintenance documentation (discussed in Chapter 8). To ignore the maintenance of the documentation will result in time being spent reinventing or reengineering the documentation each time maintenance of the software is required.

3.4 Summary

Reviews take on many forms. Each review has a specific purpose, objective, audience, and cast of participants.

Informal, inprocess reviews generally occur during the execution of each SDLC phase. They concentrate on single products or even small parts of single products. It is the intention of inprocess reviews to detect defects as quickly as possible after their insertion into the product.

Formal, phase-end reviews usually occur at the end of each SDLC phase and establish the baselines for work in the succeeding phases. Formal audits include the FA and the PA. The phase-end reviews are much broader in scope. They cover the entire family of products to be prepared in each major SDLC phase as well as the various documented plans for the project.

Documentation reviews, both formal and informal, are applicable to each software document. The most basic of the reviews is the peer walkthrough. Another basic document review is the format review, which can be either formal or informal. Requirements reviews are intended to show that the problem to be solved is completely spelled out. Design reviews verify that the evolving design is both correct and traceable back to the approved requirements. Test documentation is reviewed to ensure that the test program will find defects and will test the software against its requirements. The reviews of the user documentation are meant to determine that the documentation meets the criteria.

Other documents are often produced during the SLC and must be reviewed as they are prepared. Reviews of all these documents concentrate on the basic criteria and on the completeness of the discussions of the specific areas covered.

Design and code reviews held during the course of the various phases are usually in the form of walkthroughs and inspections. These reviews are held to get an early start on the elimination of defects in the products being examined and generally are informal.

Test reviews are much the same as code reviews, covering the test program products rather than the software products.

Implementation reviews are those conducted just prior to implementation of the software system into full use.

Reviews take place throughout the SLC and verify that the products of each phase are correct with respect to the phase inputs and the activities of the phase.

3.5 The next step

To find out how to start a review program, consult the following sources:

- *Software Reviews and Audits Handbook* by Charles P. Hollocker (New York: John Wiley & Sons, 1990).
- *Software Inspection Process* by Susan H. Strauss and Robert G. Ebenau (New York: McGraw-Hill, 1994).

ADDITIONAL READING

Boehm, B. W., *Software Engineering Economics*, Englewood Cliffs, NJ: Prentice-Hall, 1981.

Dunn, Robert, *Software Defect Removal*, New York: McGraw-Hill, 1984.

Fagan, M. E., "Design and Code Inspections to Reduce Errors in Program Development," *IBM Systems Journal*, Vol. 15, No. 3, 1976.

Yourdon, Edward, *Structured Walkthroughs*, Englewood Cliffs, NJ: Prentice-Hall, 1989.

Chapter 4

Testing

THE GOALS OF testing are to find defects and to verify that the software meets its requirements as perceived by the user. It is unfortunate that, in many cases, the testing program is actually aimed at showing that the software, as produced, runs as it is written. That is far short of the real goal of a sound testing program. Testing that is not based on challenging requirements compliance is generally a waste of time.

It has been shown that the cost of finding and correcting a defect goes up dramatically with the length of time the defect exists. That is especially true in the case of design and requirements defects. When a test program merely shows that the software runs, the design and requirements defects are going to come up in the acceptance and operation phases of the SLC. The user or customer is going to discover that the system received is not the system desired. The software will have to go back through large portions of the SDLC, and the costs will be significant.

An alternative to correcting defects is to accept the system as is and live with it or to modify the system while it is being used. Those, too, are expensive situations. The final alternatives are to throw out the system and start over or just abandon the whole project altogether. None of these "alternatives" is especially attractive. The answer seems to be to generate a testing program that will exercise the software against its requirements in such a way as to uncover as many defects as possible as soon as possible in the SDLC.

The types of testing that will be covered here are unit, module, integration, user or acceptance, and regression testing. These tests follow the natural progression of the SLC and lead from one into the next. As the testing progresses, the emphasis shifts slightly from the pure defect search to a more sophisticated demonstration of the requirements. Early testing intends to exercise as many of the software paths as is practical to find mistakes in coding, errors in design, and so on. As the SDLC matures, there is less opportunity to exercise all paths of the software, so the concentration is on the integration of the modules and subsystems into the whole and the exercise of the growing entity against the requirements. The basic goal remains the finding of defects, but there is reliance on the earlier testing for the finer, internal details of each module. Later testing deals with the system itself and its interfaces with the outside, as defined in the requirements.

It must be remembered that all testing is designed to challenge the software implementation of the approved requirements. In straightforward data processing applications this task is uncomplicated. In applications such as client-server, graphical user interfaces, or distributed processing, the approach becomes much more sophisticated. But whatever the application, the underlying rule remains requirements-based testing. The quality control practitioner must be well versed in the types of applications being tested. To expect a practitioner with specific experience in testing traditional accounting systems to step in and immediately be successful at testing a distributed processing, imbedded real-time software system is asking too much. The quality assurance practitioner will recognize such a situation as a training requirement and recommend that the tester be given the proper training before being assigned the new testing task.

The testing program begins in the requirements phase and, effectively, never ends. The regression tests continue for as long as there are changes and enhancements being made to the system. Figure 4.1 depicts this concept. Planning for such a long-lived effort must also begin in the requirements phase and be updated at each milestone along the way. The planning will include not only the tests to be run but also the resources needed, including people, hardware, support software, and scheduling.

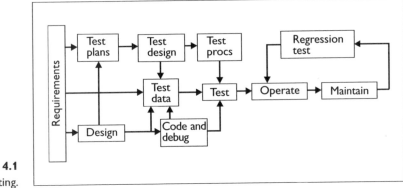

Figure 4.1
SLC testing.

4.1 Types of testing

The four most common types of testing are unit testing, module testing, integration testing, and user or acceptance testing. The tests may have different names in different organizations, but the types are basically the same.

4.1.1 Unit testing

Unit testing, the most basic type of software testing, ignores the concept that document reviews are really a type of testing. Unit testing is usually conducted by the individual producer.

Unit testing is primarily a debugging activity that concentrates on the removal of coding mistakes. It is part and parcel with the coding activity itself. Even though unit testing is conducted almost as a part of the day-to-day development activity, there must be some level of planning for it. The programmer should document at least the test data and cases he or she plans to use and the results expected from each test. Part of each walkthrough or inspection of the software should be dedicated to the review of the unit test plans so that peers can be sure the programmer has given thought to the test needs at that level.

It is worth reiterating the tenet that the tests run must be oriented to finding defects in the software, not to showing that the software runs as it is written. Further, the defects found will include not only mistakes in the coding of the unit, but design and even requirements inadequacies or outright mistakes. Even though the unit is the smallest individually compilable portion of the software system, its interfaces and data manipulation can point out wide-reaching defects. Informal though it may be, the unit testing activity is the first chance to see some of the software in action.

It can be seen that the rule of finding defects, not showing that software runs, could be in jeopardy here. In fact, a tradeoff is in play with having programmers test their own software. The expense, in both time and personnel, to introduce an independent tester at this point usually offsets the danger of inadequate testing. With high-quality peer reviews and good, though informal, documentation of the tests and their results, the risk is reduced to a low level. Software quality practitioners in their audits of the UDF and their reviews of the testing program as a whole will also pay close attention to the unit test plans and results.

4.1.2 Module testing

Module testing is a combination of debugging and integration. It is sometimes called *glass box testing* (or *white box testing*), because the tester has good visibility into the structure of the software and frequently has access to the actual source code with which to develop the test strategies. As integration proceeds, the visibility into the actual code is diminished.

As units are integrated into their respective modules, the testing moves appropriately from a unit testing—that is, debugging—mode into the more rigorous module testing mode. Module integration and testing examine the functional entities of the system. Each module is assigned some specific function of the software system to perform. As the units that make up the module are brought together into that functional unit, the module tests are run.

The testing program becomes somewhat more rigorous at the module level because the individual programmer is not now the primary tester. There will be in place a more detailed test plan, sets of data and test cases, and expected results.

The recording of defects is also more comprehensive at this stage of the test program. Defects are recorded in defect history logs, and regularized test reports are prepared. As they are found, the defects are fed back into the code and unit test phase for correction. Each defect is tracked from its finding and reporting through its correction and retest. The results of the correction are monitored and controlled by the configuration management system that is begun at this point in the SLC. That is important, since many of the errors that have been made and defects that have been discovered will affect the design and requirements documentation.

Most of the minor coding mistakes will have been caught and corrected in the unit testing process. The defects that are being found in the module tests are more global in nature, tending to affect multiple units and modules. Defects in interfaces and data structures are common, but a significant number of the defects will involve deficiencies in the design and requirements. As those deficiencies come to light and are corrected, the design and requirements baselines will change.

It is critical to the rest of the SLC that close control of the evolving documents be maintained. If the corrections to the defects found in the test program are allowed to change the products of earlier SLC phases without proper control and documentation, the software system quickly can get out of control. When a requirement or the design changes without commensurate modification to the rest of the system, there will come a time when the various pieces do not fit together, and it will not be clear which versions of the units and modules are correct.

Software quality practitioners will have reviewed the test plans and the rest of the documentation prior to the module testing. Software quality practitioners are also expected to review the results of the testing. Their reviews ensure that defects will be recorded, tracked, resolved, and configuration-managed.

4.1.3 Integration testing

Integration testing may be considered to have officially begun when the modules begin to be tested together. This type of testing sometimes is referred to as *gray box testing*, referring to the limited visibility into the software and its structure. As integration proceeds, gray box testing approaches *black box testing*, which is more nearly pure function testing, with no reliance on knowledge of the software structure or the software itself.

As modules pass their individual tests, they are brought together into functional groups and tested. Testing of the integrated modules is designed to find latent defects as well as interface and database defects. Because testing up to this point has been of individual modules, several types of defects cannot be detected. Such things as database interference, timing conflicts, interface mismatches, memory overlaps, and so on, are found only when the modules are forced to work together in integrated packages.

Integration testing uses the same sorts of conditions and data as the individual module tests. Valid data and messages are input, as are invalid conditions and situations. The test designer must be creative in coming up with valid combinations of possible circumstances but with illegal or invalid conditions. How the integrated software responds to those situations is noted, as well as the software's performance with valid inputs.

Integration testing is the level at which the quality control practitioner or tester begins to see differences between traditional systems and client-server or distributed processing applications. The greatly increased sets of inputs and initial conditions require some more elaborate testing schemes such as record and playback, automated test generation, software characterization, data equivalence, and sampling.

The reporting of test results is important in the integration test period. How the software responds is recorded and analyzed so corrections can be made that fix the defect but do not introduce new defects somewhere else. Error and defect logs should be maintained for trend analysis that can point to particularly vulnerable portions of the software and its development. Those portions can then receive additional testing to ferret out deep-seated anomalies and improper responses. Close control must be maintained of the configuration of the software system through this period so that all changes are properly documented and tracked. It is in this time frame that many software systems get out of hand and accounting is lost as to which version of which unit, module, or subsystem is the proper one to use at any point.

It is the integration test phase that will uncover many hidden defects with the design and requirements. Formal reviews and less formal walkthroughs and inspections have been used to find many of the design and requirements defects. But as the software is put into use in an increasingly realistic manner, other defects may surface that were beyond the depth of the earlier defect-finding efforts. As defects are found in the design or requirements, they must be corrected and changes to the earlier documents made. That in turn may necessitate rework of design, code, and earlier testing. Finding such serious defects at this point is expensive but less so than finding the defects in the operations phase. Thus, every effort must be made to maximize the defect-finding capabilities of the integration tests.

An important role for the software quality practitioner in this effort is the review of the integration test plans, cases, scenarios, and procedures. Software quality practitioners should make every effort to ensure that the integration tests cover the full range of capabilities of the integrated set of modules. Review of the test results and the decisions made on the basis of those results also should be reviewed and approved by the software quality practitioner before testing progresses beyond the integration phase.

4.1.4 User or acceptance testing

User testing is intended primarily to demonstrate that the software complies with its requirements. This type of testing is black box testing, which does not rely on knowledge of the software or the structure of the software. Acceptance testing is intended to challenge the software in relation to its satisfaction of the functional requirements.

Acceptance tests are planned based on the requirements approved by the user or customer. All testing up to this time has been oriented to finding defects in the software. Earlier tests also were based on the requirements, but they were designed to show that the software did not comply in one fashion or another to the requirements. By the time the acceptance testing stage is reached, the software should be in a sufficiently defect-free state to permit the emphasis to change.

One important aspect of the acceptance test is that, whenever possible, it is performed by actual intended users of the system. In that way, while it is being shown that the software complies with its requirements, there is still the opportunity to introduce anomalous user actions that have not yet been encountered. Persons unfamiliar with the system may enter data in incorrect, though technically permitted, ways. They may push the wrong buttons or the correct buttons in an incorrect sequence. The software's response to those unexpected or incorrect situations is important to the user—the system should not collapse due to human mistakes. The overriding requirement for every system is that it perform its intended function. That means that if incorrect actions or data are presented, the system will not just abort but will tell the user what has been done wrong and will provide the user the opportunity to retry the action or input. Invalid data received from outside sources also should be treated in such a manner as to prevent collapse of the system.

Another important consideration of an acceptance test is verification that the new software does not cause changes to workflow or user responsibilities that have been overlooked. While it may be shown that the software performs exactly as expected, the associated human-factor changes may make the system difficult to use or cause negative effects on the related work of the users.

The acceptance or user test is usually the last step before the user or customer takes possession of the software system. It is important that software quality and configuration management practitioners play active roles in the review and execution of the tests and the change management of the system during this period. Software quality practitioners may even have performed the full execution of the acceptance test as a dry run prior to the release of the system for the user operation of the test. Configuration management of the system at this time is critical to the eventual delivery of the exact system that passes the acceptance test.

4.1.5 Special types of tests

Four types of tests may be considered to fall into the "special" category. These tests are planned and documented according to the same rules and standards as the other types of tests, but they have specific applications. The four major special tests are regression tests, stress tests, recovery tests, and back-out and restoration tests.

Regression tests

Regression tests show that modifications to one part of the system have not invalidated some other part. Regression tests usually are a subset of the user or acceptance test. They are maintained for verification that changes made as a result of defects or enhancements during operation do not result in failures in other parts of the system. Regression tests are an abbreviated revalidation of the entire system using generally valid data to show that the parts that were operating correctly before the changes are still performing as required.

Discussions "around the water cooler" indicate that as many as 50% of all changes made to a software system result in the introduction of new defects. This figure may be low or high, but there is a significant risk to the introduction of corrections. Some, of course, are errors in the change being made, such as coding errors and change design mistakes. Others, however, come from unexpected interactions with subsystems other than the one being modified. A change to the way a database variable is updated in one module may affect the time at which another module should read that variable in its own computations.

Close configuration management control and analysis of changes and their impact on the system as a whole are imperative. Software quality practitioners must be sure that a change control board or equivalent function is involved in all change activity during both integration testing and the operation phases of the SLC. That protects the integrity of the baseline system itself and helps ensure that changes are being made to the correct versions of the affected software. Delivery of the proper versions of the modifications is also a function of configuration management that software quality practitioners must monitor.

Stress tests

Stress tests cover the situations that occur when the software is pushed to or beyond its limits of required capability. Such situations as the end of the day, when the software is required to recognize that 00:00:00 is later than 23:59:59, must be challenged. The rollover of the year field also is a situation ripe for testing. Will the software realize that the years "00" and "000" are later than the years "99" and "999," respectively?

Other stress situations occur when the software is presented with the full number of transactions it is expected to handle plus one or two more. What happens when transaction $n + 1$ is presented? Does one of the existing transactions get overwritten? Is there a weighting algorithm that selects some transaction for replacement? Is the new transaction merely ignored?

Still another case is the situation in which the software is run for a long time without interruption. Such a case could easily expose flaws in housekeeping or initialization routines.

Stress tests are an important part of any test program. The types of stress that might be exercised will become apparent as the software develops and the testers understand its construction more clearly. The requirements statement should spell out a valid way of handling these and other situations. The compliance of the software with the requirement is to be challenged.

Recovery tests

Most data centers have recovery procedures for the repair of data on a damaged disk or tape, and they also consider the case of operator errors that may invalidate some of the data being processed.

Recovery testing is conducted when a hardware fault or operating error damages the software or the data. This type of testing is critical to the confidence of the user when a data or software restoration has been performed.

Often, restoration testing can be accomplished by using the regression test software. In other cases, the full acceptance test might be required to restore confidence in the software and its data.

Back-out and restoration tests

To back out and restore is the decision to remove a new software system in favor of the older version that it replaced. Needless to say, developers usually are embarrassed by such an action. It is recognition that the new system was insufficiently tested or was so error-ridden that it was worse to use than the old system.

In a back-out and restoration situation, the new system is removed from production, any new database conditions are restored to the way they would have been under the old system, and the old system itself is restarted. In the least critical case, the database used by the new system is the same as that of the old system. More often than not, the new system provides expanded database content as well as improved processing. When the contents of the new database must be condensed back into the form of the old database, care must be taken to restore the data to the form in which the old system would have used it.

The testing required includes at least the acceptance test of the old system, which often is augmented by the running of the most recent set of regression tests used for the old system. Clearly, there must have been some planning for back-out and replacement when the new system was installed. The old system normally would have been archived, but the saving of the acceptance test and the regression tests must also have been part of the archiving process.

It is rare that a newly installed system is so badly flawed that it must be replaced. However, it is the responsibility of the quality practitioner to make management aware of the threat, no matter how remote.

4.2 Test planning and conduct

Testing is like any other project. It must be planned, designed, documented, reviewed, and conducted.

4.2.1 Test plans

Because proper testing is based on the software requirements, test planning starts during the requirements phase and continues throughout the SDLC.

As the requirements for the software system are prepared, the original planning for the test program also gets underway. Each requirement eventually will have to be validated during the acceptance testing. The plans for how that requirement will be demonstrated are laid right at the start. In fact, one of the ways the measurable and testable criteria for the requirements are determined is by having to plan for the test of each requirement. The test planning at this point is necessarily high level, but the general thrust of the acceptance demonstration can be laid out along with the approaches to be used for the intermediate testing.

Requirements traceability matrices (RTMs), which track the requirements though design and down to the code that implements them, are used to prepare test matrices. These matrices track the requirements to the tests that demonstrate software compliance with the requirements. Figure 4.2 is an example of what a test traceability matrix might look like. Each requirement, both functional and interface, is traced to the primary (P) test that demonstrates its correct implementation. In an ideal test situation, each requirements will be challenged by one specific test. That is rarely the case, but redundant testing of some requirements and the failure to test others are quickly apparent in the RTM. Figure 4.2 also indicates other tests in which the requirements are involved (I). In this way, there is some indication of the interrelationships between the various requirements. As the software matures and requirements are modified, this matrix can offer clues to unexpected and usually undesirable results if a requirement is changed or eliminated.

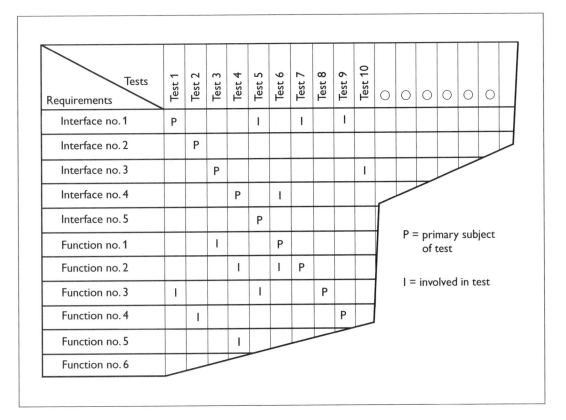

Figure 4.2 Requirements traceability matrix.

Conflicts between requirements can sometimes be indicated in the RTM, as the I fields are completed. A common example of requirements conflict is the situation that calls for high-speed processing and efficient use of memory, as in the case of real-time, imbedded software. The fastest software is written in highly linear style with little looping or calling of subroutines. Efficient use of memory calls for tight loops, subroutine calls, and other practices that tend to consume more processing time.

Figure 4.2 is an example of an RTM at the system or black box testing level since the requirements are noted as functions. As the SDLC progresses, so does the planning for the testing, and the RTM becomes more and more detailed until each specific required characteristic of the software has been challenged in at least one test at some level. Not every requirement can or should be tested at every level of the test program. Compliance with some can be tested at the white box level; some cannot be fully challenged until the black box testing is in progress.

The RTM is also important as the requirements evolve throughout the development of the software system. As the requirements that form the basis for testing are changed, added, or eliminated, each change likewise is going to affect the test program. Just as the requirements are the basis for everything that follows in the development of the software, so, too, are they the drivers for the whole test program.

Some items of test planning are necessarily left until later in the SDLC. Such things as the bases for regression testing are determined during the acceptance test period as the final requirements baseline is determined. Likewise, as new requirements are determined, so are the plans for testing those requirements.

Even though some parts of the test planning will be done later, the overall test plan is completed during the requirements phase. It is also, therefore, one of the subjects of the system requirements review at the end of the requirements phase. As the approved requirements are released for the design phase activities, the approved test plans are released to the test design personnel for the beginning of the design of test cases and procedures. Figure 4.3 depicts the flow of testing, starting with the test plan and culminating in the test reports.

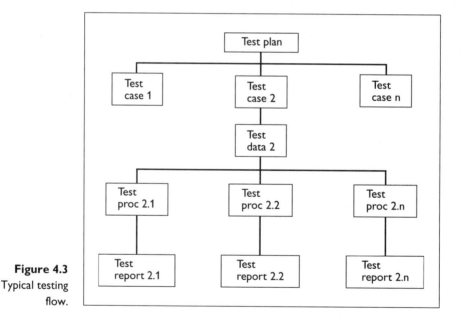

Figure 4.3
Typical testing
flow.

4.2.2 Test cases

The first step in function testing, and often in input/output testing, is to construct situations that mimic actual use of the software. These situations, or test cases, should represent actual tasks that the software user might perform.

Once the test cases have been developed, the software requirements that are involved in each test case are identified. A check is made against the RTM to be sure that each requirement is included in at least one test case. If a test case is too large or contains too many requirements, it should be divided into subtest cases or scenarios. Test cases (and scenarios) should be small enough to be manageable. Limited size makes sure that errors uncovered can be isolated with minimum delay to and effect on the balance of the testing.

Consider the case of testing the software in a point-of-sale terminal for a convenience store. The store stocks both grocery and fuel products. The test cases might be as follow.

1. *Open the store the very first time.* This would test the requirements dealing with the variety of stock items to be sold, their prices, and the taxes to be applied to each item. It also includes requirements covering the setting of the initial inventory levels.

2. *Sell products.* Sales of various products might be further divided into test scenarios such as:

   Sell only fuel. This scenario includes those requirements that deal with pump control, fuel levels in the tanks, and the prices and volume of fuel sold. It also tests those requirements that cause the sale to be recorded and the register tape to be printed.

   Sell only grocery items. Here, the sales events are keyed in on the terminal rather than read from a pump register, so there are requirements being tested that are different from the preceding scenario. The sales recording requirements are probably the same.

   Sell both fuel and grocery items. This scenario, building on the first two, causes the previous requirements to be met in a single sale. There may be additional requirements that prevent the keying of a grocery sale to adversely affect the operation of the pump and vice versa. Other requirements might deal with the interaction of pump register readings with key-entered sales data. Further, a test of the ability to add pump sale charges to keyed sales charges is encountered.

3. *Restock the store.* After sufficient items have been sold, it becomes necessary to restock shelves and refill fuel tanks. This test case might also deal with he changing of prices and taxes and the modification of inventory levels. It can be seen as an extension of the requirements tested in test case 1.

4. *Close the store for the last time.* Even the best businesses eventually close. This test case exercises the requirements involved in determining and reporting the value of the remaining inventory. Some of these same requirements might be used in tallying weekly or other periodic inventory levels for business history and planning tasks.

Should comparison of the test cases and scenarios with the RTM reveal leftover requirements, additional situations must be developed until each requirement is included in at least one test case or scenario.

Although this has been a simple situation, the example shows how test cases and scenarios can be developed using the actual anticipated use of the software as a basis.

4.2.3 Test procedures

As design proceeds, the test plans are expanded into specific test cases, test scenarios, and step-by-step procedures.

Test procedures are step-by-step instructions that spell out the specific steps that will be taken in the execution of the test being run. They tell which buttons to push, what data to input, what responses to look for, and what to do if the expected response is not received. The procedures also tell the tester how to process the test outputs to determine if the test passed or failed. The test procedures are tied to the test cases and scenarios that actually exercise each approved requirement.

The software quality practitioner reviews the test cases and scenarios, the test data, and the test procedures to ensure that they all go together and follow the overall test plan and that they fully exercise all the requirements for the software system. Figure 4.4 is a sample test procedure form.

4.2.4 Test data input

Input of test data is the key to testing and comes from a variety of sources. Traditionally, test data inputs have been provided by test driver software or tables of test data that are input at the proper time by an executive test control module specially written for the purpose. These methods are acceptable when the intent is to provide a large number of data values to check repetitive calculations or transaction processors. The use of these methods does diminish the interactive capability of the test environment. The sequential data values are going to be presented regardless of the result of the preceding processing.

TEST C/S/T ____________ TEST DIRECTOR ________________ DATE & TIME __________

HARDWARE CONFIG ID ____________________ SOFTWARE CONFIG ID ______________

SET UP __________ INITIALIZE ____________ TERMINATE ___________ RESTORE ________

	PROCEDURES	RESULTS		PASS / FAIL	
NO.	ACTION	EXPECTED	ACTUAL	P	STR

Figure 4.4 Sample test procedure form.

As the software system being tested becomes more complex, particularly in the case of interactive computing, a more flexible type of test environment is needed. *Simulators*, which are test software packages that perform in the same manner as some missing piece of hardware or other software, frequently are used. Simulators can be written to represent anything from a simple interfacing software unit to a complete spacecraft or radar installation. As data are received from the simulator and the results returned to it, the simulator is programmed to respond with new input based on the results of the previous calculations of the system under test.

Another type of test software is a *stimulator*, which represents an outside software or hardware unit that presents input data independently from the activities of the system under test. An example might be the input of a warning message that interrupts the processing of the system under test and forces it to initiate emergency measures to deal with the warning.

The final step in the provision of interactive inputs is the use of a keyboard or a terminal that is being operated by a test user. Here the responses to the processing by the system under test are, subject to the constraints of the test procedures, the same as they will be in full operation.

Each type of data input fulfills a specific need as called out in the test documentation. The software quality practitioner will review the various forms of test data inputs to be sure that they meet the needs of the test cases and that the proper provisions have been made for the acquisition of the simulators, stimulators, live inputs, and so on.

4.2.5 **Expected results**

Documentation of expected results is necessary so that actual results can be evaluated to demonstrate test success or failure. The bottom line in any test program is the finding of defects and the demonstration that the software under test satisfies its requirements. Unless the expected results of each test are documented, there is no way to tell if the test has done what was intended by the test designer. Each test case is expected to provide the test data to be input for it. In the same way, each test case must provide the correct answer that should result from the input of the data.

Expected results may be of various sorts. The most common, of course, is simply the answer expected when a computation operates on a given set of numbers. Another type of expected result is the lighting or extinguishing of a light on a console. Many combinations of these two results may also occur, such as the appearance of a particular screen display, the starting of a motor, the initiation of an allied software system, or even the abnormal end of the system under test when a particular illegal function has been input, for example, an invalid password into a software security system.

It is the responsibility of the software quality practitioner to review the test documentation to ensure that each test has an associated set of expected results. Also present must be a description of any processing of the actual results so they can be compared with the expected results and a pass/fail determination made for the test.

4.2.6 **Test analysis**

Test analysis involves more than pass/fail determination. Analyses of the expected versus actual results of each test provide the pass or fail determination for that test. There may be some intermediate processing necessary before the comparison can be made, however. In a case in which previous real sales data is used to check out a new inventory system, some adjustment to the actual results may be necessary to allow for the dating of the input data or the absence of some allied software system that it was not cost effective to simulate. In any case, the pass/fail criteria are applied to the expected and received results and the success of the test determined.

Other beneficial analysis of the test data is possible and appropriate. As defects are found during the testing or as certain tests continue to fail, clues may arise as to larger defects in the system or the test program than are apparent in just a single test case or procedure. As test data are analyzed over time, trends may appear that show certain modules to be defect prone and in need of special attention before the test program continues. Other defects that might surfaces include inadequate housekeeping of common data areas, inappropriate limits on input or intermediate data values, unstated but implied requirements that need to be added and specifically addressed, design errors, sections of software that are never used or cannot be reached, and erroneous expected results.

Software quality practitioners can play an important role in the review and analysis of test results. It is not as important that software quality practitioners actually perform the analysis as it is that they ensure adequate analysis by persons with the proper technical knowledge. This responsibility of software quality practitioners is discharged through careful review of the test results and conclusions as those results are published.

4.2.7 Test tools

Many automated and manual test tools are available to assist in the various test activities. A major area for the application of tools is in the area of test data provision. Commercially available software packages can help in the creation and insertion of test data. Test data generators can, on the basis of parameters provided to them, create tables, strings, or files of fixed data. Those fixed data can, in turn, be input either by the test data generator itself or by any of several test input tools. General-purpose simulators can be programmed to behave like certain types of hardware or software systems or units. Stimulators that provide synchronous or asynchronous interrupts or messages are available. It is more likely, though, that most of these tools will be created inhouse so they can be tailored to the test application at hand.

Another area in which tools are available is that of data recording. Large-scale event recorders often are used to record long or complicated interactive test data for future repeats of tests or for detailed test data analysis. In association with the data recorders are general- and specific-purpose data reduction packages. Large volumes of data are often sorted and categorized so that individual analyses can be made of particular areas of interest. Some very powerful analysis packages are commercially available, providing computational and graphic capabilities that can be of great assistance in the analysis of test results and trend determination.

Other valuable tools in the test area are *path analyzers*. These tools monitor the progress of the test program and track the exercising of the various paths through the software. While it is impossible to execute every path through a software system of more than a few steps, it is possible to exercise every decision point and each segment of code. (A *segment* in this context means the code between two successive decision points.) A path analyzer will show all software that has been executed at least once, point out any software that has not been exercised, and clearly indicate those code segments that cannot be reached at all (e.g., a subroutine that never gets called or a decision point that, for some reason, cannot take a branch).

Many of these tools are commercially available. Most applications of them, however, are in the form of tools specifically designed and built for a given project or application. Some development organizations will custom-build test completeness packages that software quality practitioners will use prior to acceptance testing or, perhaps, system release. Whatever their source or application, test tools are becoming more and more necessary as software systems grow in size, complexity, and criticality. Software quality practitioners should monitor the application of test tools to be sure that all appropriate use is being made of them and that they are being used correctly.

4.2.8 Reviewing the test program

An important part of the software quality practitioner's activity is the review of the test program. As discussed in Section 3.3.3, review of the test documentation is important. In fact, the full test program should be reviewed regularly for status, sufficiency, and success. Such reviews are expected to be an integral part of the major phase-end reviews, as explained in Section 3.1.2. It is reasonable to hold less formal, inprocess reviews of the test program as testing progresses and more of the software system is involved.

The development test documentation permits this review of the whole test approach as it is formulated. Without a documented approach to the problems of testing the software, the testing tends to become haphazard and undisciplined. There is a strong tendency on the part of many project managers to commit to a firm delivery date. If the project gets behind schedule, the slippage is usually made up by shortening the test phase to fit the time remaining. This also happens in the case of budget problems. A well-planned and well-documented test program reduces the temptation to shorten the testing effort to make up for other problems. Having a software quality practitioner review and approve the documentation of the test program adds even more impetus to maintain the integrity of the program.

The documentation of the test program should extend all the way to the unit and module tests. While those tests tend to be more informal than later tests, they, too, should have test cases and specific test data recorded in, at least, the UDF. The results of the unit and module tests also should be recorded. Software quality practitioners will review the results of the unit and module tests to decide, in part, whether the modules are ready for integration. There may even be cases in which the module tests are sufficient to form part of the acceptance test.

4.3 Who does the testing

Until recently, the common preference for who actually performed the testing favored the independent tester. While this is still valid in some very critical software situations, the definition of *independent* has been changing for most applications.

On the basis of the concept that everyone is responsible for his or her own work and that this responsibility also applies to groups, the task of testing is being returned to the developers. That is not to say that programmers should test all their own work, but rather that the development group is responsible for the quality of the software that they deliver.

A programmer should test only that software for which he or she has sole responsibility. Once the work of more than one person is to be tested, an independent tester, that is, someone other than the persons involved, should carry out the testing. Even at this level, though, the testers should come from within the development group responsible for the full set of software. Outside testers are necessary only at the full software system test level when all the developers have an investment in the software.

Unit, module, and most integration testing are the proper tasks of the development organization. This is consistent with total quality concepts and the idea that persons (or in this case organization) are responsible for the quality of their own work. The very early testing is in the form of debugging, and as the unit tests cover more of the software, they flow into module tests. Module tests, too, are primarily debugging in nature. Even the initial integration tests can be thought of as advanced debugging, although this is more of an organizational decision than an industrywide convention.

The characteristic of debugging that separates it from rigorous testing is that defects are generally fixed on the spot without much formal change control. At whatever time the organization institutes some level of change control, the testing is usually considered out of the debugging process and into rigorous testing. That is not to say that there is no configuration control up to this point. Configuration control is already in effect on the documentation. Any change that affects the requirements or design must be processed formally to maintain the integrity of the documentation and the system as a whole. Changes that merely fix mistakes in the code can be made with minimum control at this stage, since the only elements involved are individual units or modules or small groups of two or three closely interfacing modules prior to actual integration.

There should, however, be at least an audit trail of the changes maintained in the UDF. This trail will be used for error and defect history analysis as the development proceeds. Software quality practitioners should monitor the testing at the unit and module levels to be sure that such an audit trail is provided. Software quality practitioners are also an appropriate resource for the error and defect history analysis. Conclusions reached as a result of the analysis should be fed back, as improvements, into the development process.

As the time for full-scale integration and system testing arrives, a test team that is organizationally independent from the producers should take over the testing. Because the goal of the test program is to find defects, the objectivity of an independent test team greatly enhances the quality of the testing. The independent testers will perform the testing tasks all the way to user or acceptance testing. This team is probably the group that produced the formal test program documents. User or acceptance testing should be performed by the users themselves, preferably in the user's environment, to help ensure that the software meets the user's expectations, as well as the officially approved requirements. Table 4.1 suggests appropriate testers for each type of testing. As each organization's test program matures, the identification of the testers for each type of test will be based on the organization's experience and testing approach.

Type of testing	Tester
Debugging	Programmer
Unit testing	Programmer
Module (or object) testing	Programmer
Module (or object) integration testing	Third party
Subsystem and system integration testing	Third party
System testing	Developer test team
User/acceptance testing	User test team

Table 4.1
Who tests what

Regression tests are conducted by many different persons involved in the SLC. The developers will regressively test changes to modules and subsystems as they make changes in response to trouble reports generated during formal testing or maintenance. The test team also will have occasion to use regression testing as they verify that new modules or subsystems do not adversely affect the system as a whole. Software quality practitioners can even use regressive testing techniques as they perform some of their audit and review tasks.

The software quality practitioner's primary role in the testing process, aside from reviewing and approving the test documents, is to monitor the testing as it progresses. The software quality practitioner will audit the tests against their plans and procedures and report the status of the test program to management. There are added benefits if software quality practitioners have been doing more than just cursory reviews of the documentation as it has been produced. The cross-fertilization of the technical knowledge of the system and the test planning for the system can produce better results in both areas.

4.4 Summary

Testing has as its goals the finding of defects and verifying that the software meets its requirements. The cost of finding and correcting a defect goes up dramatically with the length of time the defect is present. The types of testing are unit, module, integration, user or acceptance, and regression testing.

Unit testing is primarily a debugging activity that concentrates on the removal of coding mistakes. Module integration and testing examine the functional entities of the system. As modules pass their individual tests, they are brought into increasingly larger functional groups. Testing of the integrated modules is designed to find latent defects as well as interface and database defects. User testing is intended primarily to demonstrate that the software complies with its approved requirements, as they are perceived by the user. Regression tests usually are a subset of the user or acceptance tests. They are maintained for the verification that changes made to the software do not result in failures in other parts of the system.

As the requirements for the system are prepared, the original planning for the test program also is started. During software design, the test plans are expanded into specific test cases, scenarios, and step-by-step test procedures.

Expected results are an important part of the test procedures. Unless the expected results of each test are documented, there is no way to judge whether the test has performed as intended. Analyses of the expected versus actual results of each test provide the pass or fail determination for that test.

A necessary part of the software quality practitioner's activities is the review of the test program. The software quality practitioner's additional role is to monitor the testing as it progresses. The practitioner will audit the tests against their plans and procedures and report the status of the test program to management.

Tests follow the natural progression of the SLC. The testing program begins in the requirements phase and, effectively, never ends, since regression tests continue for as long as there are changes and enhancements being made to the software system.

4.5 The next step

Testing takes on many forms and must adapt to every type of software, from traditional data processing applications through embedded real-time systems to client-server and distributed systems. Starting points for your testing efforts could be the following texts:

- *Software Testing* by Marc Roper (New York: McGraw-Hill, 1994).
- *Testing Very Big Systems* by David M. Marks (New York: McGraw-Hill, 1992).

ADDITIONAL READING

Beizer, Boris B., *Software Systems Testing and Quality Assurance*, New York: Van Nostrand Reinhold, 1984.

Beizer, Boris B., *Black Box Testing: Techniques for Functional Testing of Software Systems*, New York: John Wiley & Sons, 1995.

De Millo, Richard A., et al., *Software Testing and Evaluation*, Menlo Park, CA: Benjamin/Cummings, 1987.

Howden, William E., *Functional Program Testing and Analysis*, New York: McGraw-Hill, 1987.

Myers, G., *The Art of Software Testing*, New York: John Wiley & Sons, 1979.

Perry, William, *Effective Methods for Software Testing*, New York: John Wiley & Sons, 1995.

Chapter 5

Defect analysis

MOST ORGANIZATIONS use the term *quality* to mean no or few defects. Some consider quality to mean meeting users' or customers' expectations. In the context of this book, both uses are correct. Any time that the software does not perform as the user expects, a defect has been encountered. It matters little to the user whether the problem is a coding error, a missed requirement, or just a function that would be nice to have but is absent.

It is no secret that defects occur in the SLC from the beginning of the concept phase through the final removal of the software system from use. It is expected that each defect found be corrected. The recording and tracking of defects ensure that all defects found are, in fact, addressed. Defect analysis applies to all defects and is intended to lead to the correction of current deficiencies and the elimination of defects in the future. Analysis of defects is the primary road to defect reduction. It can show where we started, where we are, and where we are going.

Defect analysis is the bridge between the product-oriented software *quality control* (QC) activities and the process-oriented software *quality assurance* (QA) activities of the SQS. Defect analysis is a combination of detecting product flaws, so they can be removed, and the analysis of defect and error data, so future defects can be prevented. Defect reporting, tracking, and removal are adjuncts to configuration control (see Chapter 6).

While it is useful to analyze defects in a system as it is being developed, analysis of long-term trends also should be conducted to give clues to weak areas in the software development process. An accumulating history of defect data can indicate where modifications to the software development process can be effective. It is those problem analyses that provide the bridge from QC (detecting product errors) to QA (detecting process weaknesses).

This chapter concentrates its attention on the QA application of defect analysis and the metrics that can be developed.

5.1 Analysis concepts

Defect analysis is the discipline of measuring software development and use. The measures can come from surveys, defect data, schedule and budget plans and records, system characteristics, help line usage, and so on. Each organization will discover and determine the sources of measurements best suited to its own needs and situations.

Metrics, an essential part of any SQS, are relationships between measures that turn measurement data into applicable, quality management information. However, metrics are too often merely an exercise in collecting numbers without developing any useful information. The role of the QA practitioner is to bring to decision-making, action-capable managers the information they need to beneficially affect the software development process, and metrics are useful only when they contribute to that information base.

5.1.1 Measures

A number, for example, 6 or 1,000, is not a metric. It is merely a number, usually with no information value. When we add a dimension to the number, such as *lines of code* (LOC) or *critical errors* (CEs), we have created a measure, more descriptive than a number by itself but still without significant utility. Six CEs and 1,000 LOC are both measures, but they hold no information until we relate them to something.

5.1.2 **Metrics**

In this text, a metric is defined as the ratio of, or relationship between, two measures. Thus, a defect density of 6 CEs per 1,000 LOC (KLOC) begins to take on the characteristic of information. Ratios of metrics finally reach real information status. We might compare a defect density of 6 CE/KLOC before institution of software inspections to a defect density of 2 CE/KLOC after inspections have begun.

Defect metrics are, not surprisingly, those metrics composed of measures dealing with defects. The measures might include the number of software system failures, calls made to the help line, time spent recoding after a failure, and cost of lost sales after a bad press review based on too many errors found by the reviewer. The list could go on and on. A typical defect metric is the number of problem reports closed versus the number of new problem reports recorded.

Nondefect metrics are just that: metrics that are not based on defects. Budget overruns, schedule shortfall, size of the software system in LOC or function points, module complexity, cost of computer time, and the like, are representative of nondefect measures. Nondefect measures are combined to develop nondefect metrics. An example of a nondefect metric might be LOC developed per person-month.

5.1.3 **Product analysis**

Product analysis is the first area for most organizations to begin to measure. Error frequency, software product size, development cost, number of tests run successfully, and the like, are often the kinds of things measured in the beginning. Most of these *product metrics* can be developed directly from the *software trouble reports* (STRs) and project planning documentation. Product metrics deal with the attributes of a product, defect characteristics, and other data about the product.

Using product metrics, the software QC practitioner can locate error-prone areas of the code, design weaknesses, testing flaws, and so on. Product metrics also help the QA practitioner to identify efforts that can beneficially affect the specific product being analyzed. In the longer run, product analysis will build up a body of information that can be applied to process-oriented analyses.

5.1.4 **Process analysis**

It is the goal of the software QA practitioner to improve the process by which the various software products are produced. Process understanding and improvement depend heavily on the results of product analysis. As each product is reviewed, tested, operated, and maintained, a history of its defects and changes can be kept. By itself, the record of analysis of defect and nondefect data for a single product will not be especially useful on a process basis. It is the continuing analysis of data on multiple products that leads to the body of information that describes the process. At this point, the software QA practitioner can begin to describe the process and its behavior.

Analysis of defect detection methods and their results can give insight into their value. Comparing when and how defects are detected as opposed to when they were introduced into the software products is one view of that process. Comparison of budget and schedule actual values with estimates reflects on the estimation and management processes. Analysis of defect types gives insights into the development process strengths and weaknesses. Tracking the levels of the costs of the quality program versus its effects provides information quality process. Once an understanding of the behavior of the process is achieved, intentional modification to the process will result in identifiable changes in the products it produces. In that way, the software QA practitioner is able to suggest beneficial process changes based on data and information rather than on guesses.

For example, if defect records show that walkthroughs are finding more defects than testing, the quality practitioner may do further research to determine if the walkthroughs are finding most of the defects and that fewer exist for testing to uncover, or if the testing process is not sufficiently robust.

5.2 Locating data

The collection of data, in the form of measures, is a necessary task if we are to develop metrics. Most data come from easily available sources, such as budget and schedule reports, defect reports, personnel counts, help line call records, and the like. The data usually reflect defect experience, project planning and status, and user response to the system.

5.2.1 Defect reporting

When software systems and programming staffs typically were small, the usual method of trouble reporting was to note the location of the defect on a listing or note pad and give it to the person responsible for repair. Documentation defects were merely marked in the margins and passed back to the author for action. As organizations have grown, and software and its defects have become more complex, those old methods are inadequate. In many cases, though, they have not been replaced with more organized, reliable techniques. It is clear that the more information that can be recorded about a particular defect, the easier it will be to solve. The older methods did not, in general, prompt the reporter for as much information as was available to be written down.

Figure 5.1 depicts a typical STR. The actual format of the form is less important than the content. Also of less importance is the medium of the form; many organizations report troubles directly online for interactive processing and broad, instant distribution.

It can be seen that the STR in Figure 5.1 is a combined document/software defect report. While many organizations maintain both a document and a software defect processing system, there is much to suggest that such a separation is unnecessary. Using the same form and then, logically, the same processing system, eliminates duplication of effort. Further, all defect reports would be in the same system and database for easier recording, tracking, and trend analysis.

The STR form shown in Figure 5.1, when used to report documentation defects, would ask for data about the specific location and the wording of the defective area. It then would call for a suggested rewording for correction of the documentation defect, in addition to the simple "what's wrong" statement. In that way, the corrector can read the trouble report and, with the suggested solution at hand, get a more positive picture of what the reviewer had in mind. This is a great deterrent to the comment "wrong" and also can help avoid the response "nothing wrong." By the inclusion of the requirement for a concise statement of the defect and a suggested solution, both the author and the reviewer would have ownership of the results.

As a tool to report software defects, the STR includes data to be provided by both the initiator (who can be anyone involved with the software throughout its life cycle) and the corrector. Not only does it call for location, circumstances, and visible data values from the initiator, it asks for classification information such as the priority of the repair, criticality of the defect, and the original source of the defect (coding error, requirements deficiency, etc.). That classification information can be correlated later and can often serve to highlight weak portions of the software development process that should receive management attention. Such correlations can also indicate, at the start of new projects, potential problem areas that should be given to more senior personnel, be targeted for tighter controls, or receive more frequent reviews and testing during development.

SOFTWARE TROUBLE REPORT

CONTROL NO. _____   PRIORITY - E H M L _____ PAGE _____ OF _____

DATE _____ TIME _____   TYPE - _____ A I L D _____

SOURCE - R D C T O _____   SEVERITY - C S M T _____

PHASE - R D C T O _____   EST: HRS _____ $ _____

METHOD - Q W I D T A U _____   ACT: HRS _____ $ _____

PROBLEM APPEARS IN:

SYSTEM _____   SUBSYSTEM _____

MODULE _____   UNIT _____

DOCUMENT _____   DOCUMENT NO. _____

PAGE NO. _____ PARA _____   LINE NO. _____

PROBLEM DESCRIPTION:

PROPOSED SOLUTION:

SUBMITTED BY _____ ORG. _____ TEL. NO. _____

PROBLEM ACCEPTED ☐   PROBLEM REJECTED ☐   PROBLEM COMBINED WITH _____

DISPOSITION:

RESPONSE BY _____ ORG. _____ TEL. NO. _____

DISPOSITION ACCEPTED ☐   DISPOSITION REJECTED ☐

Figure 5.1
Sample software
trouble report.

5.2.2 **Other data**

Other, nondefect measures are available from many sources. During development of the software system, project planning and status data are available, including budget, schedule, and size estimates (LOC, function points, pages counts, etc.).

After installation of the system, data can be collected regarding customer satisfaction, functions most used and most ignored, return on investment, requirements met or not met, and so on.

5.3 Defect repair and closure

An important aspect of the trouble report, in whatever manner it is implemented, is that it provides a means to ensure that each defect is addressed and the solution recorded. The closure of trouble reports should follow a prescribed procedure. Defects that are reported but never resolved can resurface at a later, perhaps much more damaging or expensive, point in the SLC. The software quality practitioner has the responsibility to monitor all open trouble reports and keep management informed as to their status. In that way, there is less chance for a defect to escape notice and become lost. There is also a check and balance with the developers to be sure that they are not letting defects go unheeded in favor of further development activities.

The form in Figure 5.1 provides for recording the disposition of the defect. The trouble report is not considered closed until that area has been filled in. Defects can get lost in the system if they are not tracked to their closure and reported as finished. Each organization should have standards that govern the reporting and tracking of defects. One of these standards should specify the length of time a defect may remain unaddressed before further activity is halted and the defect specifically addressed. The use of online defect recording and status reporting can make that task quite easy and give it increased visibility.

Each trouble report, for either documentation or software in general, should provide a forward reference to the formal record of disposition of the defect and its resolution. As stated, the defect reports can provide for directly recording the defect dispositions. In some organizations, there is a separate report for the disposition of a defect correction or change. One format for a separate record is the *software change notice* (SCN), shown in Figure 5.2. The SCN could be used if a separate form is required to formally implement the change. In that way, the report-fix-implement-report loop is closed, and a complete trail is formed of the treatment of each reported defect.

The closure of a trouble report usually describes the action taken to correct the defect. Of course, not all trouble reports are correct themselves. There can be instances in which what was perceived as a defect was not a defect at all. Perhaps an incorrect keystroke caused a result that looked like a software defect. The trouble report still exists, however, and even though there is no change spelled out, the report must be formally closed. As a side observation, should later correlation of defect data show a high number of "no-defect" trouble reports, some attention may be needed to the topic of defect reporting itself.

SOFTWARE CHANGE NOTICE

SCN #:	DATE:	AUTHORIZED BY:	
		INSTALLED BY:	
		CM APPROVAL:	

STR / DTR #	MODULE/ DOCUMENT TO BE CHANGED	REGRESSION TEST BY:
		PAGE _____ OF _____

Figure 5.2
Sample software
change notice.

In projects under formal *configuration management* (CM), trouble report closures that require CM processing, especially approval of the change before implementation (see Section 6.3.2), will reflect any CM action involved. The defect tracking activity will show when the defect and its planned solution were presented for CM processing, what was done, and the results. Once CM approval has been obtained, the defect returns to the regular processing path for implementation.

Figure 1.6 depicted a typical defect reporting, tracking, and closure procedure. Each organization will have some version of this procedure that is suited to its own situation, but all aspects of this procedure should be present. In some of the topics covered in this text, the breadth of application of the topic within a given organization or project is left up to the discretion of the organization or project. Defect reporting and tracking are sufficiently important topics that only the actual technique used for each of the activities is seen as discretionary. The presence of a complete defect reporting and tracking system is not optional in an effective SQS. Figure 5.3 is an example of a typical defect processing, with its forms and connections to other SQS functions.

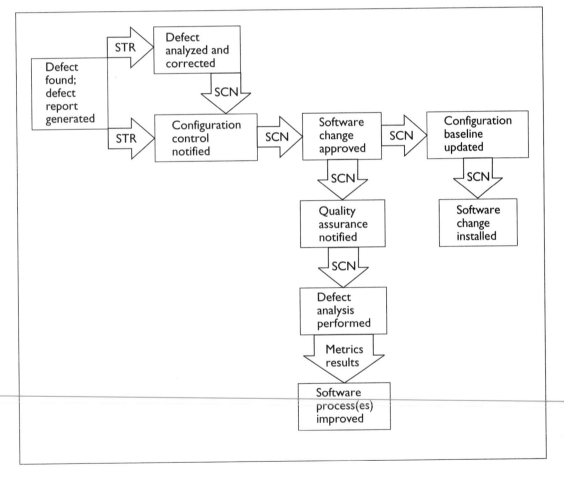

Figure 5.3   Defect processing example.

5.4 Selecting metrics

The goals of the SQS lead to questions about defects and their effects. Those questions, in turn, lead to metrics that may provide defect information. The metrics lead finally to the measures that must be collected.

5.4.1 Available metrics

It is possible to create any number of metrics. In the most trivial sense, every measure can be combined with every other measure to create a metric. Metrics, in and of themselves, are not the goal of a beneficial SQS. Just because one organization uses a metric does not mean that metric will have meaning for another organization. An organization that does not use CICS will not be interested in a metric expressing CICS availability. One that uses LOC as their size measure will not want to compute function points per person-month.

Other metrics may be too advanced for some organizations. Organizations just starting to develop metrics will likely be ready to monitor open and closed problem reports. They are not likely to use metrics that attempt to express the validity of the software system development estimation algorithm until they have been using metrics for some time. In the case of estimation, a new metrics-using organization may not even have a repeatable method of estimating the size and cost of software systems development.

The selection of specific metrics to develop is a function of the goals of the SQS. This text does not intend to imply that there are certain metrics that all organizations should use. This section merely introduces a few sample metrics that some organizations have found useful. (A more detailed discussion of specific metrics is given in Section 5.4.3.) The metrics identified here are not all-inclusive by any means. They are intended to give the new defect analyst or SQS implementer ideas of what metrics to use and what questions to ask.

5.4.2 Applicable metrics

Most metrics are either product oriented or process oriented.

Product-oriented metrics

Of significant interest to software QA practitioners is the product defect experience of the current software development project and its predecessors. For a given software product, defect experience can indicate its progress toward readiness for implementation. Some metrics can lead to identification of error-prone modules or subsystems. Other metrics indicate the reduction in defect detection as the defects are found and removed.

Rework generally is considered to be any work that is redone because it was not done correctly the first time. Most frequent causes of rework are corrections needed to resolve defects or noncompliance with standards. Monitoring rework metrics can help the software QA practitioner demonstrate the advisability of better project planning and closer attention to requirements.

Process-oriented metrics

Of historical interest are much the same set of metrics, but for the body of software products already completed rather than for just the current project or products. Long-term defect experience helps us understand the development process and its stability, predictability, and level of improvability. The software QA practitioner will track trends in defect detection and correction as indicators of process maturity.

Productivity metrics give indications of process effectiveness, quality of estimation techniques, quality of defect detection techniques, and the like. Some are based on defects, some on nondefect data.

Trend analysis is the long-term comparison of measures and metrics to determine how a process is behaving. Statistical process control, error detection rates, output over time, cost of quality, and help line usage are all examples of measures and metrics that can be studied over a period of time. Such study looks for trends that will describe the development process or its reaction to intentional change. The use of process control charts for software can help describe the behavior of the development process. The charts can also help us to identify process behavior changes in response to intentional changes made to the process.

Cost of quality

The *cost of quality* (COQ) is often used as a measure of the value of the SQS. By combining the costs of resources expended to prevent errors from happening and to appraise the quality of a product, we can find the *cost of achieving quality* (COA). This value is added to the costs of resources expended because quality was not achieved—the *cost of failure* (COF). The sum of COA + COF represents the cost of quality.

Prevention costs include such items as training, the purchase of a methodology, the purchase of automated tools, planning, standards development, and other similar items. These are costs incurred to reduce the likelihood that an error will be made in the first place.

Appraisal costs result, for the most part, from reviews and testing. These costs are those incurred in the search for errors once the product has been produced.

Failure costs are incurred when a product manifests an error. It is important to recognize that only the first review of a product or the first test of a piece of code counts as an appraisal cost. Any rereviewing or retesting required because a defect has been found and corrected is a COF. This is a cost that would not have been incurred had the task been done correctly the first time.

Failure costs include the cost of rework, penalties, overtime, reruns of applications that fail in production, lawsuits, lost customers, lost revenues, and a myriad of other costs. The COF in most companies may be found to contribute half to three-quarters of each dollar spent on the overall COQ.

Table 5.1 presents some typical components of the COQ.

COQ category	Representative contributing costs
Prevention	Training and education, configuration management, planning, standards
Appraisal	Reviews (until defect found), testing (until defect found)
Failure	Rework (rewriting specifications and plans, rereviewing after defect correction, retesting after defect correction, scrapping project, customer complaint handling, lost customers, missed opportunities

Table 5.1
COQ
contributors

5.4.3 SQS goal-oriented metrics

There is an unending list of metrics that can be developed. It is important that the organizational goals and those of the SQS be understood before metrics are haphazardly chosen and applied. The metrics types mentioned so far are reasonably considered by an organization just beginning to use metrics in its SQS. As each organization grows in experience with its SQS, additional goals, questions, and metrics will become useful. More advanced metrics will come to light as the SQS is applied over time.

Table 5.2 suggests possible goals of the SQS and some representative metrics that could apply or be beneficial in reaching those goals.

None of the metrics suggested in Table 5.2 is to be construed to be required or even desirable for all organizations. No text on metrics could cover the vast array of potential metrics available to the developer of an SQS. Even less likely is that a text could guess the exact set of metrics that would apply to every possible organization. The intention of this chapter is to identify typical metrics so that the implementing organization will see the types of concerns that its SQS could address.

SQS goal	Applicable metric
Improved defect management	COQ changes/SQS implementation schedule Cost of rejected software (scrap)/total project cost Cost of defect corrections/cost of defect detection Defect density/software product Defect density/life cycle phase Defects found by reviews/defects found by testing User-detected defects/developer-detected defects STRs closed/total STRs opened STRs remaining open/STRs closed STRs open and closed/time period Mean time between failures Software product reliability Help line calls/software product
Improved requirements	Changed requirements/total requirements Implemented requirements/total requirements Requirements errors/total errors
Improved defect detection	Tests run successfully/total tests planned Defects found by reviews/defects found by testing Defect density/software product User-detected defects/developer-detected defects
Improved developer productivity	KLOC or function points/person-month Schedule or budget "actuals"/estimates Budget expenditures/schedule status Mean time to repair a defect Defects incorrectly corrected/total defects Software product defects/software product complexity
Improved estimation techniques	Schedule or budget "actuals"/estimates Mean time to repair a defect Budget expenditures/schedule status
Increased data center throughput	Incorrect corrections/total corrections Mean time to repair a defect User-detected defects/developer-detected defects

Table 5.2
Goals and metrics

5.5 Collecting measurements

Once it has been decided which metrics are to be used, attention can be turned to the collection of the necessary measures. From the point of view of the SQS, most measures will be related to defects.

5.5.1 Classification of defects

As defects are detected, analyzed, and corrected, many data are available that are of use to the software QA practitioner. Classification of defects aids in the use of defect data to guide defect resolution now and to identify software development process weaknesses or predict problem areas in the future. That is the connection, or bridge, between software QC—finding and fixing defects—and software QA—analyzing and improving the development process. Defects can and do occur in any phase of the SLC. The data gathered with respect to defect classification can direct additional testing of software, point out inherent anomalies in requirements or design, call attention to needs for enhancements to operational software, and give guidance in the correction of current defects.

Defects can be classified according to their various basic characteristics (see Figure 5.1), which should include, at least:

- Severity of the defect if it is encountered in operation;
- Priority of immediate repair;
- Source (life cycle phase) of the defect;
- Type of defect;
- Phase (life cycle phase) in which the defect was found;
- Method by which the defect was found;
- Estimated and actual costs to repair the defect.

The severity of a defect is an indication of the impact of not fixing it immediately. A defect that presents a life-threatening situation or could result in the loss of property if not fixed is a severe defect indeed. On the other hand, some defects may result in a wrong answer from a calculation but not hold up further testing until they are corrected. Such defects would be fairly nonsevere until they began to affect the test program itself. (This shows that some factors are a function of situation as well as immediate impact.)

Related to and sometimes dependent on the severity of a defect is the repair priority assigned to it. Usually a life-threatening defect will be addressed immediately, and a noninterfering defect will be addressed when there is time. That rule, of course, is not hard and fast. There will be occasions in which a severe defect can be isolated so that work can continue in other areas. Some defects may be of such complexity or wide-reaching effect that they cannot be repaired without extended study or serious impact on resources. These defects may be addressed immediately but require a solution that is a long time in coming. Recognition that work can continue while the defect in question is being solved can give it a lower priority. Other factors may affect the priority as well, not the least of which is visibility. A relatively minor defect in the screen format may become a top priority if it is in a highly visible demonstration that will affect the future funding of a software project.

A piece of classification data that often is overlooked is the source, or genesis, of the defect. This is an indication of where the original error was made and where the defect entered the product. It also points up areas in the SDLC that may profit from increased attention by software quality practitioners. When later correlation of defects shows a high concentration of defects that can be traced back to the requirements, it is probably wise to spend more effort in the generation and review of requirements in future projects. Likewise, a preponderance of coding errors may indicate the need for better programmer training. By looking at the data collected on multiple projects, the QA practitioner can suggest to management changes that affect the process of software development. New data from projects begun after the process changes have been made can provide information of the effectiveness of those modifications.

The type of defect encountered is one indication of weakness in design, implementation, or even support software. Input/output defects are those that involve the transfer of data into or out from the object, module, or other part of the software system. Those transfers may be internal to the system or external to the software, as with a key entry or printer action. Input/output-type defects, when seen frequently, may suggest an operating system that is difficult to use. Arithmetic defects are problems in computations that may indicate weak support routines or less than desirable coding practices. Arithmetic defects are also caused by incorrect requirements, such as specifying an equation incorrectly. Control defects occur primarily in decisions within the software. Indexed loops, wrong exits from decision points within the software, and improper transfers of control between objects or modules are examples of the control type of defect. Control defects often are indicative of design or requirements deficiencies.

Two additional characteristics are less defects-based and more indicative of the benefit of the detection techniques being used. Where they are found, that is, in what part of the SLC, can be compared with the source to evaluate the various review methods being used. How they are found permits direct comparisons of the efficiency of the different methods and can also indicate those defect detection methods that are more successful against the various types and sources of defects.

Finally, the estimated and actual costs to repair lead to evaluations of the estimation techniques employed and can be useful in the calculation of COQ.

5.5.2 **Other defect measures**

Certainly not all the measures will be restricted to defect classifications. Countless other defect-related measures can be made. The following list is not intended to be complete but just to suggest some potentially useful measures.

- Number of defects;
- Defect frequencies;
- STRs open and resolved;
- Time between defect detections;
- Defects resulting from correction of previous defects;
- Size of change;
- Incorrect defect reports (incorrect information on STRs).

The number and frequencies of defects can be used to detect defect-prone products or processes. Those measures usually are taken with reference to specific parts of the system of its documentation. Once the system is in production, those counts may be used to monitor the maturity of the system or its need for maintenance. Modules or documents with higher than average defect counts may be in need of redesign or rewriting. In addition, high defect counts or frequencies in a particular product may permit us to redeploy our defect detection efforts.

Defects tend to clump. A QC adage is that if you find a defect, look in the same area for more. Since our defect detection resources are always limited, this adage can give us clues as to where to concentrate QC activities. High counts or frequencies spread more or less evenly across the products may indicate a development process problem. The QA practitioner should always be alert to process flaws that may be indicated by inordinate defect experience.

Open and resolved STR counts can be used to determine defect detection and correction productivity, identify poor defect analysis and isolation methods, detect flawed defect correction techniques, and so on. The number of resolved STRs can be compared to the number of newly opened or still open STRs to monitor correction activities.

The time between defect detections, either directly indicated by date and time or via mean time to failure, can be used in several ways. Longer times may indicate a reduced defect level. They may also indicate reduced defect detection success or effort. Stable or shorter times might indicate the addition of defects during modifications. They could also be indicative of increased defect detection efforts or improved detection processes.

Defects resulting from the resolution of other defects are known to be frequent. This measure will aid in the identification of poor defect resolution processes or insufficient QC of software modifications.

The size of the change is often one of the comparative measures used to develop various metrics. In combination with other measures, size can be a normalizing factor. We do not want to compare data from small, short projects with data from large or long schedule projects. Such comparisons are often invalid and can lead to erroneous conclusions. For example, if two projects both have 10 STRs opened per day, we might presume that the defect levels were about equal. When we see that the first project is only a three-month project involving two people, and the second is a three-year project with 25 participants, we probably come to a rather different conclusion about the projects' respective defect levels.

Not all reported defects are defects. In some cases, the detected operation of the system is not wrong, just unexpected, for example, incorrect expected results in the test case or an inexperienced user. In other cases, the data entered on the STR may be incorrect: wrong module name, incorrect document reference, wrong version, and so on. The QA practitioner will want to determine what causes the incorrect STRs. Training of users or defect reporters may be necessary, or better user documentation might be the answer. In any case, it is not productive to try to correct defects based on incorrect reports.

5.5.3 Nondefect measures

Defect analysis depends on defect data, but defect data alone are not sufficient for most metrics. Nondefect data are usually the basis for product and process metrics. In some cases, they form the whole metric, as was noted in Section 5.4.2.

Some nondefect measures are readily available and are in "hard" numbers; for example, project size, budget and schedule figures, clock and processor time, and the number of people involved in an activity. These measures can be taken directly, and no interpretation of them is usually needed.

For the software quality practitioner, some measures are not available in hard numbers but rely on quantification of subjective data. These "soft" measures might include customer impressions, perceived quality on some subjective scale, and estimates of quality. Soft measures should be used with care, for there is often no precise way to quantify or validate them.

Derived measures include those that we cannot determine through either hard or soft means. An example of a derived measure might be *quality*, which ranks as *good* (a soft measure) since *90 users out of 100* (a hard measure) do not return survey forms and thus must not be dissatisfied. Great care must be exercised with measures such as these. Only organizations with significant experience in metrics should consider using derived measures.

5.6 Quality Tools

The representation of measures and metrics can take many forms. Even their collection must be considered. The following tools are most often used for measure collection and measure and metric use.

- Tally sheet;
- Scatter diagram;
- Graph;
- Histogram;
- Pareto diagram;
- Flowchart;
- Cause and effect diagram;
- Statistical control charts (process control charts).

None of these tools is new. Hardware quality practitioners have been using them for many years. Some, such as the tally sheet and the scatter diagram, have been used in software quality activities regularly. Others, like the cause and effect diagram and statistical control charts, are relatively new to software quality applications.

5.6.1 Tally sheet

The tally sheet is the simplest form of data collection. Each occurrence of some event or situation is tallied as it happens or is detected. The example in Figure 5.4 depicts a collection of data for defects detected in several modules of software being reviewed. Note that this is merely a collection of "detected defects" data. Taken by itself, the collection gives little or no information about the modules beyond pure defect counts. It is usually beneficial to chart or graph the numbers for comparison.

Module	Defect count (x five)		Total
1	IIII		20
2	HHT I		30
3	HHT HHT	Plus 4	54
4	HHT	Plus 2	27
5	HHT III		40
6	HHT HHT	Plus 2	52
7	HHT HHT HHT III		90
8	HHT II		35
9	HHT III	Plus 3	43
10	II	Plus 2	12
11	HHT I	Plus 1	31
12	HHT HHT	Plus 3	53

Figure 5.4
Sample tally sheet.

5.6.2 **Scatter diagram**

Figure 5.5 presents the data from the tally sheet in a more "mathematical" form. The numbers are the same, but some people find this representation more understandable. The scatter diagram gives a visual comparison of the numbers from the tally sheet. Sometimes it is useful to plot the trend line or least squares curve, which summarizes the scattered points. The dashed line represents an estimate of the data trend.

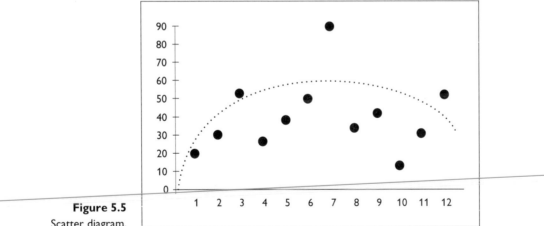

Figure 5.5
Scatter diagram.

5.6.3 **Graph**

In its simplest form, a graph is just a scatter diagram with the points connected. Continuing the defect count example, Figure 5.6 is a graphical representation of the numbers on the tally sheet. Graphs are often preferred for observing the progress of a process or activity with respect to time. Continuing the example, modules 1–12 may have been completed in the time sequence shown. More information, such as calendar dates or complexity can be shown in a graph. We might discover that module 7 was highly complex, while module 12 was completed near year's end.

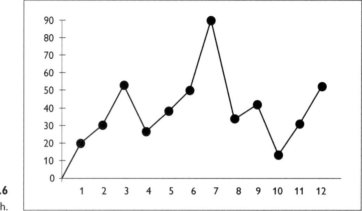

Figure 5.6
Graph.

5.6.4 **Histogram**

A histogram is similar to a graph, but instead of the points being connected with a line, they are shown as vertical (or horizontal) bars whose lengths represent the numbers. Figure 5.7 is a histogram of the tally sheet data. Histograms are often precursors to Pareto charts. Histograms are sometimes expanded to have the width represent an additional condition such as size or effort.

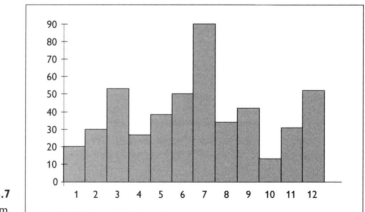

Figure 5.7
Histogram.

5.6.5 **Pareto diagram**

In the nineteenth century, economist Vilfredo Pareto determined that approximately 80% of his country's wealth was controlled by about 20% of the population. Thus was born the *80/20 rule*. Although originally directed toward economics, the 80/20 rule has come to be used in many applications, including software quality management. The 80/20 rule in software quality management suggests that we pay attention to the products that account for 80 or so percent of the defects. Admittedly not mathematically precise, it serves as a good guide to the application of quality effort.

The Pareto diagram is the histogram arranged in (usually) descending order of bar height. Figure 5.8 is the Pareto representation of the tally sheet numbers. Also indicated is the approximate 80% point. The software quality practitioner could use a Pareto diagram to prioritize an examination of the causes for the defect numbers associated with each module.

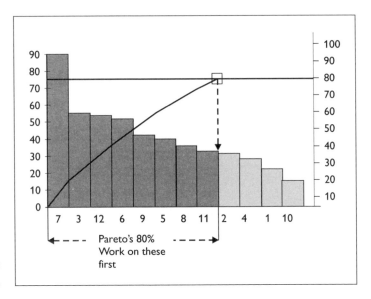

Figure 5.8
Pareto diagram.

5.6.6 Flowchart

Flowcharts are diagrams that permit users to describe processes. They are not used to represent data but rather the way in which things are done. Manufacturing, sales, banking, military, software, in fact nearly all processes have been described with flowcharts. The software QA practitioner will use the flowchart to depict the various processes used in software development, maintenance, operation, and improvement. As the metrics begin to suggest flaws in one or another process, the flowchart can help isolate the part of the process that is flawed. Figure 5.9 depicts the format for a typical flowchart.

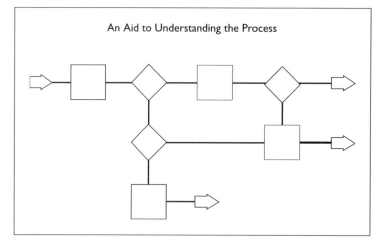

An Aid to Understanding the Process

Figure 5.9
Flowchart.

Continuing our example, the development process for each module might be flowcharted in a search for differences that might account for the variations in the defect rates. Alternatively, the defect detection processes might be flowcharted in a search for their variations and the reasons for their differing results.

5.6.7 Cause and effect diagram

Another diagram used to locate process flaws is the cause and effect diagram. Defect detection and correction is responsible for eliminating the defect. Cause and effect diagrams are used to determine the actual cause of a defect. In that way, not only is the defect itself eliminated, but the situation that permitted it to be introduced is also eliminated, so it will not occur again.

The cause and effect diagram, an example of which is shown in Figure 5.10, is also called the Ishikawa diagram, after Professor Kaoru Ishikawa, who introduced it in Japan, and the root cause diagram. Note that neither the flowchart nor the cause and effect diagram is not used to depict data. Rather, they help describe processes and analyze defect causes.

In our example, based on the high defect rate for module 7, the software quality practitioner might use the cause and effect diagram to seek out the specific causes for the high defect rate, rather than just guessing.

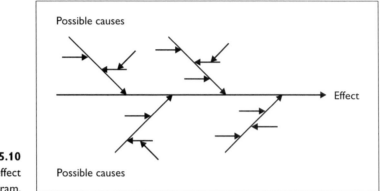

Figure 5.10
Cause and effect
diagram.

Coupled with the knowledge of the module's complexity, the time of year of its creation, the type(s) of defect detection methods applied, flowcharts of the development and defect detection processes, and, perhaps, its cost and schedule variations from expectations, the cause and effect diagram can assist the quality practitioner in the analysis. One arm might represent all the potential effects of calendar dates, another the effects of schedule or budget changes, still another the effects of requirements changes, and so on. The user of the cause and effect diagram tries to examine each potential cause until the actual root cause of the situation is discovered. The diagram serves to document each potential cause examined and its relationship to other potential causes.

5.6.8 Process control charts

Walter Shewhart, in 1931, applied the laws of statistics to production processes and discovered that the process behavior can be plotted. He then showed how the process can be controlled and that control monitored.

Run charts

Run charts depict the statistical behavior of a process. Shewhart intended that a run chart be used to show when a process was stable or "in control." It is not based on the intended or target behavior of the process but its actual behavior. Figure 5.11 shows a basic process control chart. The center line is the mean level of the described characteristic (perhaps the error rate for a given software system). The upper line is the upper control limit (UCL) and indicates the presence of special causes of defects. The lower line is the lower control limit (LCL) and also reflects special causes, this time because the product is better than it has to be. Shewhart set the UCL and LCL as functions of the mean and standard deviation for the population being plotted.

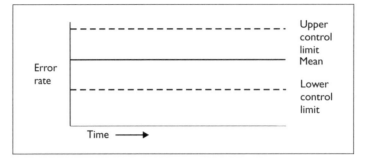

Figure 5.11
Basic run chart.

The idea of evaluating process behavior using a run chart is depicted in Figure 5.12. A process that has an error rate falling consistently between the control limits (as in the first section of Figure 5.12) is said to be in control. An occasional point outside the limits identifies a special case, a target for cause and effect analysis. In general, however, the process is considered sound and repeatable. The second section of Figure 5.12 shows the case in which the points falls randomly around the mean. That process is said to be out of control. Changes to the process are not likely to be identified with changes in the results. The third section of Figure 5.12 shows a process in control but drifting. In the manufacturing world, we might conclude that a tool was getting worn. In software, we might suspect that a defect detection technique was improving (the drift implies we are finding more defects) or that the development process was degenerating (and letting more defects into the products).

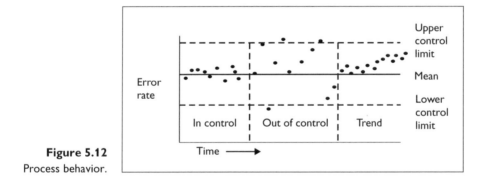

Figure 5.12
Process behavior.

Continuous process improvement might be depicted as in Figure 5.13. Based on the Japanese concept of *kaizen*, the process is continually improved. As a result, the control limits, still functions of the mean and the standard deviation, tend to move closer to the mean.

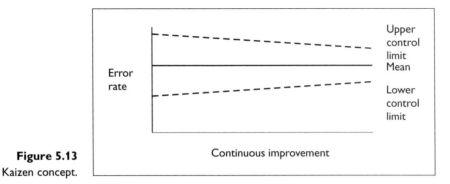

Figure 5.13
Kaizen concept.

Acceptance control charts

Acceptance control charts are not based on statistical determination of the mean and control limits. These charts use the desired value, called the target, as the center line. The UCL and LCL are chosen based on permissible variation, not statistical variation.

In software terms, when depicting defects, we would like all three lines to lie on the zero-defects line. And that is the ultimate long-term goal of the SQS. In the meantime, and in the real world, there are other pressures that slow our attainment of the zero-defect goal. Just as in the hardware world of Shewhart, costs and risks will define the realistic levels for the target and the control levels. In economic terms, we might say that the UCL is the level at which the customer will no longer accept the product, and the LCL the level at which the costs of finding further defects exceed the costs incurred if the defect occurs in the use of the software. Stated still another way, the UCL defines "how bad I dare to make it," and the LCL defines "how good I can afford to make it."

Acceptance control charts are not as statistically valid as run charts, but they do not require the large sample and population sizes on which run charts usually are based. Acceptance control charts are more easily adapted to the uses of the software QA practitioner, however. Figure 5.14 combines the acceptance control chart, the kaizen concept, the desire for zero defects, and economic reality into a typical software process control chart. In this chart, the LCL is set as close to zero as is economically feasible. The centerline, the target defect rate, starts at the current experienced value and slopes downward at the goal rate of the SQS. At the same time, the UCL is more sharply sloped to motivate process improvement.

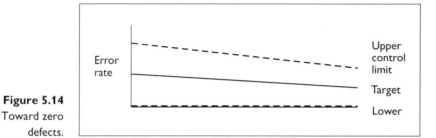

Figure 5.14
Toward zero
defects.

5.7 Implementing defect analysis

The creation of a metrics program starts with the determination of the requirements or reason for measuring something. Just as in the development
of software, defining the problem we wish to solve is the first step. Once we
know what information we might want, we can begin to determine what
measures can lead us to our objective.

It is unfortunate that there are few, if any, metrics in common use in
the industry. Even those measures that many organizations use, LOC, function points, error counts, time, and so on, are not defined industrywide. In
effect, each organization that counts something counts it in its own way.
For that reason, when one company claims to have one error per thousand
delivered LOC, another company may have no idea as to how they compare. The reason is that there is no commonly accepted definition of either
"error" or "lines of code."

The solution may be for a given company to design its metrics program for its own situation. When the company has a metrics set that is pre-
senting the company with information about its software processes, it
might offer those measures to the industry as guidelines. At some point,
other companies may adopt and adapt those metrics, and a de facto standard may be born. The IEEE has published a standard covering the establishment of a metrics program (IEEE Standard 1061-1992). It would
certainly be a starting point for a company just starting to develop their
own program.

5.7.1 Rules

There are a few simple but important rules to be observed in the design
and implementation of a defect analysis and metrics program. Many programs are started, but most fail in the first year or so. The primary reason
for failed programs is failure to observe the following vital considerations:

- The program must be instigated and supported from the top of the organization down.
- The metrics must support quality as quality is seen from the customers' perspective.
- The measurements must not interfere with the performance of assigned work.
- The people being measured must have a role in defining the measurements and methods.

Support from top management is necessary, because as measurements are begun they must be seen to be of interest to top management. If management does not use the metrics, ignores the results of the program, does not provide for the costs of data collections and metrics development, and is not visibly committed to the success of the metrics program, the rest of the organization will soon conclude that metrics do not matter.

Metrics that are developed for the sake of metrics usually will not be used. Metrics that are not used become targets for elimination. The metrics developed must be based on defects and other data that will lead to better customer satisfaction. If the program does not result in increased customer satisfaction, the costs eventually will be determined to be wasted. That is almost always the end of the program.

Even when top management supports the defect analysis or metrics program, if it gets in the way of job performance, the workers will not cooperate. The persons conducting the data gathering must remember that the rest of the people are busy with the jobs to which they are assigned. They are being paid to do their work, not the measurer's. When pressures mount, the assigned task gets attention, not additional side tasks that do not appear in the worker's job description.

It should not be a surprise that if you are going to measure my productivity, the defect history of my work, and things of that nature, I want some influence over or at least a full understanding of what is measured, how the data are collected, and what the metrics and their use will be. Perhaps even worse than non-customer-focused metrics are those that are used for personnel evaluations and comparisons. Especially damaging to the metrics program is defect data that are construed to reflect the performance of the workers. When that is the case, the program will not survive as a useful activity. It must always be remembered that "you get what you measure." If my defect data are going to be used against me, I will make very few accurate defect data available to the software quality practitioner or management.

5.7.2 **Designing the program**

A defect analysis or metrics program should be treated exactly the same as the development of software. It is a project, has requirements, must be designed, "coded," tested, implemented, and maintained. A simple five-step approach can be used to define and start the program:

1. Define the goals of the program.

2. Ask questions about the use of the program and metrics.

3. Identify the metrics to be developed and used.

4. Identify the measures that must be made to gather the data for the metrics.

5. Plan the data collection, metrics development, and metrics application.

It has been stated that the defect analysis or metrics program must have established goals before anything else is done. That is analogous to the setting of vision and mission statements for the organization. The goals of the program lead to questions about customer attitude, product quality, defect experience, process improvement opportunities, and the like. The answers to the questions give insight into what kinds of metrics will be of value. If we are just interested in defect analysis, one set of metrics may emerge. If we are interested in improved quality and processes, a larger set of metrics will be recognized. In every case, the organization must perform these steps in the context of its own maturity, business, and capabilities.

Once the metrics that will be needed have been defined, the data and required measurements can be defined as well. It was noted earlier that some data consists of hard numbers that are collectable directly. Other data are soft, or subjective, in the form of opinions, guesses, feelings, and so on. The soft data must be quantified for use with the hard data. The organization must determine the quantification methods and how precise they believe the quantifications to be.

Throughout the process of defining goals, asking questions, and identifying metrics and measures, the people whose work and products will be the subjects of the measures must be involved. Acceptance of the program is not the only thing requiring the participation of the people being measured. The persons doing the work are the closest to all the things being measured—their effort, products, processes, defects, and so on. They often can suggest metrics and measures that have even more utility than those conceived by the software quality practitioners. If the program is to succeed, it is imperative that the voice of the workers be solicited and heard.

5.7.3 Metric characteristics

If the SQS and the metrics program have requirements, so have the metrics themselves. Measures and their resulting metrics must be easy to gather and develop. Measures that require extensive investigation or complicated collection methods will tend to be poorly collected (at least at the beginning of the program). Section 5.4 suggested that many useful metrics comprise easily collected measures. Those measures and metrics should form the basis of the beginning metrics program. As experience and maturity are gained, more sophisticated metrics and measures can be adopted. In the beginning, "keep it simple" is a good motto.

Metrics also must be easy to understand and apply. It may be possible to determine the number of defects per thousand LOC written from 10:00 PM to 11:00 PM on a cloudy Friday the thirteenth by developers in Bangalore, India, compared to the same data for developers in Fort Wayne, Indiana. Whether there is useful information in that metric is another question. If there is information, of what use is it? As metrics become more sophisticated, their understandability often becomes more difficult. Many of the metrics being converted from hardware to software quality applications must be redefined for use on software. Those metrics generally are applicable after their adaptation but frequently require very large sample sizes to be meaningful. Again, the new metrics program must be useful. Utility of the metrics being developed is more important than whether they are the most complete set of metrics.

Validity of the metrics is another key point. Do the metrics correctly reflect their target situation? An example was given in Section 5.5.2 of the need to consider the size of the project in a given situation. Metrics that are sensitive to parameters other than those in the direct equation may not reflect the real situation. Software is tested to determine if all its requirements have been corrected addressed. Metrics, too, need to be tested to ensure that they present the information we want and do so correctly and repeatably. Careful definition of each of the data terms being used, specification of exact data collection methods to be used, and precise equation for the metrics can only reduce the likelihood that the metric is developed incorrectly. The real question being asked is whether the metric is the correct one for the desired application. It must be shown that the metric actually applies to the situation in which we are interested. Is the metric in support of the original goals of the program? Does it address the organizations concerns? Does it give us information we need and do not have elsewhere? The comparison of defects between Bangalore and Fort Wayne may be available and precise, but if we really don't have a need for that comparison or know what to do with it, it is not beneficial to develop it.

5.8 Summary

Defects can and do occur in any phase of the SLC. The recording and tracking of defects in the software make sure that all found defects are, in fact, addressed. An important aspect of the trouble report, in whatever manner it is implemented, is that it provides a means to ensure that each defect is addressed and the solution recorded.

Changes require careful control. Every time a change is made, there is the chance that a new defect will be introduced with the change. In projects under formal CM, trouble report closures that require CM processing, especially formal change approval, will reflect any CM action involved.

Classification of defects aids in the use of defect data to guide defect resolution now and to identify software development process weaknesses. Future problem areas also can be predicted by using error or defect trend analysis.

As defects are found and eliminated, a body of data about the defects can be accumulated. These data become input for QA analysis. Such analysis as trends and metrics can be conducted to help depict the development process in use and its potential weaknesses. While finding and fixing defects is the QC role, and defect analysis aids in the repair of defects, the QA practitioner needs defect data to help identify potential process flaws. The defect data also are useful as empirical information that can aid decision-making, action-capable management in its process modifications.

5.9 The next step

No text can cover the entire scope of software metrics, but these two are good starting points:

- *Practical Implementation of Software Metrics* by Paul Goodman (New York: McGraw-Hill, 1993).
- *Practical Software Metrics for Project Management and Process Improvement* by R. B. Grady (Englewood Cliffs, NJ: Prentice-Hall, 1992).

ADDITIONAL READING

Blakemore, John, *The Quality Solution,* Melbourne: Information Australia, 1989.

Feigenbaum, Armand V., *Total Quality Control*, New York: McGraw-Hill, 1991.

Humphrey, Watts S., *Managing the Software Process*, Reading, MA: Addison-Wesley, 1989.

Jones, Capers, *Applied Software Measurement*, New York: McGraw-Hill, 1991.

Kan, Stephen H., *Metric and Models in Software Quality Engineering*, Reading, MA: Addison-Wesley, 1995.

Logothetis, N., *Managing for Total Quality*, Englewood Cliffs, NJ: Prentice-Hall, 1992.

McConnell, John, *The Seven Tools of TQC*, 4th Ed., Manly Vale, Australia: Delaware Books, 1992.

Musa, John D., Anthony Iannino, and Kazuhira Okumoto, *Software Reliability Measurement, Prediction, Application*, New York: McGraw-Hill, 1987.

Chapter 6

Configuration management

C M IS THE DISCIPLINE that ensures that the state of the software at any given time is known and reconstructable. CM is a discipline that covers hardware as well as software, but in this text CM will be limited to software unless specifically stated otherwise.

CM comprises three basic elements: *configuration identification* (CID), *configuration control* (CC), and *configuration accounting* (CA). While each element may be invoked without the others, CM is incomplete in the absence of any of them.

CID provides a method for specifically and uniquely identifying each instance (e.g., release, version) of a given software product or set of products. By the use of a standard naming convention that allows for the identification of every instance of the product, each new draft of a document or each new compilation of a unit can be specifically identified.

CC is the element that ensures that each change to an instance of the product is known, authorized, and documented. CC includes the activities of the *change control board* (CCB), which reviews and authorizes changes to the documents and code as increasingly formal control is placed on the developing software system. The software library may also be included as a function of CC.

CA serves to maintain track of the status of each instance of the product. This function becomes increasingly important as units and modules are integrated into subsystems and systems. It is obvious that the specific parts of a given system must be known so the system itself can be known. CA is also the element that assigns and tracks the status of each baseline of the requirements, design, code, and so on, as the software effort proceeds. Another growing requirement for configuration accounting is the case of a basic product that is adapted for use in multiple installations, each with slight variations in the total requirements set.

Figure 6.1 presents an overview of CM processing.

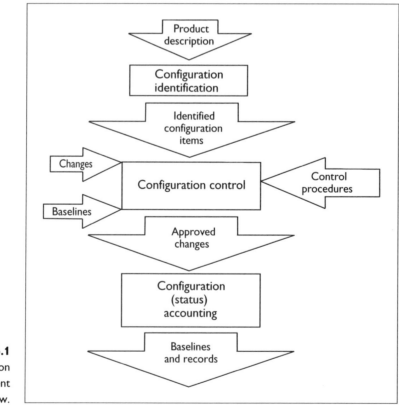

Figure 6.1
Configuration
management
overview.

6.1 Configuration management components

Traditionally, CM has included identification of the items to be configuration managed, control of the changes to the identified items, and maintenance of the status of each item.

6.1.1 Configuration identification

Configuration identification permits unique and uniform naming of each component and product of the total software system down to the lowest separable level.

Any system, including a software system, is separable into smaller and smaller parts down to some desirable, manageable level. In this text, the lowest level of a software system—that is, the smallest component that can be assembled or compiled—is called the *unit*. Increasingly larger components are the *module*, the *subsystem* (there may be more than one level of subsystem, depending on the size of the system), and finally the system itself. The documentation goes through a similar separation, from the original requirements statement to the individual module and unit design specifications, the code, and the test procedures.

Each of these subdivisions, code components, and documents will go through multiple issues as they are developed. The primary issue usually is called a *release*. This is a formal issue and usually represents a baseline. After a release has been issued, updates to the release are made, often called *versions*. Versions represent significant changes to the release but not wholesale modification or replacement. Finally, in some large systems, there may be reissues of versions that may be little more than recompiles or document updates to make editorial or minor corrections. These low-level issues may be called *editions*. The actual terms used are up to the individual organizations. As in most areas of software engineering, there are no industrywide standard names for these levels of products. Figure 6.2 shows an example of a hierarchical structure of these product levels.

It is clear that the management of all of the subdivisions and issues is critical to the development and delivery of a quality software system. The first step in the CM of all the various subdivisions and issues is to give each a unique identifier. That is the role of CID.

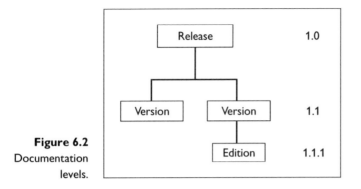

Figure 6.2
Documentation
levels.

As each product—a component of code or a document—comes into being, it must be assigned an identifier that will depict its instance, its "parent" (the next larger component of which it is a part), and its "age" (when it was created). In that way, users of the product can be sure they have the exact issue that is appropriate for their use. As shown in Figure 6.2, each level carries the name of its parent for continuity in identification. Not all identification schemes carry this information, as will be seen in Section 6.2.1.

6.1.2 **Configuration control**

CC ensures that all—and only—approved changes are made to the baseline.

Once a baseline has been established, all changes to it must be acted on with increasing formality and control. Early in the development, there normally are few products to consider as changes are made. There is, for example, usually only one requirements document. Changes to that one document early in the requirements phase may be easy to track and record and so may require less formal control than the entire system during acceptance testing. As the system becomes more and more subdivided into its lower level products or component parts, defects become more expensive to correct. Therefore, control of changes becomes more stringent.

When the software system is under formal CM, changes are proposed in a formal manner, for example, a change request form or an STR. These requested changes are reviewed by a software CCB, which evaluates such things as impact on other software components, cost, and schedule. Approved changes are then prepared and tested, and, if successful, they are implemented into the affected component by means of an SCN (as described in Section 6.3.3). The SCN gives formal notice that the software or a document has been changed. The SCN is also notification to the CA element that a change has been made to the current baseline.

It is the intent of all of CM, but especially CC, to be sure that the software products (the code and the documentation) stay in step with one another and that no changes are made without proper consideration and approval. It is one role of the software quality practitioner to verify that the CM program is sufficient to accomplish that task and that it is being followed.

6.1.3 Configuration accounting

CA maintains and records the status of each baseline and its history. It may also be called on to account for multiple instances of the products, such as those in Figure 6.2.

Baselines

The establishment of a baseline generally occurs as the result of a major phase-end review. The importance of a base line is that it represents the starting point for all changes as the product evolves. As shown in Figure 6.3, there are five commonly recognized baselines that should be established. These baselines and their phase-end reviews are:

- Functional baseline (SRR);
- Allocated baseline (PDR);
- Design baseline (CDR);
- Product baseline (TRR);
- Operational baseline (FA/PA).

Informal inprocess baselines are established if they are necessary for a particular development consideration.

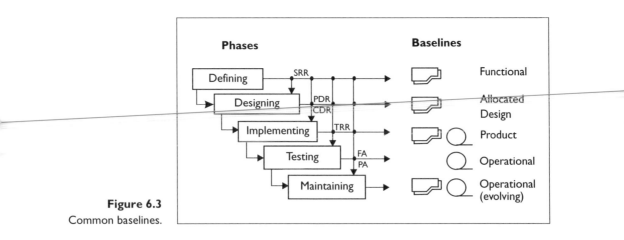

Figure 6.3
Common baselines.

Instances

Instances of a product may occur when changes occur, variations evolve, or the software product exists in multiple forms.

The simplest instances are those that happen each time a product undergoes any change. Quite often, especially during the development of drafts of a document, those instances are not recorded and "disappear." Only when CM is required do the instances take on names and recorded existence. New instances arising from the modification of an existing product—usually as a result of a correction or an enhancement—are called *successors*. Figure 6.4 depicts the creation of a successor.

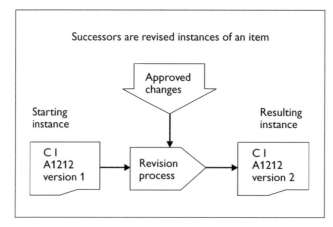

Figure 6.4
Successors.

When different installations of a software system require minor variations in the functional or other requirements, but the basic system is intact, *variants* are created, as depicted in Figure 6.5. CM of variants is extremely important in situations such as the same software running on various platforms and having to perform identical functions with slightly different, platform-dependent differences. Another instance of variants might be weapon system software running on identical computational platforms but on different weapons platforms such as aircraft versus shipboard installations. Graphical user interfaces and client-server installations often need slight modifications to permit implementation on multiple hardware configurations without affecting the users' perception of software performance.

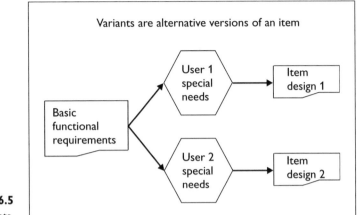

Figure 6.5
Variants.

Equivalents are multiple instances of a product in which the content is identical. Equivalents normally are associated with multiple copies of a product, such as purchased applications that are reproduced on disks or other media. Equivalents also are created when a document or software application is copied from a floppy to a hard disk, for example. The specific medium of the equivalent is not a factor, other than to those customers who want a specific medium. The key to equivalence is identical content, not medium. Figure 6.6 shows equivalents on various media.

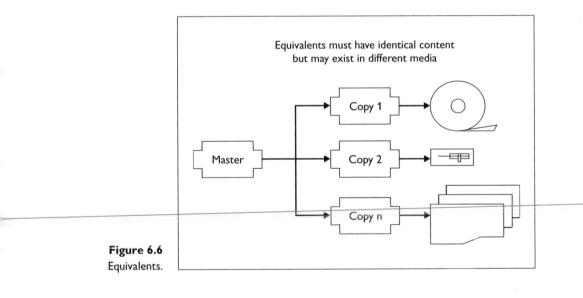

Figure 6.6
Equivalents.

CA keeps track of the instances of individual products and their relation to the established baselines. It also records which smaller or lower level components make up each higher level component; that is, which specific units go together to make up which specific module. Further, CA records all approved changes made to the current baseline. Accounting for all approved, but outstanding, changes also is provided. In that way, the CM requirement for providing reconstructability is met.

6.2 Configuration identification

CID involves selecting the items to be configuration managed and giving each of them a unique identifier or name.

6.2.1 Configuration item

Each component of the software is a manageable configuration item (CI). Each project will decide the level of component that will become the lowest managed item.

A CI is any product—any component of the software, documentation, code, and, in some cases, storage medium (e.g., memory chip)—that has a unique CID. Thus, CID can be applied to everything produced during the SLC. In fact, for most large-scale software systems, that is true. Compilers and assemblers usually are constructed so as to append an updated CID to each new assembly or compilation.

Each CI must have a unique identifier to differentiate it from all its predecessors and successors. The identifier should show the CI's parent; that is, the next higher level of configuration and the specific issue at that level. There must also be a clear indication of the status of the CI. The CID must show at least the release, the version, and, if used, the edition of the CI. In documentation, that generally is a simple document name followed by an issue indicator. For code CIs, it is much more important to show the sequence of compilation or assembly, so that work can be performed on the most recent or up-to-date instance of the CI. As integration proceeds and delivery is made, the situation be comes more critical. The software system being tested must be exactly known, down to the unit level, so that when changes are made, only the correct instance of each component is affected.

In the simplest form of identification, each CI is sequentially numbered, starting with 1 and continuing until the last CI has been created. This system fulfills the requirement of unique identifiers for each instance of each CI, but there is little "intelligence" contained in the name. Clearly, a table of numbers versus the CIs would be needed to indicate which product was which. This base-level naming scheme would be suitable for only the smallest of software projects. In a slightly more informational scheme, a date-and-time-of-creation tag could be used. This scheme presumes that two CIs cannot be created at the same instant. As in the case of the sequential numbering approach, though, a table showing the correspondence between a specific name and the exact CI to which it applies would be required.

Figure 6.7 depicts two examples of those simple schemes as well as a much more elaborate identification scheme that is more likely to be of the type most software projects would use. In the third scheme, each level of the system has its identifier included in the name. With some care, a certain amount of intelligence can be built into such a naming approach. The characters chosen for each level name can be related to the level so the user can recognize products without an elaborate cross-reference table. Of course, if the number of CIs is large, a reference list may be necessary just to keep track of what the codes in each field stand for.

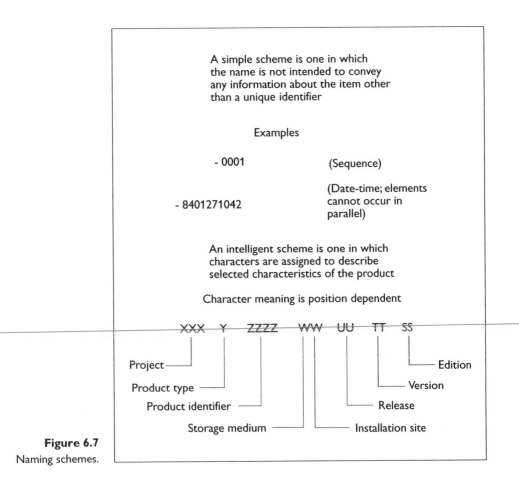

Figure 6.7
Naming schemes.

In any case, the CID must be suited to the software system being developed. Clearly, very large software systems will require more elaborate naming schemes than very small systems. Further, the CID should, to the extent possible, be based on a standard CID method throughout the organization. Using a single scheme throughout the organization makes it easier for the CM practitioner to operate on more than one project at a time. Having a separate naming approach for each project, or even groups of several projects, increases complexity unnecessarily.

6.2.2 **Release**

A release is a major instance or issue of a product. A release usually occurs at a milestone and often is the baseline of the product as defined at that milestone. Once the software is placed into operation, a release represents an entire new issue of the software product. The term release is usually applied to the reissue of a product at its highest level.

6.2.3 **Version**

Each time a component is formally reissued, recompiled, or assembled for inclusion in its parent, a new version of all higher level components is created.

The concept of version is usually rather subjective and reflects the needs of the organization and the project. In general, a new version is created any time there is a major update to a component. A revision to a document is usually considered to be a new version. (This is a smaller case than the release, which is the issuance of the document with all revisions to all components fully integrated.) A new compilation of a code component for inclusion in the next higher level component is also generally considered to be a new version.

Each component of a system, down to the unit level, can be considered to be a replaceable part of the whole. A code CI at the unit level is a part of a code CI at the module level. A module is a part of a subsystem, and so on. There is a less clear inclusive relationship between documents, but the same principle applies. A design specification describes the detailed response to some portion of the requirements. Design changes may be an affect related requirements. In a document, a chapter or major section is clearly a part of the whole document.

When a large (large is a subjective term, sometimes determined by an arbitrary standard suitable to the software of the organization) number of changes is made as a group, a new version is created. This is often associated with a set of changes to a functional aspect of the software. For example, if a new module is introduced into a subsystem, a new version of the subsystem is created. If a new chapter or major section is inserted into a document, a new version of that document is created. Changes that correct defects but do not change the basic design or functional intent of the component might not warrant the designation of a new version.

6.2.4 **Edition**

Some organizations may find it useful to define a third level of product instance, called the edition. Each time any component of a system is recreated, a new edition is formed.

The creation of a new edition is any action that changes any component of the system. While this is a true statement, not all projects or organizations use this concept for CID. On small projects, it is sometimes not worth the extra effort to manage the configuration at that level. In most cases, though, the information is available if it is wanted. Most compilers and assemblers now include type of new edition indication as a part of their normal processing, even if it is only a date and time record.

The use of the edition is important with larger systems since several editions of the whole system may exist at any one time. Remember that any variation in any component is also a variation in every superior level of which that component is a part. Thus, if a change is made to a unit, that change must be reflected in the CID of every level above that unit all the way to the system level if integration is in progress.

At some point, there are sufficient editions present within a version to make the creation of a new version appropriate. Thus, a new issue of the component will be made with the version identifier increased and the edition identifier reset to its starting point. The new version will also cause ripples up through the system, since its change must be reflected by all components of which it is a part. Whether the superior components become new releases, versions, or editions is a decision based on the overall CM philosophy for the project or the organization.

6.3 Configuration control

CC is that part of CM concerned with the processing, approving, and installation of changes to the software products.

6.3.1 **Change processing**

Without an effective change processing mechanism, the software easily can become unidentifiable and unmanageable. Change processing mechanisms

must be effective ("effective" does not necessarily mean complicated or bu-
reaucratic). Figure 6.8 presents a simple process for incorporating changes.

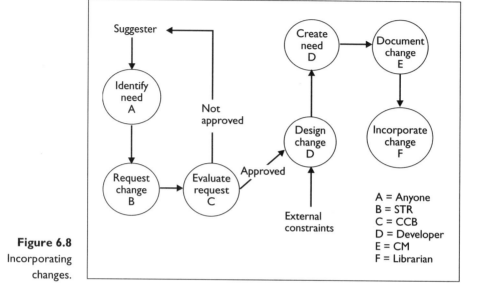

Figure 6.8
Incorporating
changes.

Changes come from two sources: defect corrections and enhancements. To the change processing system, it matters little which source is involved. Each change must be requested, prepared, tested, approved, and
implemented. It is the change processing activity that ensures that all required steps have been taken.

Once the software is baselined, all changes are referenced to the baseline in effect. It is important that all changes be controlled so that their
effects can be tracked. The control of the changes depends on the stage in
the SLC, various organizational factors, standards, and project priorities.
The customer, who may have to pay for the changes, also is interested in
change processing. The trail of the change, from its inception as the result
of a defect or an enhancement request, must be clear. All steps in the
change process are important; ignoring or skipping one or more of them
can introduce mistakes, thus necessitating further changes.

Defects make changes necessary. Obviously, changes are the methods
by which defects are corrected. The full defect tracking process was discussed in Chapter 5, so suffice it to recognize here that the change process
is not limited to defect correction alone.

Enhancements are a major source of changes as the deployed software
matures and new capabilities are needed. There are many cases in which
the software system is implemented in a phased manner, starting with a

smaller capability and gradually adding functions until the full required system is available. These changes are processed in the same manner as defects; that is, they are proposed, designed and tested, approved, and implemented.

The software CCB can be seen here as playing an important role. It is the CCB that makes the final determination as to whether the change is made at all and, if so, when it will be made. The CCB is responsible for making sure that changes are carefully analyzed and that all associated software effects are considered. The software quality practitioner is usually a member of the CCB and so can report on the quality aspects of the change and whether the quality requirements have been met.

Figures 5.1 and 5.2 showed examples of forms designed for the purpose of initiating and tracking a change through its processing. Change processing also often uses automated tools, such as spreadsheets, database management systems, and full CM systems, to assist in the management of changes.

6.3.2 **Change control boards**

The software CCB is the final approval authority for the implementation of software changes. Coordination of changes and their intercomponent effects is the responsibility of this body.

The size and membership of the CCB depend on the standards of the organization and the needs of the project. All affected functions should be represented on the CCB so it can adequately review requested changes. In most cases, members come from each functional area (usually at the subsystem level), CA, CC, and the hardware areas involved, if appropriate. In addition, the software quality practitioner is expected to be a member of the CCB. In some organizations, a representative of the internal audit group is also an appropriate member.

Size is a factor in the efficacy of the CCB. If the group is too large, things may not get done in a timely manner. If, on the other hand, the proper areas are not represented, changes may be approved that adversely affect other parts of the system.

It is the responsibility of the CCB to review all proposed changes for their correctness and their effect on the baseline. Interactions with other parts of the software system are considered, as well as impacts on the schedule and cost. Especially in the case of cost and schedule, the customer is a necessary member of the CCB. There also may be cases in which a change will affect the system requirements. In those cases, the customer or user must be present to agree that the change and its impact are permissible.

The impact of the change on the documentation is also considered by the CCB. Any change that affects higher level components probably also affects the documentation of that level. Some changes may affect documentation all the way back to the requirements of the system. If the documentation is not updated as changes are made, the task of the software maintainer is made much more difficult. If the documentation is not up to date, the maintainer must regenerate it before beginning useful work on the next change.

There are instances where multiple CCBs are convened. That may be especially true in the case of very large or multiple-contractor projects. At the software development level, an informal CCB may review changes within subsystems and the overall system as the changes are proposed. These informal boards serve to prepare the changes for the more formal software CCB to which the changes will be submitted for final approval. At the same time, there is likely to be a hardware CCB working with the proposed changes to equipment involved in the system.

In the case of large systems involving hardware as well as software, there will be hardware CCBs paralleling the software CCBs. In addition, there will be an overall system CCB to review changes that affect performance, cost, schedule, hardware-software interface, and other global concerns beyond the scope of the lower CCBs. In the case of multiple CCBs, it is imperative that a written description of the relationships among the CCBs be prepared. That will ensure that there are no conflicts over authority and that no areas of concern are left unheeded.

The software quality representative to the CCB must make certain that all software quality system requirements for the project are being met. Of particular interest to the software quality representative will be the test plans for a change and the regression tests on the rest of the system to ensure that no unexpected impacts are being felt. Changes are to be tested to the same, or even greater, rigor as original development.

6.3.3 Software libraries

Ultimate access to configuration-controlled code is through the software library.

The software library is the repository of the official issues of all documents and code. The librarian is responsible for the control of the baselined system and all current issues of the documents and code. There must be formal procedures for the entry of a particular issue of a component into the library. Equally formal procedures are used to gain access to the official issues of the components.

Provisions will be made for authors and programmers to access working copies of the official issues but not to enter them back into the current library. There will also be procedures for maintaining cognizance of which working copies are being used, so that two changes are not being made to the same component at the same time without knowledge of the changers.

Once the formal change procedures have been followed, and the CCB has authorized the implementation of a change, an SCN will be generated that tells the librarian to update the current official issue of the affected component. In a well-controlled library, the SCN is the only way to effect a change to the baselined system. Finally, it is the library that prepares the full system for formal delivery to the customer. Along the way, the library will prepare official issues for testing and operation. (Figure 5.2 suggested a format for an SCN.)

As reuse of existing software products becomes more prevalent, the software library's responsibilities usually are increased to include the management and control of reusable items. Not only the item or product itself but the applicable documentation describing the item and its appropriate usage must be available and configuration managed. Reuse of items usually requires some sort of modification to the item so that it correctly fits its new use. Those modifications create variants of the item, which will be managed and controlled just like the original. It is worth repeating that each instance of any CI or product must be carefully managed and its status and baseline records maintained.

It is frequently the additional task of the library to be the repository of all documentation for the software system. In some cases, even contracts and correspondence between the organization and the customer are kept in the central library. The use of the library as a documentation center is an effective way of ensuring that copies of requirements and design documents are available when needed and are of the most current issue.

6.4   Configuration accounting

Baselines mark major CI status levels of the software. However, while the creation of baselines is of major importance in CA, the baselines only form the basis for the actual accounting process.

6.4.1   Baselines

As shown in Figure 6.3, several baselines can be identified, but three of them are most common. Each baseline usually is associated with a major review marking the end of an SDLC phase. Again, there is no industrywide standard for the names of the baselines. The names used here are common in the defense arena.

The functional baseline is established at the SRR. At that point in the SDLC, the requirements have been documented and reviewed, at the end of the requirements phase, for compliance with the criteria discussed in Chapter 3. The functions that will perform the processing necessary to achieve the requirements in a hardware/software system are analyzed and assigned to the hardware and the software as appropriate. Documenting of the software requirements specifies the tasks assigned to the software and what the software is going to do in performing those tasks.

The requirements are then allocated to functions and the design process determines how each requirement is going to be fulfilled. This phase is typically called preliminary design and may not be necessary for simple software projects. When it is included in the system development methodology, it culminates in the PDR. The conclusion of the PDR results in the allocated baseline.

At the end of the full design phase, the "code-to" design has been completed. It is validated in the CDR, which determines the design baseline. It is the design baseline that determines the specification for the coding activities.

Prior to acceptance testing on which user approval of the product is based, an analysis of the results of all preceding testing is performed. On the satisfactory completion of the TRR, the product baseline is established. The product baseline is that instance of the software that will undergo acceptance testing.

At the end of acceptance testing and installation of the software and on completion of the FA and PA, the operational baseline is established. The operational baseline identifies the software as it is going to be delivered to the user or customer. It is occasionally called the "as-built" baseline, since it represents the actual system being delivered. (This is frequently not the system that was originally specified in the initial requirements documentation.) After installation of the software system, the operational baseline will continue to evolve as the software is maintained and enhanced throughout its useful life.

Other baselines have various names and are instituted for specific purposes within the organization. There are no hard and fast rules about how many baselines there should be (other than those that are called out in software development contracts). Each project or organization will determine the applicable level of control needed for the project and will then impose those baselines that fulfill the control needs.

Baselines are defined so that change control may be instituted. The baseline determines the point of departure for all changes to a given status. It is a fixed reference point and all changes are made to that reference point. As CM is imposed with increasing rigor, the baselines become more important as well. It is obvious that if the basis for changes is not known, there is a good chance that the wrong component or instance of the component will be changed. There is also the danger that two changes may be made to the same part of a component without the knowledge of each other.

6.4.2 **Accounting**

Given the baselines and the imposition of CC, the CA element keeps track of the status of the software as it goes through the SDLC and operation. Records of all changes, reviews, and action items affecting the configuration of the software are maintained by CA.

CA must monitor such things as the baselines themselves, where and how they were established, and by whose authority. CA maintains the records of changes made to the current baseline and notes the date of the change request, action of the CCB, status of the change in progress, and data about the ultimate installation of the change.

Instance coordination

An important record maintained by CA is the exact composition of each instance of each software component. The name, release, version, and edition of each product and each of its subordinate components are closely monitored so that when changes are made, all CIDs of affected components can be updated. Not only is this important in the changing of software components, but it is critical to the coherence of the testing and delivery activities. To test and accept one version of a component and then deliver a different version is not conducive to quality software development or installation.

Figure 6.9 depicts a situation in which different versions of products were delivered. In this case, without more information, the user would not know whether the products were internally consistent. Rigorous CA will lessen the likelihood that incompatible instances of related software products will be delivered and used.

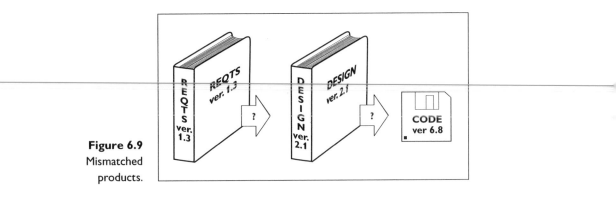

Figure 6.9
Mismatched products.

Instance tracking

As newer technologies, such as client-servers, are implemented, the role of CM, especially CA, becomes even more important. In the mainframe environments still in use throughout the world, most software products exist in only one or two instances. CM is important but not as heavily taxed as in the newer, distributed information processing installations. It is critical to keep track of environmental software such as operating systems, languages, database managers, and so on, so that applications will be subject to the environments for which they were prepared.

Multiple application instances are also frequently present in distributed systems. CM, particularly CA, must ensure that the expected instances of processing applications are called by the user. Maintenance of the environments and applications also depend on CM to ensure that modifications are correct for the product concerned and are applied to the intended products. Coordination of modifications between variants of products becomes a serious concern.

6.5 Summary

CM is the discipline that ensures that the state of the software at any given time is known and reconstructable. It is composed of three basic elements: identification, accounting, and control.

CID permits the uniform naming of each software component and product, down to the lowest separable level.

Baselines, specific points of departure for a new set of development activities and changes, are constructed by the CA portion of CM. CA maintains and records the status of each baseline and its history. Baselines mark major CI status levels during the SLC. They are usually associated with major milestone events (such as formal reviews) in the development cycle.

CC ensures that all approved changes are made to the software. It has the equally significant obligation to ensure that no changes that have not been properly approved are made.

A CI is any product of the software development process that is to be configuration managed. Each CI must have a unique identifier to differentiate it from all the other software development products and other instances of the item itself.

Ultimate access to the SLC products, so that changes can be made, is through the software library, which is the repository of the official, approved issues of all documents and code. Changes to the products of the software development process come from two main sources: defect correction and enhancements. Without an effective change processing mechanism, the software can easily become unidentifiable and unmanageable.

Coordination of changes and their intercomponent effects is the task of the CCB. The CCB is responsible for determining that all effects of the proposed change have been anticipated and reconciled. Especially important is the control that the CCB exercises over the creation of new instances or versions of the various software system products. Once CM has been imposed on the project, it is the CCB that has the authority to approve changes and to permit the updating of the various issues of the products. It is the responsibility of the software quality practitioner to monitor the functioning of the CCBs.

6.6 The next step

To begin your CM program or to see if it is up to date, consult the following texts:

- *Software Configuration Management* by H. Ron Berlack (New York: John Wiley & Sons, 1992).
- *Implementing Configuration Management: Hardware, Software and Firmware*, 2nd Ed., by Fletcher J. Buckley (New York: IEEE Press, 1995).

ADDITIONAL READING

Babich, W. A., *Software Configuration Management Coordination for Team Productivity*, Reading, MA: Addison-Wesley, 1986.

Compton, Stephen B., and Guy R. Conner, *Configuration Management for Software*, New York: Van Nostrand Reinhold, 1994.

Daniels, M. A., *Principles of Configuration Management*, Advanced Applications Consultants, North Babylon, NY, 1985.

Pressman, Roger S., *Making Software Engineering Happen: A Guide to Instituting the Technology*, Englewood Cliffs, NJ: Prentice-Hall, 1988.

Chapter 7

Associated quality concerns

S OME ISSUES, while of concern to the software quality practitioner, are usually outside the practitioner's direct responsibility and authority. Nonetheless, they have no less impact on the quality of the software system. This chapter discusses four important software quality issues.

The role of the software quality practitioner with respect to these issues is to ensure that decision-making, action-capable management is aware of their importance and impact on the software system during its development and after its implementation. These important issues are security, education of developer and users, management of vendors, and maintenance of the software after implementation.

7.1 Security

Security is an issue that is frequently overlooked until it has been breached, either in the loss of or damage to critical data or in a loss to the data center itself.

Security has three main aspects. Two of these aspects deal primarily with data: the security of the database and the security of data being transmitted to other data centers. The third aspect is that of the data center itself and the protection of the resources contained therein.

The software quality practitioner has the responsibility not to protect the data or the data center but to make management aware of the need for or inadequacies in security provisions.

7.1.1 Database security

The software quality concern of data security is that the data used by the software be protected.

Database security is twofold. The data being processed must be correct, and, in many cases, restricted in its dissemination. Many things affect the quality of output from software. Not the least of those is the quality of the data that the software is processing. The quality of the data is affected in several ways. The correctness of the data to be input, the correctness of the inputting process, the correctness of the processing, and, of interest to security, the safety of the data from modification before and after processing are all database security issues.

Data modification can be in the form of inadvertent change by an incorrectly operating hardware or software system outside the system under consideration. It can be caused by something as simple to detect as the mounting of the wrong tape or disk pack or as difficult to trace as faulty client-server communication. From a security point of view, it also can be the result of intentional tampering. A disgruntled employee who passes a magnet over the edges of a tape to scramble the stored images and the hacker who finds his or her way into the system and knowingly or unknowingly changes the database can be a threat to the quality of the software system output. Large distributed computing installations often are victims of the complexity of data storage and access activities. While usually not responsible for the design or implementation of the database system, the quality practitioner should be aware of the increasing security concerns as the systems become more widely disbursed or complex.

The physical destruction of data falls into the area of data center security, which will be discussed later. Modification of the data while they are part of the system is the concern of data security provisions.

Database security generally is imposed through the use of various password and access restriction techniques. Most commonly, a specific password is assigned to each individual who has access to the software system. When someone attempts to use the system, the system asks for identification in the form of a password. If the user can provide the correct password, he or she is allowed to use the system. A record of the access usually is kept by a transaction recording routine so that if untoward results are encountered, they can be "backed out" by a reversal of the actions taken. Further, any damage to the data can be traced to the perpetrator by means of the password that was used.

This scheme works only up to a point. If care is not taken, passwords can be used by unauthorized persons for access to the system. For that reason, many systems now use multiple levels of password protection. One password may let the user access the system as a whole, while another password is needed to access the database. Further restrictions on who can read the data in the database and who can add to it or change it often are invoked. Selective protection of the data also is used. Understanding databases and the logical and physical data models will help the quality practitioner recommend effective security methods.

A typical system of data protection is shown in Figure 7.1. The first control is an unlisted telephone number that accesses the computer. A user who has the telephone number and reaches the computer must then identify himself or herself to the computer to get access to any system at all. Having passed that hurdle and selected a system to use, the user must pass another identification test to get a specific system to permit any activity. In Figure 7.1, the primary system utilizes a remote subsystem that also is password protected. Finally, the database at that point is in read-only mode. To change or manipulate the data, special password characteristics would have to have been present during the three sign-on procedures. In that way, better than average control has been exercised over who can use the software and manipulate the data.

Another concern of database security is the dissemination of the data in the database or the output. Whether or not someone intends to harm the data, there are, in most companies, data that are sensitive to the operation or competitive tactics of the company. If those data can be accessed by a competitor, valuable business interests could be damaged. For that reason, as well as the validity of the data, all database accesses should be candidates for protection.

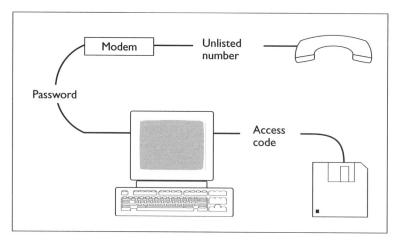

Figure 7.1
Dialup data
protection.

7.1.2 Teleprocessing security

The data within the corporate or intercompany telecommunications network also are a security concern.

Data contained within a database are vulnerable to unauthorized access but not to the extent of data transmitted through a data network. Data networks include such things as simple, remotely actuated processing tasks all the way to interbank transfers of vast sums of money. Simple password schemes are rarely satisfactory in these cases. To be sure, they are necessary as a starting point, but much more protection is needed as the value of the data being transmitted increases.

Two concerns are of importance in regard to telecommunications. The first concern, usually outside the control of a company, is the quality of the transmission medium. Data can be lost or jumbled simply because the carrier is noisy or breaks down, as depicted in Figure 7.2. Defenses against that type of threat include parity checking or check sum calculations with retransmission if the data and the parity or checksums do not coincide. Other more elaborate data validity algorithms are available for more critical or sensitive data transmissions.

Unauthorized access to the data is the other main concern of transmission security. As data are being transmitted, they can be monitored, modified, or even redirected from their original destination to some other location. Care must be taken to ensure that the data transmitted get to their destination correctly and without outside eavesdropping. The methods used to prevent unauthorized data access usually involve encryption to protect the data (Figure 7.3) and end-to-end protocols that make sure the data get to their intended destination.

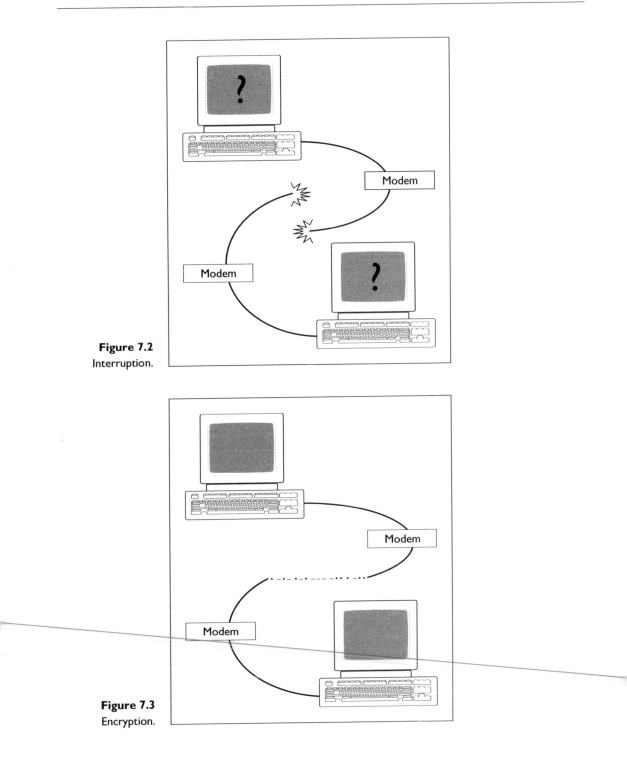

Figure 7.2
Interruption.

Figure 7.3
Encryption.

Encryption can be performed by the transmission system software or by hardware specially designed for that purpose. Industries in the defense arena use highly sophisticated cryptographic equipment, while other companies need only basic encryption algorithms for their transmissions.

As in the case of prevention of loss due to faulty network media, the use of check sums, parity checking, and other data validity methods are employed to try to ensure that the data have not been damaged or tampered with during transmission.

Prevention of the diversion of data from the intended destination to an alternative one is controlled through end-to-end protocols that keep both ends of the transmission aware of the activity. Should the destination end not receive the data it is expecting, the sending end is notified and transmission is terminated until the interference is identified and counteracted.

It is the responsibility of software quality to monitor data security provisions and keep management informed as to their adequacy.

7.1.3 Viruses

A recent entry into the threat scenario is the computer virus. A virus is software that is attached to a legitimate application or data set. It then can do relatively benign, nuisance acts like blanking a screen or printing a message announcing its presence. It also can be intended, like some more recent viruses, to be malignant, in that it intentionally destroys software or data. Some viruses can even erase a full hard disk.

A virus usually is introduced as an attachment to software that, often in violation of copyright laws, is shared among users. Downloading software from a bulletin board is one of the more frequent virus infection methods. Data disks used on an infected system can carry the virus back to an otherwise healthy system, as shown in Figure 7.4.

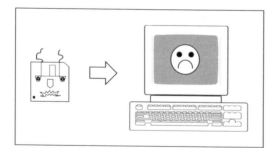

Figure 7.4
Virus introduction.

Some viruses do not act immediately. They can be programmed to wait for a specific date, like the famous Michelangelo virus, or, perhaps, some specific processing action. At the preprogrammed time, the virus activates the mischief or damage it is intended to inflict.

Many antiviral packages are available. Unfortunately, the antiviral "vaccines" can fight only those viruses that have been identified. New viruses can cause damage before antiviral software is available.

The best defense against viruses, although not altogether foolproof, is to use only software fresh from the publisher or vendor. Pirated software—software that has not been properly acquired—is a common source of infection.

7.1.4 Risk analysis

The best software systems in the world are not useful if they cannot be run. That may seem like a rather basic concept, but the security of the data center itself is often the last concern of an organization. The data center is at constant risk from fire and water damage; any precautions taken usually are in that area. Beyond that, most data centers overlook the potential for interrupted processing due to severe damage. Unfortunately, few data centers make provisions for temporary processing facilities in case of damage to the center.

A formal risk analysis will expose the various types of damage to which a specific data center is vulnerable and the degree of protection that is appropriate.

Many physical risks may threaten a particular data center. Fire, of course is the most widely acknowledged threat, and provisions are nearly universal for prevention, detection, and extinguishing of fire. A second commonly recognized threat is water, usually from above, in the form of rain leakage or a burst water pipe. There, too, provisions for detection and protection are common. Unfortunately, protection frequently stops there because other risks are not recognized or given credence. A risk analysis can point out additional threats against which protection may be required.

A risk analysis may show the potential for severe weather damage that is a real factor in hurricane and tornado regions and in areas where heavy snow can damage roofs. The potential for fire damage may be shown to exist not only within the data center but immediately outside it, such as in adjacent warehouses or office areas. The proximity of landing aircraft or railroad sidings presents the possibility of damage from accidents outside the center. Electrical power transmission lines in the immediate vicinity could break in a storm and fall onto or into the data center.

Intentional damage is a real threat, as well. One data center was flooded by a recently discharged employee who went to the top floor of the building and opened the fire hose connection. That occurred on a weekend, when the bulk of the building was deserted. By the time the basement data center first noticed the presence of water, there was sufficient water on the way to flood the center to a depth of five feet. A risk analysis per formed prior to the installation of the data center may have warned against its being placed in the basement, where water would have nowhere else to go. A second data center had no thought of intentional damage being done to it until a terrorist bomb destroyed a nearby data center. Again, risk analysis could have shown the danger of building the data center in that particular location.

Not all risks are preventable. In fact, some are inevitable, so no real prevention can be provided. Others will cause such little negative effect as to be ignored. Each risk must, however, be identified before such judgments can be made. Risk analyses help the diligent data center determine the best places to spend its protection dollars. Determining that a particular factor is of little or negligible risk is as important as finding those factors that do present risk. Once the risks and their costs of occurrence are known, preventive or protective action can be taken.

7.1.5   Disaster recovery

A specific plan of recovery should be developed and tested to ensure continued operation in the case of damage to the data center.

Even the best risk analysis, prevention, detection, and correction are not always enough to avoid damage that can prevent the data center from operating for some period of time. Many companies are now so dependent on their data processing facility that even a shutdown of a few days could be life threatening to the organization. Yet the majority of companies have done little or no effective planning for the eventuality of major damage to their data centers. Sometimes a company will enter into a mutual assistance agreement with a neighboring data center. Each agrees to perform emergency processing for the other in the event of a disaster to one of them. What they often fail to recognize is that each of them is already processing at or near the capacity of their own data center and has no time or resources to spare for the other's needs. Another fault with that approach is that the two companies often are in close physical proximity. Although that makes assistance more convenient from a travel and logistics viewpoint, if the disaster suffered by one of them was the result of a storm or serious accident like a falling airplane, the odds are high that the backup center also suffered significant damage. Now both of them are without alternative facilities.

One answer to these threats is the remote, alternative processing site. A major company may provide its own site, which it keeps in reserve for an emergency. The reserve site normally is used for interruptable processing that can be set aside in the case of a disaster. However, because a reserve site is an expensive proposition, many companies enroll in disaster recovery backup cooperatives. These cooperatives provide facilities of varying resources at which a member company can perform emergency processing until its own center is repaired or rebuilt.

Two conditions must be in place to augment the backup processing center approach. The first condition, usually in place for other reasons, is the remote storage of critical data in some location away from the data center proper. That way, if something happens to a current processing run or the current database, a backup set of files is available from which the current situation can be reconstructed. The backup files should be generated no less frequently than daily, and the place in which they are stored should be well protected from damage and from unauthorized access as a part of the overall data security scheme.

The second necessity in a disaster recovery program is a comprehensive set of tests of the procedures that will enable emergency processing to commence at the remote backup site. All aspects of the plan, from the original notification of the proper company authorities that a disaster has occurred through the actual implementation of the emergency processing software systems at the backup site should be rehearsed on a regular basis. Most backup cooperatives provide each member installation with a certain number of test hours each year, which need to be augmented by a series of tests of the preparations leading up to the move to the backup site. Notification procedures, access to the backup files, transportation to the backup site, security for the damaged data center to prevent further damage, provision for the acquisition of new or repaired data processing equipment both for the backup site and the damaged data center, provisions for telecommunications if required, and other types of preparations should be thoroughly documented and tested along with the actual operation at the backup site.

Software quality practitioners are natural conductors for the tests, since they must ensure that the disaster recovery plan is in place and that the emergency processing results are correct. Further, software quality is the reporting agency to management on the status of disaster recovery provisions.

Education

Education of personnel in the proper performance of their tasks is important to the production and use of quality software systems.

Education, while rarely provided by the software quality group, is a necessary step in the provision of a quality product. The software quality practitioner has as one responsibility the monitoring of the educational activities that surround the development and use of software systems. Education is one of the elements of the SQS that is most often delegated to another group in the company. While software quality practitioners will monitor and report on the educational status with regard to each development project, they rarely are the educating facility. Most companies utilize an inhouse education group, video courses, outside instructors, outside seminars, and hands-on or on-the-job education and training methods.

Programmers must be taught the proper use of programming languages and software development facilities for their assignments. Users must be taught the proper ways to use the software system and its results. The operations personnel need to learn the correct procedures for running the system. And, finally, the various support groups, including software quality, must be educated in the proper performance of their tasks.

7.2.1 Developer education

The production of a quality software system depends heavily on the performance of the producers.

Developers—the designers, analysts, coders, and testers—must know their jobs in order to contribute to the production of a quality software system. All the participants must have the proper training and background to permit them to do their jobs correctly. Inadequate education, missing experience, and lack of training all can contribute to lower than acceptable performance and, thus, lower than acceptable quality in the end product.

It is obvious that a system designer who knows little about the system being designed can bring little insight into the solution of the problem. To expect a designer well schooled in accounting systems to be a top performer on a radar guidance system without specific education in radar theory and practice would be an invitation to a product with questionable reliability.

New techniques for design and programming are being developed at a rapid pace. While not every new technique can or should be applied to every project, the more experience and education in the various techniques that a staff has, the more likely it is that the best approach will be taken. Some techniques, like structured design and programming, have been widely accepted as the standard approach to be taken in all cases. Newer techniques are beginning to show that, while it is a fine methodology in many situations, structured design and programming are not always the best methods. Techniques such as rapid prototyping, automated design, and program design languages are being shown to be superior in a growing number of applications. Better techniques usually mean better results and higher productivity. Education of the development staff can lead to the implementation of that software development methodology best suited for the specific application.

Equally important to the development of quality software systems is the fluency of the programming and coding personnel in the language in which the system is being written. One of the more important education concerns of the software quality practitioner is that the developers be knowledgeable in the language to be used for the system. While emphasis generally is on the coders, it is also important that the designers and testers be well trained in the language. That way, the designers can express design considerations in terms more understandable to the coders and help the testers understand the intricacies of the code itself.

Another area of educational concern is the background environment to be used during the development. Such things as operating systems and database management systems greatly affect the design and implementation of the software and should be well understood by the developers. Failure of the developers to recognize the various characteristics of the software environment can cause many headaches later in operation and testing. Even the operation of the desktop terminal cannot be overlooked in the educational process. Software development is a labor-intensive activity, and many tools, techniques, and methodologies are coming forth. Computer-aided software engineering; object-oriented techniques; client-server and distributed processing; local-, wide-, and municipal-area networks; value-added networks; test tools; database management applications; visual development languages; graphical user interfaces; and the like are all areas of challenge to the information technology developer. The quality of the development and the productivity of the developers depend to a large extent on the level of education, training, and experience of the developers.

7.2.2 Support training

Support includes both the development environment that must be maintained and the ancillary activities such as software quality, configuration management, testing, and security.

As already mentioned, developers need to be schooled in the programming environment, such as the operating system and the database management system. They need to know how the environment is going to affect the software being developed and vice versa. Care must be taken, though, that the personnel charged with the creation and maintenance of that environment are well educated in their tasks. In addition, the developers must be well educated in the specific development methodology to be used on a given project. Development methodologies such as structured and object-oriented analysis and design techniques and fourth-generation languages require detailed understanding if they are to be applied beneficially.

As Figure 7.5 shows, the development staff is at the center of and is supported by a much larger environment. Failures in any of the surrounding fields can seriously affect the ability of the developers to accomplish their assigned tasks.

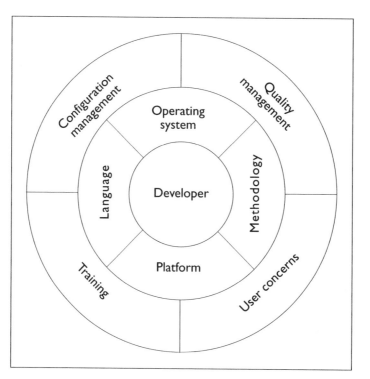

Figure 7.5
Developer's world.

The area commonly known as systems programming includes the operating systems and various language systems. Without them, there is no software development at all and effectively no maintenance. The software quality practitioner is responsible for ensuring that an adequate and ongoing education program is provided for the systems programming staff.

Database administration, security measures, and telecommunications are also present in most organizations. Poorly trained or inexperienced personnel in those groups also must receive the necessary training and education to keep them able to cope with the advances being made in those disciplines and the growing dependence of the total organization on them.

The testing group is a frequently overlooked area for education. The test group should be knowledgeable in the system as a whole, the programming language being used, and the programming environment. Armed with such information and knowledge, the testers are able to see areas of potential weakness in the code and can test for those weaknesses.

Finally, software quality practitioners cannot ignore themselves in ensuring that all software personnel have adequate education and training for their jobs. The software quality people must know how to review documents, the standards being imposed on the various projects, how to communicate their findings upward to management, how to accomplish the various audits for which they are responsible, and all the rest of the SQS tasks.

7.2.3 User education

The best system will not perform well if incorrectly used. It is worth restating that if the users of a system do not have full knowledge of how to use the system, the system will not perform up to its capabilities. The system may be underused, which effectively wastes some of the effort put into its creation. It may not work at all, making the whole system a waste. Worst of all, incorrect use of the system may negatively affect other systems being run; sometimes even to the extent of bringing a halt to the whole processing activity. It should be clear that user education is at least as important as developer education.

The two main areas of user education are the inputting of data and the use of the outputs from the system. Data input includes starting the system and telling it what it is required to do for any particular processing exercise. Some systems need only be started, and they then perform a series of preset functions. Such things as process control or standard data reduction systems may fall into that category. Knowing how to start the system is the important point. Other systems require parameters or additional data to be provided. Payroll systems, for example, need to have time records input and may have to have parameters, such as special bonus equation values, entered. The proper provision of existing databases is important in both cases. Finally, some systems are interactive, and the user must respond to the system while it is running, perhaps by providing additional input or by giving directions based on the system's computations or questions. A simple example is the word processing package on which this text was generated. The user entered text into the package, and the package occasionally asked for directions on what to do in certain situations, like reaching the limit of the working memory allotment.

The use of the produced information is of equal importance. If a security system detects an attempted breach of the secure area, the user must have full instructions as to what action to take. That is true whether the breach attempted is of a data security system or of a building. If the system has not been designed to respond with some action on its own, the user must take the appropriate action.

More often, though, the output is in the form of business or scientific data in one format or another. Business users and users of scientific data must understand what they are receiving and what to do with it. At other times, education in the use of the output will be as simple as informing the user to whom a particular printer report is to go. Whatever the specific system requires, though, with respect to inputs and outputs, the user must be properly trained in its usage.

Other user educational considerations include such things as the limits of the system. These may involve valid input data limits, number of entries that the system can accept at one time, speed of input, limits on the size or type of outputs, access control passwords, frequency of usage in a particular time period, and so on. Each user must be aware of the capabilities built into the system so those capabilities are not violated or underused. Asking more of the system that it can provide may lead to crashes, while under-utilization may lead to underestimation on future projects.

Dr. W. Edwards Deming was a strong proponent of employee training and development. Implementation of new software products and systems normally brings change to the way users perform their jobs, or the environment in which they work. New jobs and tasks may be created, while existing jobs and tasks may be vastly altered or even eliminated. Management of this type of change offers many educational and development opportunities.

The software quality practitioners' role in user education is much the same as their role in developer education; that is, the monitoring of the user education plans and progress so the proper education is provided. Software quality practitioners may even take the education themselves as a part of the acceptance test procedures. By exercising the system in the same manner as the intended users, the test team often can find flaws not only in the software but also in the educational programs.

7.2.4 Operations training

If a system is not run properly, results are suspect and users cannot rely on the information provided.

Operation includes everything from computer power-up to report delivery. Virtually anything and anyone outside the user at the terminal at his or her desk can be thought of as the domain of the operations organization. Operations loads the data media, starts the various applications, monitors throughput, puts paper in the printer, delivers the reports to their intended recipients, and keeps the operational environment sufficient for the processing load being demanded by the developers and users. Training in this area encompasses an extremely wide range of activities. And, of course, there is a correspondingly wide range of potential problems if the personnel are not properly and completely trained in their functions.

In the early days of computer centers, the operations group had to contend with only the running of jobs. The jobs generally were run in the order in which they were submitted, and the reports were placed in a mailbox-like slot for someone to retrieve. As the computing industry has matured, the complexity of the computer center activities has increased manyfold. Multiple processors are running multiple jobs, many of which are submitted at the same time with multiple priorities. Those processors in turn may be generating multiple outputs on multiple media. Operations personnel must be knowledgeable in job sequencing, computing hardware operation, data entry and validation, report distribution, remote job entry and computing, security, job control languages, defect reporting and correction, long-range and short-range facilities planning, space allocation, safety, and a multitude of other considerations. Training must be provided in most of these fields, since on-the-job training often takes too long for a new person to become proficient and productive.

In some cases, generally in very large and very small data centers, on-the-job training is feasible. In a large shop, new employees are assigned to small, specialized tasks such as tape or disk loading and unloading. They are then rotated through the various tasks. A small shop usually has a simple small-scale computer whose operation can be learned quickly. A small shop also has a correspondingly small set of applications with which to deal. The bulk of computer centers, however, include multiple central processing units and several types of data media. When experienced personnel cannot be hired, they must be trained by the organization.

The software quality practitioners should monitor the operations activity and the levels of training present within it. Close coordination with the manager of the operations area will ensure that the proper training is provided to the operations personnel.

7.2.5 Education delivery

Various educational needs are met in different ways, but there are five major methods of delivering the needed education. Each method is applicable to one or more of the education and training needs discussed so far. These methods are:

- On-the-job or hands-on training;
- Formal classes;
- Seminars;
- Video tapes;
- Demonstrations.

Developer education should include all the methods that are suited to the individuals' needs. On-the-job training is the slowest method for most development tasks, but it can be of value to the new employee who has had some formal education in computer programming, computer science, or the specific application area being developed. Formal classes, either in an actual classroom atmosphere or through video tapes, are valuable to both the learning of new applications areas and the gaining of familiarity with features of new development environments. Languages are best learned through a formal classroom experience coupled with hands-on exercises. New design techniques are often the subject of seminars and video tapes. Demonstrations can be used to show how new equipment, such as workstations or desktop terminals, is to be utilized.

Support personnel have much the same education needs as do the developers, though in different areas, of course. The methods that seem to best serve support education are similar to those for developers. Classrooms are appropriate for operating system and language familiarization as well as database operation. For highly experienced personnel, seminars and video tapes are sometimes sufficient. If the subject to be learned is an extension of a system already in place in the organization, hands-on experience and demonstrations can be used.

User education can sometimes be provided with demonstrations or in-house seminars, even on-the-job learning if the system is simple or similar to or an extension of existing systems. New, large-scale systems frequently need formal classroom education when the range of user opportunities is wide or there is much user system interaction. In the latter case, hands-on experiences are justified as well. Video tapes are less useful unless they are an adjunct to demonstrations or formal classroom presentations.

Operations training almost always is a series of demonstrations of the proper way to perform a particular task. This method is usually enhanced by hands-on or on-the-job training. For new equipment, formal classroom and video tape presentations are often appropriate. When new environment systems (operating systems, languages, database management systems, and the like) are being installed, more formal training is needed, and the classroom may again be the preferred method. Finally, hands-on experience and demonstrations will be an almost regular part of the routine in a large data center as additional data storage media are installed and enhancements to the environment are made.

Once more, it should be emphasized that the role of the software quality practitioner in the training of personnel is monitoring and reporting the status of the various training situations. The actual delivery of the education and training is normally the responsibility of the education department or the individual group, such as development or operations. The software quality practitioner keeps management aware of the need for education and training and their status. Table 7.1 suggests typical types and sources of training and the recipients for whom they may be suited. There are no hard and fast rules; each organization must use the means at their disposal.

Training need	Recipient	Training source
Application area	Developer	Classroom
Design methods	Developer Quality group Developer	Classroom Demonstration Vendor
Operating system	Developer	Vendor
Database management system	Data administrator	Vendor
Language	Developer	Classroom
Testing	Tester	Seminar, on-the-job training
SQS	Quality group Developer	Seminar Demonstration
Operations	Operator	Demonstration
Application use	User Customer service	Demonstration, classroom Classroom
Networks	Developer User	Seminar, demonstration Demonstration

Table 7.1
Training needs
and sources

7.3 **Vendor management**

Purchasing software often is a risky business at best. While there are many reasons for an organization to buy software rather than write it inhouse, the role of the software quality practitioner often is reduced. Thus, the risks increase that the software will not meet its requirements.

When software is purchased, much, if not all, control over development is lost. The risks run from slightly more than those for inhouse development all the way to "what you see is what you get." The role of the software quality practitioner changes when software is purchased. Since visibility into the development process is diminished, if not lost altogether, other avenues must be found to investigate and ascertain software quality. The software quality practitioner must be innovative in selecting quality methods to apply and firm in insisting that those methods be applied.

There are many packages and methodologies that can help with software product acquisition, but the basic quality concerns remain the same.

Three basic types of software purchase are available: off the shelf, tailored, and new development. Each type presents a different challenge to the software quality practitioner. Visibility and influence over the development process change as each type of purchase is exercised. Table 7.2 gives examples of purchased software and quality approaches that could be applied to them.

Type	Source	Quality approach
Graphics application	Off the shelf	Vendor reputation, trial use period
Database manager	Off the shelf	Vendor reputation, trial use period
Operating system	Vendor	Trial use period, vendor maintenance
Tailored application	Application customizer	Partial purchaser SQS, test records, vendor maintenance
Contracted application	Third-party developer	Full purchaser SQS, vendor maintenance

Table 7.2
Quality
approaches to
purchased
software

Each type of purchase presents different maintenance situations. Who will maintain the purchased software is an important consideration for the software quality practitioner in evaluating purchased software.

7.3.1 Off-the-shelf software

Purchasing off-the-shelf software allows little or no insight into the processes involved in its development.

Software purchased off the shelf, for example, an operating system, a compiler, or a database management system, whether for a mainframe or a portable computer, usually comes as is. Usually there are no guarantees and sometimes blunt denials of any liability on the part of the vendor. This type of software offers the greatest challenge to software quality practitioners.

Few traditional quality assurance steps can be taken with off-the-shelf software. Often, the only evidence of a vendor's software development process is its reputation in the marketplace. The quality and the availability of documentation can also provide clues. However, even in the best of cases, visibility into the development process is dim and unreliable. Software quality practitioners must resort to emphasis on other aspects of software development in order to do their job.

The primary step is to clearly identify the requirements for the software package that is needed. Software quality practitioners must make every effort to determine what the organizational needs are for a software purchase. For example, many database packages exist for personal computers. If a company or organization decided to provide its employees with personal computer workstations, including a database package, software quality practitioners would have to urge as much specificity in the requirements of the database as could be determined. Once the actual, intended usage and application of the database package were determined, evaluation of candidate vendors and their products could commence. At this point, the process is no different from traditional software development. Until the software requirements are known, software development or, in this case, purchase should not begin.

Having settled on the requirements, vendor and product evaluation can begin. Vendors with the reputation of developing sound packages and packages that best appear to meet the requirements will be identified. When one or more possible packages have been identified, two more SQS activities should take place: the specific testing of the packages and consideration of future maintenance. Either or both of these actions may be impossible for a given vendor or product. In that case, the product should be dismissed.

The vendor should provide for a period of real-world use of a potential package. Most acceptable vendors will allow a trial use period in which the buyer has a chance to see if the product really meets the requirements for it. Unless there are serious, overriding conditions, software quality practitioners should counsel against purchase of off-the-shelf software from a vendor who will not allow such a test. Test or demonstration portions of many packages also are available for trial use. Some vendors sell the demonstration package and give credit for the demonstration package price against the purchase of the full software package.

When permitted by licensing terms or provisions, reverse engineering techniques can be applied to establish design methods or data models. These can then be assessed for compliance to the approved requirements. Such techniques, however, must be undertaken only when the vendor grants permission. The quality practitioner should alert management that carrying out such activities without permission may result in legal action on the part of the vendor for copyright infringement.

The second action is the review of vendor software maintenance provisions. A package that provides for vendor support, free updates when latent defects are found and corrected, reduced cost for new versions offering enhanced capability, and the like, should receive special attention. Vendors who agree to nothing, once the package has been bought, should be viewed with a suspicious eye by software quality practitioners. The most likely case is a negotiated agreement as to the costs involved in various kinds of maintenance situations. Again, the marketplace reputation of the vendor should influence that activity.

All in all, purchase of off-the-shelf packages is risk intensive. Of course there are situations when it is the proper method of providing software capability to the users. Software quality practitioners must recognize the risks involved, however, and act to reduce those risks with whatever means are available.

7.3.2 Tailored shells

Software often can be purchased as a *shell*, which is generic and off the shelf. Its advantage is that the purchaser's unique needs are custom built into the shell and the total package tailored to the specific application.

As in pure off-the-shelf software, software quality practitioners will have little influence over the generic shell portion. The shells usually are prebuilt and act as a foundation for the customized software that will be added. The software quality practitioner should encourage negotiation of development control over the customized portions.

The reputation of the vendor often is a good clue in this type of software purchase, just as it is for off-the-shelf software. During early evaluation of potential vendors and shells, software quality practitioners can review marketplace reports to help identify leading vendors for particular applications.

After-purchase maintenance also must be considered. Unlike most off-the-shelf software, a purchaser may be able to take over some or all of the maintenance of a tailored package. Cost of source documentation for the shell, postpurchase vendor maintenance announcements, and the buyer's ability to maintain the software should be investigated by the software quality practitioner and corresponding recommendations made to management.

It is entirely acceptable to request that the vendor's proprietary source code be placed in escrow against the possibility that the vendor becomes unwilling or unable to continue maintenance of the software. In such an event, the customer would receive the code from the escrow and take over maintenance at that point. In some cases, the source code would become the property of the customer after some contractually agreed period of time. In that way, the vendor's proprietary property is protected, and the customer is at less risk of loss of maintainability of important software.

Testing of the tailored portion of the software is commonplace, so the software quality practitioner's main concerns in this area are the quality of the software requirements and the adequacy of the test program. Software quality practitioners must urge the adequate statement of requirements for the software and then ascertain that the test program will, while finding defects, give confidence that the software meets the requirements.

Finally, software quality practitioners should encourage management to secure warranties or guarantees with respect to at least the custom portions of the software.

7.3.3 Contracted new development

Purchase of total software packages, developed as new software for a specific buyer, provides the greatest opportunity for involvement of the purchaser's software quality practitioners.

The purchase of or contract for the development of a new software package is similar to an inhouse development effort. All the same activities in the software development process must be accomplished under the auspices of the software quality practitioners. It is expected that the buyer's software quality requirements will cause the invocation of at least as stringent software quality requirements on the vendor as are followed by the buyer. Even when more strict software quality requirements are placed on the vendor, the buyer's software quality practitioner's visibility is probably hampered.

Remembering that the purchase of new software permits (in fact, requires) the buyer to specify all the software requirements, the software quality practitioner should be certain to have all the quality program requirements included in the contract. Not only should the vendor be contractually required to provide a strong software quality program, the buyer's software quality requirements must demand visibility into that program and its conduct. The buyer must have the right to conduct regular scheduled and unscheduled reviews and audits of the vendor's development process and controls at the vendor's facility. Too often, these reviews and audits are held at the buyer's facility and amount to little more than "dog and pony shows" at which the buyer is assured that everything is fine. Only later does the buyer discover that costs are overrun, schedules have slipped, and the software doesn't work. The buyer's software quality practitioners must be provided the contractual right to visibility into the vendor's activities.

Maintenance of the software continues to be a concern of software quality practitioners. If the vendor will be contracted to maintain the software, software quality practitioners should continue their regular level of visibility into the vendor's processes. When maintenance will become the responsibility of the buyer, software quality practitioners must be sure that training, documentation, and the inhouse facility to maintain the software are in place prior to delivery of the new software.

Finally, software quality practitioners should be sure that all new software being purchased is subject to rigorous, requirements-based acceptance testing prior to approval and acceptance by the buyer.

7.4 Maintenance

A frequently quoted "fact" of the software industry is that something like 70% of the SLC is devoted to maintenance. There may be empirical data somewhere to back this up, or it may just be someone's off-the-cuff observation. The important thing is that it indicates that many companies expend a large share of their software resources in maintenance activities.

The heavy majority of effort in the SLC is expended in the maintenance phase. While maintenance is considered to be composed of both defect correction and enhancements to the original system, most maintenance is the result of requirements or design deficiency or planned obsolescence. (Planned obsolescence is usually termed "phased implementation.") Certainly there will be occurrences of latent coding defects that remained hidden through the testing process, but the majority of defects usually are found to be faulty requirements and design.

Two points about maintenance should be made. First, except for the very simple correction of a very simple coding defect, maintenance is usually a repeat of the SDLC activities. Second, the cost of maintenance is almost never clearly known or recorded.

The role of software quality practitioners is also twofold: (1) monitoring the SDLC-type activities the same as was done in original development, and (2) trying to help management realize the true cost of the maintenance effort. Once management can see and understand the cost of maintenance, the task of justifying the SQS activities will become much more achievable.

7.4.1 Types of maintenance

The four broad categories of maintenance are repairs, polishing, enhancements, and adaptations.

Repairs are necessary to resolve latent defects that survived the best efforts of the testing program and improvements to make the system do those things that were wanted but were left out of the original requirements or design. As shown in Figure 7.6, repair of actual defects that were found after the system was placed in full operation account for about 20% of the maintenance activity. Another percentage is the result of additions made to bring the system up to the level of capability originally desired, which might be called polishing. Little definitive data exist to express the degree of effort expended in making those changes, but at least a portion of the enhancement number will include requirements corrections as well as new requirements.

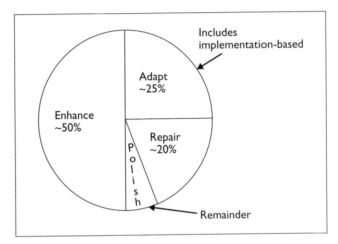

Figure 7.6
Maintenance types.

Enhancements, shown as the largest category in Figure 7.6, are those changes to give the system capabilities that were not originally foreseen. Often, enhancements come at the request of the user, who finds that additional capabilities would be desirable. While new requirements and needs frequently do arise over the life of a software system, it is likely that many corrections are identified as enhancements. Requirements that were overlooked or ignored during the original development often come back as enhancements. That may happen even though they probably were caused by errors in the requirements analysis or design portions of development. Maintenance that is termed an enhancement should not include any change that helps the system perform as it should have originally.

Adaptations, another large category, are generally in response to changing environmental conditions or the outside world. Environmental conditions might include a change to a different computer or a new operating system. Outside conditions could include a change in government regulations relating to an insurance or banking system.

Software quality practitioners must be closely involved in the maintenance activity to ensure that proper control of the software and documentation configurations is enforced. In a protracted maintenance period, the loss of control of the configuration can mean the introduction of new defects as the existing ones are found and corrected. Software quality practitioners will monitor and audit the defect reporting and tracking system reports and ensure that the configuration management function is in operation throughout the maintenance period.

Repairs

Repairs reflect defects from all sources. Repairs are the changes made for every defect, from the simplest latent coding mistake, such as a misspelled data name, to a requirements deficiency. While repairs consume a minority percentage of the overall SLC costs, they do represent the most expensive tasks. Defects that must be repaired in the maintenance phase almost always affect more than just the code. Those requirements that were known but not addressed should be categorized as defects and processed as repairs.

Each repair will result in the reentry of the development cycle, as shown in Figure 7.7. Each repair must go through the full life cycle as the requirements of the repair are determined: design, code, test, and implementation. The type and the impact of the defect will determine how far back into the development products the repair will reach. In the large majority of cases, the ramifications go back through code to design and sometimes requirements. That in turn means corrections to documentation, sometimes corrections to other parts of the system to accommodate the repair, testing of the changed areas, and regression testing of the entire system. The cost of repairing a requirements defect in the maintenance phase is often 90 to 100 times the cost to repair the defect if it had been found in the requirements phase.

Estimates are that about a third of all corrections themselves introduce new defects. Introduction of new defects is the case especially when short cuts are taken in the repair process. If configuration management procedures are skipped or testing is slipshod or incomplete, the chances of introducing a new defect are greatly magnified.

Polishing

Polishing may be some of the most difficult of maintenance to perform. Most polishing is performed to increase the operating speed of an application or to reduce its memory requirements. Quite often, these changes can be extremely far reaching, as loops are removed from the code to increase speed added to the code to reduce size. When both goals are present, large-scale reengineering of the system may be required. The software quality practitioner should be sure that all participants in the polishing maintenance activities are aware of the breadth of the effects their changes may have.

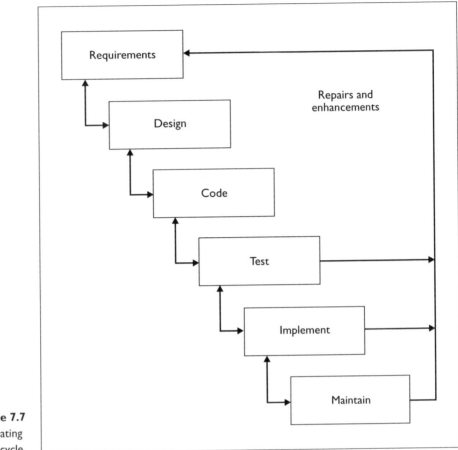

Figure 7.7
Repeating
the life cycle.

Enhancements

Enhancements usually follow the full SDLC. Enhancements occur because the original requirements did not address some need of the user or customer. They are limited to those needs that become visible or recognized after the system has been installed and running. Enhancements cover the addition of new capabilities and the removal of obsolete capabilities.

Again, Figure 7.7 shows the return path to the SDLC. Enhancements always reenter the SDLC at the requirements phase, since new requirements almost always are involved, and the entire SDLC traversed. New development planning must take place, which must include planning for the transition to the improved system once it is ready. There also may be some consideration given to provision of the needed capabilities until the software is ready to support them. The entire SDLC is then followed, just as in the original development. Testing and configuration management play a large role in the enhancement process, just as they do in the repairs process. Regression testing is especially important, as well.

The software quality practitioner has the same set of functions in the repair and enhancement processes as in the original development. Since the SDLC is being followed, so must the SQS procedures.

Adaptations

Adaptations are the modification of capabilities to meet changes from outside the original system. Activities include changes to meet new government regulations, modifications to company procedures, inclusions of new products, and similar conditions that did not exist at the time of the development of the original system.

Adaptations also include those changes made to accommodate implementation approaches. A typical type of implementation approach is phased implementation, which usually is done when the schedule or the complexity of the system will not permit implementation of the entire capability of the system all at once. The adaptations are the changes to the "edges" of the implemented software to interface with the next phase of software being implemented. Since some of the total software system has been missing up to this point, something has been done to allow the existing software to operate until the new software is added. Those allowances must be removed when the next software is ready for implementation.

Most often, the problem is in the development planning for the system. Resources, generally schedule resources, are miscalculated and run out before the system is ready for implementation. In that case, the system is partitioned into functional groups that can be implemented one or a few at a time. Some subset of the system is installed, and then, at a later time, additional system partitions are installed piecemeal until the full system is in place. This has the advantage of permitting more attention to the various phases of the SDLC, but it usually is a repair in the context of this chapter.

Only in those cases where there was good reason at the outset to plan for a phased implementation can an adaptation not be considered a repair. One case would be an experimental system in which each step is a major evaluation—and possible termination—point of the development. Other cases would be those in which the system has a large number of outside interfaces that become available at inconvenient times or where the complexity of the system dictates that smaller sections be installed one by one. It is probably appropriate to exclude these cases from the realm of maintenance altogether, since they were planned to occur from the beginning of the project.

Adaptations carry significant risk in some cases. There is small risk when the adaptation takes the form of a simple change to a job entry routine or a spreadsheet formula. They become more threatening when they entail modifications as great as database reconfiguration. Software quality practitioners must monitor adaptations as closely as the other types of maintenance.

7.4.2 Documentation

Regardless of why or where the SDLC is reentered, it is essential that the system documentation be maintained. It cannot be stressed too much that the documentation of the system is the key to the ease of repair or enhancement. The better the documentation, the more easily the maintenance personnel can find and correct a defect or properly install an enhancement. If the needed documentation is lacking, the maintainer must either recreate it or try to find the affected portion of the system through detective work. When the issues of the documents for the various phases are out of step, the maintainer has more work to do in the documentation of his or her work as well.

If more than one change is in progress at the same time, such as both an enhancement and a repair, poor documentation practices may allow the two activities to operate on different issues of the system or to conflict with each other. If the documentation is up to date and correct, both maintainers can recognize any areas of overlap in their work and can work together during the change process rather than creating another defect that must be repaired.

Software quality practitioners perform an important monitoring and reporting function in the maintenance phase by keeping management informed as to the quality and status of the documentation.

7.4.3 Regression testing

The software quality practitioner has an additional concern in the maintenance phase, that of ensuring that regression testing is accomplished. While the software quality practitioner must monitor the regular SDLC testing function, the maintenance phase introduces the regression testing activity. Although the SDLC is used to create repairs and enhancements, they normally affect only a portion of the entire system. Once the change has been tested for its own correctness, the full system must undergo overall testing to ensure that the changes have not had some unexpected negative effect on the operation of the system as a full entity.

Regression testing should be a part of the overall test plan developed for the system during its original SDLC. As the system acceptance test is designed, and data for the test are prepared, a subset of the acceptance test data should be preserved for future regression tests. The expected and actual results also should be preserved. In that way, the correct performance of the original system is known. When regression testing is needed, the same test data that were used for the acceptance test are used. The original results should be received from unchanged parts of the system, showing that unintentional changes have not been made or new defects introduced.

For those changed portions of the system, new regression test data must be prepared for use in future change activity. The software quality practitioner has the responsibility of ensuring that the regression tests are prepared in the beginning, and that they are kept up to date during the full SLC. Further, the practitioner must ensure that all differences from the expected results of the regression tests are accounted for.

7.5 Summary

Security has three main aspects; the database, data transmission, and the physical data center itself. Most companies could not last long without data being processed. Should the data become corrupted, lost, or known outside the company, much commercial harm could result.

The failure of the data center, no matter what the cause, can also have great negative effect on the viability of the enterprise. A disaster recovery plan should be developed and tested by the organization, with the software quality practitioner monitoring the plans for completeness and feasibility.

As systems increase in size and complexity and as companies rely more and more on their software systems, the security aspects of quality become more important. The software quality practitioner has the responsibility to make management aware of the need for security procedures.

Education, while rarely provided by the software quality practitioner, is a necessary step in the provision of a quality product. It is one of the elements of the SQS that is most often delegated to another group within the company.

Fluency of the programming and coding personnel in the language in which the system is being written is very important. So, too, is familiarity with the background environment to be used during the development.

Training for the support environment must not be overlooked. Systems programming (the operating systems and compiler-assembler software), database administration, and the testing group should be thoroughly trained in their tasks. The software quality practitioners must not forget themselves in ensuring that all software personnel have adequate knowledge in their responsibilities.

If the users do not have the proper education in the system's use, the system may perform inadequately and be seen as less than acceptable. The operations staff, too, must be schooled in the operation of the system for it to supply the expected outputs.

The software quality practitioner must keep management aware of the needs for training and education.

All purchased software presents risks that are not present in software developed inhouse. Software quality practitioners must be innovative in identifying the various risks attendant to the different types of software purchase. Software quality practitioners must be equally innovative in finding ways to meet and blunt those risks.

There must be an awareness not only of the developmental risks, but also of the maintenance requirements for the software after delivery. Training of the maintainers, suitable maintenance-oriented documentation, and the hardware and software facilities to support software maintenance must be available. Placing the vendor's proprietary source code in escrow should be considered. The software quality practitioner has the responsibility to ascertain the availability and sufficiency of software maintenance needs. Should there be a lack in that area, it is the task of the software quality practitioner to make management aware of any needs.

The heavy majority of effort in the SLC is expended in the maintenance phase. Repairs make up a significant portion, if not the majority, of the maintenance effort. Repairs include fixing latent defects that survived the testing program and implementing enhancements or improvements required to make the system perform those tasks that were wanted but were left out of the original requirements or design. True enhancements are those additions or modifications that enable the software to perform functions not originally wanted or needed.

Software quality practitioners must be closely involved in the maintenance activity to ensure that proper control of the software and documentation configurations is enforced and that regression testing is fully performed. The software quality practitioner has the responsibility of ensuring that the regression tests are prepared in the beginning and that they are kept up to date during the full SLC.

Software quality practitioners perform an important monitoring and reporting function in the maintenance phase by keeping management informed as to the quality and status of the documentation and code.

7.6 The next step

To find out more about several of the topics in this chapter, see *Implementing Software Engineering Practices* by Fletcher J. Buckley (New York: John Wiley & Sons, 1989).

ADDITIONAL READING

Bryan, W. L., and S. G. Siegel, *Software Product Assurance*, New York: Elsevier, 1988.

Guide International, *Quality Assurance of Purchased Packages—GPP 145*, Guide International, Chicago, IL, 1986.

Lobel, Jerome, *Foiling the System Breakers*, New York: McGraw-Hill, 1986.

McConn, Charlotte Eudy, *Business Computer Systems: Design, Programming, and Maintenance With Case Studies*, Englewood Cliffs, NJ: Prentice-Hall, 1989.

Westwater, Keith, *The Earthquake Business Plan*, Ministry of Civil Defence, Wellington, NZ, 1990.

Chapter 8

Software documentation

D OCUMENTATION IS the record of the translation from the user's needs to the software that satisfies those needs and instructions for the operation and use of the software.

A vast portion of the software being developed lacks adequate records of how it got where it is. The original requirements are poorly stated, design just evolved as it went along, code tends to simulate the design rather than implement it, testing is based on showing that the code works rather than that it meets the requirements, and user documentation is incomplete to a fault. The SQS can play a large role in the improvement of this situation.

Documentation is like the markers along a highway. Looking ahead, it provides a trail to follow toward the destination. Looking back, it provides a record of the trip thus far. Each phase of the SDLC prepares the "directions" for the next phase in the form of some sort of documentation. Those same documents are the record of what has happened during the phase itself. The requirements phase is directed by the statement of needs from the concept exploration phase. The design phase is directed by the requirements document, which is a record of the activities of the requirements phase. In turn, the design documentation directs the coding phase while recording the design phase, and so on. In parallel with the development phases, the testing documentation is prepared, leading to the testing effort the way requirements documentation leads to coding.

Software documentation comprises management, development, test, and user documentation. It is intended to follow the evolution of the software as it progresses through the SLC.

It is important to note that once a document has been written and approved, it still can—and must—change. As the development proceeds, errors, defects, incomplete specifications, and necessary additions and deletions will become known. If the documentation is to serve its purpose on a continuing basis, it must be kept current. Many software projects have suffered serious problems, not because the documentation was poorly written in the first place, but because it was allowed to fall behind the actual situation as development continued. In the later phases, when it was needed to support testing or maintenance, it was no longer current and thus not useful. The actual approved requirements were no longer reliably documented, the design specification had fallen behind the actual code implementation, and there was no way to accurately trace the code back to the requirements. In almost every case like that, the user winds up with a software system that does *something*, but not what was actually needed or wanted.

Finally, the documentation is the basis for CM. If the documentation starts out poorly or is allowed to degenerate with respect to the ongoing development activities, the software is out of control. CM loses visibility into what was required and how that has changed. Once the software development effort is out of control, the end result of that development usually is not predictable, verifiable, or maintainable.

Table 8.1 offers recommendations for minimum documentation for various project sizes. Other project factors, such as visibility, criticality, and complexity, will influence the selection of documents in each case. (Appendixes A through I include outlines for the primary documents.)

Project size	Recommended documents
Small project	Requirements specification Design description (as-built design) Test report Plans: software development, SQS, CM
Medium project	All small-project documents Preliminary design Detailed design (build-to design) Test plan
Large project	All medium-project documents Test cases (and scenarios) Interface requirements and design
Any size project	Database requirements and design User manual Operations manual Maintenance plan Training plan

Table 8.1
Software
documentation
recommendations

8.1 Management documents

Every software development project is going to be managed in some way. A plan will be prepared, in one form or another, that lays out the expected schedule and resources. Effort will be expended to review and test the software, at least at the end before delivery, and the components of the software will be identified so that the delivered software and its components are known.

The following management documents are common to all software development projects:

- Software development plan;
- SQS plan;
- CM plan.

These documents are the overall software development process control documents. Their size and depth of detail will vary with the size and complexity of the system being developed. They may even be merged into a single document for small projects. Even so, the content, describing how the development project will be managed and controlled, must be present for each software development project. It should not be surprising that the more formal the planning and its documentation, the more complete and effective it will be. Thus, creation of the *software development plan* (SDP), the *SQS plan* (SQSP), and the *CM plan* (CMP)is a necessary part of each software development project.

These plans for a project leading to 500,000 LOC probably would cost more than a whole 500-line project. Therefore, the level of detail and control included in each plan must reflect the size and complexity of the project at hand.

8.1.1 Software development plan

The SDP is the document that lays out the management approach to the software project. In its most basic form, the SDP will include the schedule and resource needs for the project. The milest ones for tracking the progress of the project will be specified, probably as a pictorial of the SDLC. The personnel loading also will be shown so that the required expertise and skills can be available when they are needed. The SDP should specify hardware and environmental needs, such as computer time, special test facilities, compilers and linkers, and other systems.

For simple systems, the material covering the SQS and CM may be included as separate sections in the SDP. As system complexity grows, so does the SDP. More and more detail is required to cover the larger scale of the software development activity. Schedules must contain intermediate checkpoints or milestones, personnel loading will become more varied and complicated, and test support facilities will become more elaborate. The SDP will also begin to address software quality and CM to a level of detail that precludes their inclusion as SDP sections.

The more elaborate the software system, the more it probably interfaces with other systems and the outside world. While any interfaces are presented in requirements documentation, provision for their involvement in testing must be ensured and scheduled in the SDP.

Larger systems may require enough people or facilities to justify special offices or test laboratories. If so, those must be presented in the SDP, to ensure their availability.

Budget control becomes more important as the size of the system grows. The SDP is the appropriate place to present budget considerations and to specify control mechanisms in support of the normal, companywide cost accounting system.

While the software quality practitioner obviously does not generate the SDP, the practitioner has the responsibility for reviewing it against SDP standards and ensuring that all appropriate information is present. Deficiencies detected by the software quality practitioner and any other SDP reviews should be corrected before the project is permitted to commence.

The software quality practitioner also monitors the software development activities against the SDP. Deviations are reported so management can take corrective action.

Most corrective action will be to correct the software development process where it has strayed from the plan. Some corrections will be made to the SDP to keep it current with changes in the project. The software quality practitioner will review those changes to ensure that contracted requirements are not being violated and that the plan still complies with the standards for it.

See Appendix A for a sample SDP outline.

8.1.2 SQS plan

The SQSP addresses the activities to be performed on the project in support of the quest for quality software. Being careful not to exceed the requirements of the customer, company standards, or the SDP, the SQSP will discuss all the activities to be performed on all of the various SLC products. A sample format for an SQSP is shown in Appendix B.

Remember that a software quality group is not necessary for the SQS functions to be performed. Thus, the various software quality functions will be assigned, through the SQSP, to be the organizational entities that will perform those functions. All activities to be accomplished in the software quality area should receive the same personnel, resource, and schedule discussion as in the overall SDP, and any special tools and methodologies should be discussed. The SQSP may be combined with the CMP for medium-sized efforts.

Whatever the format of the SQSP, it is important that the document (or its information if in another document) be complete and approved by management and the producers. The SQSP becomes the charter for the SQS functions for the particular project when approved by management. It lays out the entire SQS and how it will be implemented.

Without the involvement of and approval by the software developers, the SQSP can be a recipe for ineffectiveness and frustration on the part of the software quality practitioners. Without the cooperation of the developers, software quality practitioners can be severely hampered in their attempts to conduct the review and monitoring activities for which they are responsible. Involving the development organizations in the generation and approval of the SQSP can encourage their cooperation as the project progresses.

The software quality practitioners also must monitor their own plan and their activities according to that plan. Any deviation from the plan or any indication of inadequacy of the plan must be corrected. The software quality practitioner will monitor all the software management and development activities. It is certain that management and the developers will be watching the software quality practitioners to be sure they perform according to the plan, the whole plan, and nothing but the plan.

8.1.3 Configuration management plan

CM, as discussed in Chapter 6, is a threefold discipline. Each of the three activities should be discussed in its own section of the CMP. The methods, requirements levied on the producers, contracted requirements, and tools to be used for software CM all should be spelled out. (See Appendix C for a sample format for a CMP.)

If the project is small, the necessary information may be included in the SDP. On medium-sized projects, it may be appropriate to combine the CMP information with the SQSP in a single, dual-purpose document.

While some of the information may be in the personnel and resource sections of the SDP, CM-specific information must be presented in the CMP. Schedule s for baselining, major reviews, and auditing should be shown either on the overall project schedule or on the CM schedule.

Any special tools or resources needed to support CM must be called out in the CMP. Another topic that may appear in the CMP is the operation of the software development library, which is the repository of all software product master copies. If not discussed elsewhere (e.g., the SDP or SQSP), the library, its responsibilities, functions, and so forth, should be presented in the CMP.

As with the SDP, the software quality practitioner has the responsibility to review the CMP before its release and adoption. The software quality practitioner should make sure that the CMP is complete and appropriate for the project as well as that it meets any specified format and content standards. Software quality practitioners must also review the CM activities on an ongoing basis. The reviews will ascertain whether the activities described in the plan are being performed and if they are still appropriate for the project.

8.1.4 Additional plans

As software becomes an increasingly critical part of our lives, additional plans may be required for some software system development efforts. Such plans might include the systems engineering plan, risk management plan, safety plan, and maintenance plan. These plans certainly are not required for all development projects. It is the responsibility of the quality practitioner to evaluate their necessity for each new project and to recommend their preparation when appropriate.

8.2 Development documents

Each SDLC phase produces development-oriented documentation. These documents are the statements of the increasingly complete solution for the user's needs as development proceeds. Development documentation covers the SDLC and tracks the software from the requirements that grow out of the concept exploration phase through the installation phase. This series of documents, each serving as the basis for the succeeding level, permits the producers to determine when they have completed the task and the testers to determine whether the software complies with the intended requirements.

The primary development documents are as follows:

- Requirements specification;
- Preliminary design;
- Detailed design (build to);
- Design description (as built);
- Database specification(s);
- Interface specification(s).

There are many formats for each of the basic development documents. The format for each basic SLC document is less important than the content of the document. Further, the necessity for some specific documents depends on the size and complexity of the specific project. In some cases, the required information can be provided in a higher level document. Thus, the actual format and content specifications will be a function of the individual organization and the documentation standards that have been adopted.

The requirements document is intended to fully define the overall function to be performed or problem to be solved. It is a mandatory document, without which the project should not even be started. Until the customer or user has clearly stated what is to be provided, the producer has insufficient information with which to start work. Without a clear statement of what is wanted of the software, there is no way to determine completion or how completion is to be achieved.

Design documents, both preliminary and detailed, describe in increasing detail the method by which the problem or function is being addressed. Prior to coding, the design must be such that the coder does not need to make any "I think they meant this" decisions. After coding and testing, a final design document should be published, which is the "as-built" document that will be used by the software maintainers after installation.

8.2.1 Requirements specification

The requirements specification is the keystone of all software documentation. It is the statement of what the software system is to provide. It describes the problem to be solved, any restrictions or constraints on performance or environment, time and size restraints, specific requirements levied on inputs and outputs, and any other information that is necessary for the complete specification of the problem or function. Without this complete specification of what the software is to accomplish, the producer is put in the position of having to make requirements decisions as the design progresses. That removes some of the control of the system from the customer and may result in the customer not receiving what was expected. Viewed another way, the producer is also in the position of being unable to provide anything acceptable to the customer who says, "That's not what I asked for." Appendix D shows a general format for a requirements document.

There are many ways that errors or faulty requirements creep into the requirements document. It is the role of the software quality practitioner to carefully review the requirements document, both for adherence to the format standards for the document and for the correctness of its content. The latter may pose a problem to some practitioners who do not have the appropriate expertise to adequately review the document for technical content. In those cases, outside reviewers may be used, or the development group may be called on to provide a review of the requirements before they accept the development task.

In addition to being correct, requirements must meet at least five other critical criteria: they must be necessary, complete, measurable, unambiguous, and consistent (both internally and with external interfaces).

Correctness

Correctness of the requirements is of primary concern, both to the customer and to the producer. The description of what is wanted and the surrounding needs and constraints must be stated correctly if the development is to result in an acceptable product. The use of an equation that is not correct for the situation or addressing a government regulation incorrectly will result in a system that does not meet the needs of the customer, even though it might comply with the requirements as stated.

Necessity

A requirement that places unnecessary restrictions or demands on a software system also raises the cost in time and money at no advantage to the system. Such things as overly stringent timing, unnecessary precision in calculations, unjustifiably tight memory restrictions, excessive processing capability, and the like, sometimes creep into requirements. They may sound nice or seem necessary at the outset, but unnecessary requirements can cause poor development later on. The requirement for a check processing capability of 200,000 per day may sound fine, but if it is for a small bank that actually needs to process only 50,000 checks a day, it will add unnecessarily to the cost of the system and provide capability that will not be used.

Completeness

Completeness may seem to be an obvious criterion for requirements, but it is no less important for that. When a published requirements document does not address the whole problem to be solved, the developer is usually in store for surprises. Either a situation will arise during design or coding that has no basis in the requirements, or the customer may ask where a desired feature is after the producer thinks the job is done. At the very least, the producer may be put into the position of having to add or to modify requirements, actions that rightfully are the responsibility of the customer.

Measurability

Measurability is the key to testing. A requirement that cannot be measured cannot be demonstrated by the test program. For example, a requirement for "rapid response time" clearly is faulty. What exactly does "rapid" mean? Another example is a requirement to "process multiple targets." "Multiple" is undefined and therefore cannot be measured or demonstrated. Requirements that cannot be measured introduce opportunities for conflict at all points in the SDLC, particularly at system demonstration and acceptance time.

A two-second response time that seems adequately "rapid" to the developer may be unacceptably slow in the eyes of the customer. "Multiple" may mean 20 to the developer but only 10 to the customer, who does not want to pay for the extra capability.

Unambiguity

Unambiguous requirements leave nothing to the imagination of the producer. There is no need to guess what the customer really meant or wanted. A requirement for a response time of no more than two seconds sounds like a good, measurable requirement. It is ambiguous, however, in that it does not state the point at which the measurement of two seconds is to begin or to end. A major source of ambiguity is such familiarity with a subject that one forgets that others may not know all the jargon or have insider information. Sometimes the requirements writer presumes that "everybody knows that." Another source of ambiguity is weak wording.

Requirements must be worded in terms of the imperative verb *shall*. Verbs such as *should*, *may*, or even *will* might show desire, but they do not demonstrate intent. To say that a system "should" compute the square root of 3 implies that it might not.

Consistency

Finally, the criterion of consistency must be considered. Requirements must be consistent within themselves and also with the world outside with which they must interface. For example, the requirement in one section to process 1,000 checks per hour is inconsistent with the requirement in another section that calls for 10,000 checks in an eight-hour day. And both those requirements are inconsistent with the outside world if the check handling machinery to be used is capable of processing only 900 checks per hour.

8.2.2 Design specifications

Preliminary and detailed design specifications depict how each requirement will be approached and satisfied by the software. Detailed design specifications are of two types. The final design specification prior to coding can be considered the "build-to" design. It presents what the designers believe to be the correct solution and response to the approved requirements. The design description, which reflects the software as it was actually completed, is often referred to as the "as-built" design.

As with the requirements, the design must demonstrate the criteria for correctness, necessity, completeness, measurability and testability, lack of ambiguity, and consistency. Further, the design must be traceable back to the requirements. Each element of the design must be able to be shown as satisfying some part of the requirements. In return, each requirement must be able to be traced forward into the design. In that way, there is confidence that the designers have not added or omitted anything during the design process.

Regular formal and informal reviews of the design as it progresses are held to ensure that the design is not straying from the requirements. The reviews are also intended to show that the design is sound and adheres to the various criteria. The software quality practitioner plays an instrumental role in these reviews by ensuring, first of all, that they are, in fact, held. Software quality practitioners do not necessarily have to attend informal reviews, such as peer reviews, but the practitioners must be sure that the reviews are taking place and are fruitful in the search for design defects. Formal reviews may be chaired by software quality management, although some organizations find it better to have someone from the project as the chair. Software quality practitioners do have the responsibility to attend the formal reviews and report on their actions. The software quality practitioner also is responsible for making sure that any and all action items resulting from the reviews are fully addressed and closed and that full reports are filed with management for any managerial action that may be necessary.

Preliminary design specification

The preliminary design (sometimes called the functional, architectural, or external design) provides the initial breakdown of the requirements into functional groups for further design efforts. Each functional group represents a major portion of the overall software system. The preliminary design must specify the approach to be taken in the performance of the function, the database requirements, and the interfaces with the other functional groups in the system. It must also specify the interfaces with the external world, such as terminals, other computers, other software systems, and so forth. Appendix E shows a sample format of a preliminary design document.

Build-to design

The detailed design is a specific statement of how each part of the preliminary design will be implemented in code. The detailed design is often called the *build-to* specification, since it is the input to the programming staff for translation into the compiler language for implementation on the target computer. This document must completely describe the design so that programmers are not in the position of having to make design decisions as they make the translation into compiler language. An example of a format for a detailed design document is given in Appendix F.

As-built design

A final version of the detailed design document should be prepared after the completion of the coding and testing processes. This usually is called the *as-built* design or design description and represents the statement of the design that was actually translated into code. It is an important document for the future maintainers of the software system. It serves as the product baseline from which all changes will be made for corrections of defects found in operation of the system and for the addition of enhancements to the software as they become necessary.

8.2.3 Other development documents

The larger the system, the more documentation is appropriate. Database design and interface design documents may be needed.

Some documents are not always required as separate entities. The required content of the database design and the interface design documents may be incorporated into the preliminary and detailed design documents for small or noncomplex systems.

The role of the software quality practitioner is much the same whether the database or interface discussions are part of larger documents or volumes unto themselves. Software quality practitioners still must ascertain that format and content standards are met. They also will ensure that the documentation criteria are met and that the information is consistent with itself and among documents.

There will be projects that have special documentation needs. Two that arise most often are those projects that have many or complex interfaces, and those that involve the development of or significant interaction with a database. When the system's interfaces, either within the software system or with the external world, are many or complicated, the preparation of interface requirements and interface design specifications should be considered. These specifications can eliminate misunderstandings of the interfaces that arise when each interface is described from one side in one document and other sides in other documents. By combining all aspects of each interface in a single place, all parties can see the full set of the interfaces' descriptions

Database specifications are needed when the system being developed either creates or causes significant modification to the database(s). Even when a new or highly modified database is not the case, significant interaction with the existing database(s) may benefit from a specialized database document.

It should be remembered that the purpose of documentation is to describe how the user's or customer's requirements are being met and to ensure that the correct solution is being developed and implemented.

8.3 Test documentation

Test documentation includes all test program documents from the overall test plan through the final test report. Test documentation is a parallel effort, as shown in Figure 8.1. It starts with the original requirements statement, like the development documentation. On the basis of the requirements, test plans, cases, scenarios, procedures, data, and results documentation are generated as the SDLC progresses. (Chapter 4 addressed the topic of test documentation more fully.) Testing is documented through a series of increasingly specific documents, starting with the test plan and including test cases, test scenarios, detailed test procedures, test data, and test results. Test documentation spells out the sequence of events by which compliance of the software with its requirements ultimately is demonstrated.

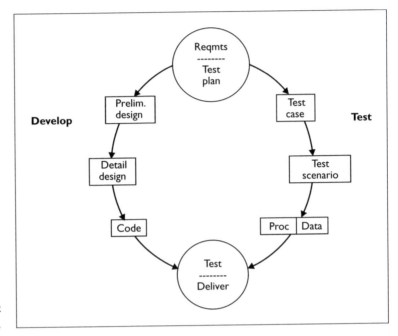

Figure 8.1
Software test
development.

Software quality practitioners play a major role in the whole testing process. They may, in fact, actually conduct the testing at the acceptance level. Nonetheless, the software quality practitioner must carefully review all of the test program to make sure it is sufficient to exercise the software in a manner that will maximize the defect-finding capability of the tests. Remember that the goal of testing is the finding of defects. Software quality practitioners must be sure that goal is being met. The second goal is to demonstrate that the software performs as the approved requirements demand. Software quality practitioners, together with the user or customer, must review the testing and ascertain whether the software does perform as required. When deficiencies are found, either in the tests or in the results, the software quality practitioner is responsible for making sure the deficiencies are recognized by management so that appropriate action is taken.

8.3.1 Test plan

As shown in Figure 8.1 (and in Figure 4.3), test documentation begins with the test plan (see Appendix G), which is based on the original requirements. In fact, the initial test planning is performed during the requirements phase. That not only gets the test activities off to an early start but helps to ensure the measurability and testability of the requirements themselves. The test plan will grow and evolve, just as the requirements grow and evolve, throughout the development life cycle, but it is important to begin at this point to keep pace with the development of the code. Plans are made for the expected test tools, data generators, simulators, and so on, that are anticipated to be needed.

8.3.2 Test cases

As the design begins to mature and functions are identified, test cases (see Appendix H) are correspondingly identified. These groups of individual tests will be applied to major sections of the software. They are usually based on logical groupings of requirements in much the same way as the functional design is approached. Test scenarios are optional subsets of the test cases. They provide for the simplification of complicated or lengthy test cases.

8.3.3 Test data

Initial test data requirements are also identified at this time. Test data must be provided, not to show that the software works as it was written, but that it works as was intended by the requirements. That means that the test data must cover as wide a spectrum of both legal and illegal values as possible. Nominal values, as prescribed in the various design documentation, will show only that the software meets nominal conditions. The object of testing is to uncover defects in the software, so the test data must be carefully chosen to present abnormal and incorrect inputs as well as expected inputs to determine the response of the software to unexpected, borderline, and erroneous conditions.

8.3.4 Test procedures

As the design and coding progress, test procedures (see Figure 4.4) are prepared. Test procedures are the step-by-step actions to be taken during each test. Every operator action, every data entry, and every expected response is specified in a sequence of steps for a given test. In that way, the exact conditions of the test are controlled, and each actual output or response of the software can be compared against the expected result. Each difference between the expected and actual results is recorded as a probable defect and is analyzed to determine whether the software is performing as required.

8.3.5 **Test reports**

The test reports (see Appendix I) record what actually happens during each test. They specify the expected and actual results and the conclusions drawn from the results. Anomalies and the final disposition of the anomalies are recorded. Test reports are the key factor in determining when testing has reached its beneficial conclusion.

8.4 User documentation

The best software is not useful if the end user does not know how to use it. User documentation may include, in addition to the user manuals, maintenance, operator, training, and other project-specific documents, such as the version description document. User documentation provides instructions to the end user of the software system. It addresses proper preparation and presentation of inputs, operating instructions, and directions for the interpretation of the output data. It also may present operating instructions, training needs, descriptions of differences from one version to the next, and maintenance information.

User documentation shows and tells the user how to make use of the software system. It should discuss the system, specify the format and content of the inputs, and describe the outputs that are the result of the system processing.

The software quality practitioner must take an active role in the review and evaluation of user documentation. If the software cannot be used properly, it matters little if it is a "quality" product. The user documentation must make proper use possible. Software quality practitioners should make a test run of the user manual to see if the instructions make it possible to actually use the system as it was meant to be used. That can sometimes be made a part of the final acceptance or demonstration testing or may be an individually conducted exercise. The important thing to be accomplished is the verification that the user documentation does make proper operation and use of the software possible.

8.4.1 **Input requirements**

With respect to input, the user documentation will tell the user what information the system requires. It will present data formats, ranges of legal values, schedules of input, and other information concerning the input data. Such things as methods of input (e.g., hardware registers, keyboard entries, data from other systems), where the data are to be submitted (e.g., remote job entry, via a terminal), when the input is required (e.g., every Thursday, when prompted), and other appropriate information specific to the particular system must be available to the user in the user manual.

8.4.2 Output description

Another important part of the user documentation is instructions on how to interpret the results of the processing. Full descriptions of all outputs are necessary. The documentation must, of course, contain instructions on how to understand the displays or printouts that are created. In addition, it must provide a complete and understandable description of all nonstandard outputs, such as error messages, abnormal halts, loss of system "sanity," and so on. Each of these situations or outputs will be described and the proper response spelled out. If the system is running in a central or remote data center, instructions for the distribution of hard-copy output will be provided.

8.4.3 Operation instructions

The user documentation should include the operation instructions, as well as pure user information; that is, it should contain details on how to actually make the system operate. Such information as how to load the system, what storage media are required, special peripherals such as high-speed printers or mass storage devices that are to be online, and how to bring the system down when processing is complete may be included in the operators' instructions. Whether this information is in the user manual or in a separate document is usually a function of the size of the system and where it is run (e.g., on a desktop computer or in the central data center). Some installations may have documentation standards that specify where this information is to be provided.

An operator manual or similar document is often needed for complicated systems that require the involvement of computer center personnel. This involvement may be the mounting of tapes and disk packs, handling of output forms or reports, sequencing of several systems into the proper executional order, and so on. Many systems are self-sufficient once they are initiated. In those cases, there may be few or no operator instructions. Larger systems may, however, justify a separate operator manual to provide detailed information concerning the operation of the software system.

The software quality practitioner has the responsibility to review operator documents for format and required content both at the initial release and during the operation and maintenance phases of the SLC.

8.4.4 **Maintenance**

Good maintenance documentation helps keep the software running and up to date. The primary tool of the software maintainers is the body of software documentation. Without clear and complete documentation of the software, the maintainers must recreate the data on which they will base enhancement and correction actions. Of course, the single most important document is the listing of the source and corresponding object code of the software. Without that, maintainers must work backward from the object code to recreate the source code or work in object code itself.

The next most important document is the final design description (or as-built) document. This document, or its equivalent, together with the up-to-date requirements and flowcharts or processing diagrams, explains to the maintainer exactly what the software is supposed to contain and how it is constructed. It is with these documents that maintainers study defect reports and requests for system enhancements. The flow diagrams (in whatever form is the standard for the specific installation) and the as-built design document present the software system design and implementation and describe what it does and how. The requirements describe the full environment into which the change must fit.

The maintenance portion of the user documentation contains information of importance to the persons or persons who are to maintain the software system. This portion usually contains the as-built design information, descriptions of phased implementation modifications made and pending, records of software changes made since implementation, and the like. Anything that will make the work of software maintainers easier is appropriate for inclusion in the maintenance portion of the user documentation.

In the evaluation of maintenance documentation, software quality practitioners must be sensitive to the environment of the maintainer and the documentation needs involved. Reviews of the maintenance documentation should be attended by and heavily influenced by representatives of the maintenance organization. Deficiencies noted in the maintenance documentation will be then be brought to the attention of management for resolution.

8.5 **Training documentation**

Training documentation, when required, will address both developer and user training. The more complicated and involved a system becomes, the more likely it is that there will be people working on it who do not have prior experience in one or more aspects of their tasks. Languages, programming environments, and technical subjects are all areas in which developers may need new or further education and training. Likewise, the customer or the user of the system may need to be trained.

Training documentation should be prepared any time there is a need for formal or extensive informal training. The format and content of the documents will vary according to need and application.

Software quality practitioners should evaluate the developer and user training needs and be sure that training documentation is appropriate, provided, reviewed, compliant with existing standards, and applicable to the project. Software quality practitioners probably will not perform the training or write the documents, but they must make management aware of any training needs.

8.6 Documentation standards

A wide variety of documentation standards are available. In many companies and organizations the first thing that is standardized is documentation. That may be because documentation is the least favorite activity of most software developers. It is the only product produced by a large portion of the SLC and is usually the object of most of the complaints about a system. Or perhaps it is the easiest to standardize since there are so many standard examples from which to choose.

Industry organizations have published or are developing standards for documentation, not only in the software field but also (and for a longer time) in the hardware arena. For example, the IEEE has standards for several software development documents (see Table 2.1). These standards represent the consensus of a large portion of the computing industry. The DoD and various other government agencies, such as NIST, have promulgated documentation standards both for general applications and for use in particular situations or special computing environments.

In some cases, externally prepared standards can be used directly. Otherwise, they can be modified to fit the needs of an individual organization. Some standards often include very specific content and format instructions so that very little is left to the author except the information to be documented. Others provide generic requirements or guidelines on which an organization can build. Some companies are willing to share their documentation standards or at least give guidance in the area.

As in the case of standards in general (see Section 2.2), each company or organization must develop or tailor documentation standards to meet its own specific needs. Documentation standards, like anything else, must serve the users of those standards, or they will be improperly followed or ignored all together. It is incumbent on the software quality practitioner to review documentation standards periodically to be sure they are up to date and appropriate for the organization. When they become inadequate or obsolete, the practitioner should prompt the standards coordinator to take action to improve them.

8.7 Summary

Software documentation is composed of management, development, test, and user documentation. It is intended to follow the evolution of the software as it progress through the SLC. Each SDLC phase has a product or products, which are the statements of the increasingly complete solution for the user's needs as development proceeds.

Documentation is like the markers along a highway. Looking ahead, it provides a trail to follow toward the destination. Looking back, it provides a record of the trip thus far. Each phase of the SDLC prepares the "directions" for the next phase in the form of some sort of documentation. These same documents are the record of what has happened during the phase itself.

The SDP is the document that lays out the management approach to the software project. In its most basic form, it will include the schedule and resource needs for the project. The methods, requirements levied on the producers, contracted requirements, and tools to be used for software CM should be defined and explained.

The SQSP addresses the activities to be performed on the project in support of the quest for quality software. All activities to be accomplished in the software quality area should receive the same personnel, resource, and schedule discussion as in the overall SDP. Whatever the format of the SQSP, it is important that this document (or its information if in another document) be complete and approved by management and the developers.

The requirements document is the keystone of all software documentation. Preliminary and detailed design documents depict how each requirement will be approached and satisfied by the software. The preliminary design provides the initial breakdown of the requirements into functional groups for further design efforts. The detailed design is often called the *build-to* specification. It is the input to the programming staff for translation into the compiler language for implementation on the target computer. The final version of the detailed design is sometimes called the *as-built* document, since it describes the software as it actually was delivered.

Test documentation includes all test program documents from the overall test plan through the final test report.

User documentation tells the user how to make use of the software system. The user documentation may include the operators' instructions as well as strictly user-oriented information.

The larger the system, the more documentation is appropriate. Database design and interface design documents may be needed. Maintenance and training may deserve separate and extensive treatment. Finally, there may be a need for a separate operations manual.

8.8 The next step

Few texts written have been written about software documentation as a subject unto itself. However, since all software development, testing, and maintenance processes depend on the requirements, you can start with *Software Requirements: Analysis and Specification* by Alan M. Davis (Englewood Cliffs, NJ: Prentice-Hall, 1990).

ADDITIONAL READING

Buckley, F. J., *Implementing Software Engineering Practices*, New York: John Wiley & Sons, 1989.

Guide International, *Quality Requirements—GPP 217*, Guide International, Chicago, IL, 1989.

Hatley, Pirbhai, *Strategies for Realtime System Specification*, New York: Dorset House, 1987.

Shumate, Ken, and Marilyn Keller, *Software Specification and Design: A Disciplined Approach for Real-Time Systems*, New York: John Wiley & Sons, 1992.

Vincent, James, Albert Waters, and John Sinclair, *Software Quality Assurance: Volume 1, Practice and Implementation*, Englewood Cliffs, NJ: Prentice-Hall, 1988.

Chapter 9

Quality system implementation

C HAPTERS 1 THROUGH 8 described the individual elements of the SQS. Those elements must be assembled into a manageable whole that will become the SQS. Figure 9.1 shows that all the elements are connected and that the connections are formed through the overall SQS. As it begins to implement the individual elements into the SQS, each organization must select the method and order of implementation and ensure that sufficient support is present for a successful implementation and that the SQS will become part of the new quality culture.

The key concerns in the implementation of the SQS include:

- Planning;
- The quality charter;
- Organizational culture change;
- The roles of the organization;
- Implementation and improvement.

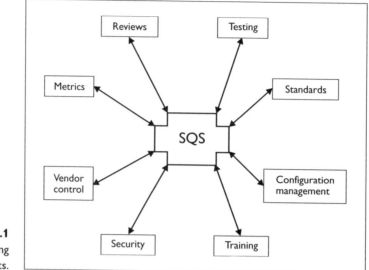

Figure 9.1
Connecting
the elements.

9.1 Planning the implementation

The planning of an SQS should involve consideration of all the elements discussed so far in this text. Many of the concerns of the SQS are depicted in Figure 9.2. Prior to beginning any actual implementation, careful consideration must be given to each step that will be taken. Those SQS elements that are already in place or that are partially implemented must be recognized and built on to the maximum extent compatible with the overall system. Each activity must be assigned to the appropriate organizational entity for execution. A period of training must be planned both for the implementers of the various portions of the plan and for the data processing organization as a whole. Inclusion of each group to be monitored in the planning process will benefit the overall system by instilling a sense of system ownership in the whole organization.

The actual implementation of the SQSP requires careful planning and scheduling. Starting with the definition of the charter of the software quality practitioners and ending with the SQS implementation strategy and execution, each step must be laid out and accomplished with the maximum involvement of the affected groups. Even the best conceived system can fail if it is implemented in the wrong way.

Figure 9.2
Software quality
system concerns.

9.2 The quality charter

Without clear direction and support from management, an SQS faces an uphill struggle.

Early in the planning stages of the SQS, a statement of what the system will accomplish is necessary. In other words, the requirements for the system must be established. Following that, the software quality group itself must be recognized with a specific charter of its role, responsibilities, authority, and organizational placement for the specific software development project.

The sample charter in Appendix J defines the limits of the software quality group's activities. It describes the expectations of and degree of support by management for the group and its efforts. In so doing, the charter formally demonstrates the commitment that management is making to the software quality group and its system. The charter can also be the instrument that describes the allocation of SQS functions and the organizational groups to which they are assigned, although that often is a part of the implementation plan, which comes later.

In summary, the charter is the written statement of management's intention to proceed with the SQS. With this document in hand, the software quality group can go forward with a clearly defined role in the total organization. Without it, there is no recourse when one or another of the SQS activities is challenged or ignored.

9.3 Changing the organizational culture

Implementation of a successful SQS requires a change in the culture of the organization with respect to quality. The key component of any culture change is commitment, in this case, the commitment of the entire organization.

9.3.1 Culture change

Changing a cultural is a four-step process.

Step 1 is the realization that the current situation, whatever is to be changed, is no longer desired. This is the first step, because if the current situation is desired, there is no basic motivation to change at all. An example might be that all projects have excessive postimplementation defect rates.

Step 2 is the determination that there is a situation better than the current one. If the current situation is undesirable but is the "least worst" of all available situations, the motivation to change still is not present. Since the testing of the project prior to implementation is at the state of the art of the organization's testers, a preferred situation in the example might be full user testing prior to implementation.

Step 3 is the determination that the preferred situation (found in Step 2) is attainable. In some cases, there is a preferred situation, but "you can't get there from here." At this point, even though the motivation to change is present, the change cannot be completed. Continuing the example, it is noted that full user testing is not feasible; they refuse, for whatever reason, to do it.

Step 4 is taken when Steps 1 through 3 have been successful. There is dissatisfaction with the current situation, and a better situation exists and is attainable. Step 4 is the application of the commitment to attaining the preferred situation. In the case of implementing an SQS, it is the combined commitment of management and the rest of the organization to expend the required effort and to aim for doing things right the first time.

9.3.2 Management commitment

A management involved in the planning and implementation of a program is more likely to commit itself to that program.

Management is going to be asked to commit resources to the SQS. No matter who carries out the individual activities represented by the eight basic elements of the system, there is a resource cost involved. Management usually is sensitive to those costs and the payback that can be expected for them. If there has been little or no management participation in the planning and development of the SQS, there will be little or no understanding of the value to be expected from the expenditures.

The costs involved in an SQS include, in addition to the actual SQS resource costs for personnel and so on, nontrivial costs to the project development. Software quality activities will have an impact on the time and resources required to develop the software product. In the experience of this author, those costs could range from as little as 5% for a minimum SQS application to as much as 20% for a fully applied SQS. Note that probably not all the costs will be new costs. It is to be expected that at least some resources were being expended for testing, configuration management, and defect reporting and correction even before there was a formal SQS. In any case, the costs to be incurred must be explained to management. If management is a part of the planning for the system, they will have a much better understanding of where these costs come from and what they will accomplish. Management must be given the opportunity to have direct inputs into the SQS planning and must be recognized for those inputs.

Without management commitment, any program is unlikely to succeed. The charter is the demonstration of management's commitment to the SQS.

9.3.3 Organizational commitment

It often is observed that a quality program will not succeed without the commitment of management. While management commitment is necessary, it is not sufficient. Also required is the full commitment and support of the organization, which must change its work habits to enable the success of the SQS and the software quality program. The cultural orientation of the organization must become one of "do it right the first time." The software quality practitioner must remember that the full set of changes cannot be made in one fell swoop. "Do it right the first time" will take effect in smaller steps of "do it more correctly sooner." As this habit becomes entrenched, the organizational culture will begin to change.

As Figure 9.3 shows, there can be involvement without much effort, but commitment requires much stronger support.

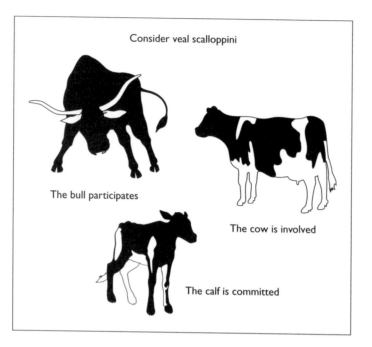

Consider veal scalloppini

The bull participates

The cow is involved

The calf is committed

Figure 9.3
True commitment.

9.4 Organizational considerations

Software quality management is the discipline that maximizes the probability that a software system will conform to its requirements, as those requirements are perceived by the user, on an ongoing basis.

Like a hardware quality system, the SQS is a measuring and monitoring function. It is a set of activities intended to encourage and, to a degree, enable conformance of the software to its requirements. Throughout this text, reference has been made to the role of the software quality practitioner. In general, this role has been one of monitoring the status of the software development or some aspect surrounding that development. The several aspects of the SQS, testing, education, security, and the others, are all factors that influence the capability of the software to conform to its requirements. The software quality practitioner's role is to monitor the status and progress of the organization with respect to those factors. Its findings are reported to the level of management that has the authority to take any necessary corrective action.

Two points are important here. First, software quality practitioners may, but usually do not, perform all the various activities that the SQS comprises or on which it reports. The software quality practitioner does not write the documentation, perform the testing, teach the programming courses, install disaster recovery procedures, and so forth. Those tasks should be performed by that part of the organization best capable of performing them. The role of the software quality practitioner is to ascertain that those activities are being performed and whether that performance is sufficient to permit the software to conform to its requirements.

The second point is that software quality practitioners are not an enforcement agency. A software quality practitioner reviews, inspects, evaluates, measures, and then reports. The organizational level at which software quality practitioners report can strongly affect the perceived value of the reports that they generate and the influence they can exert over the software development process. The task of enforcement is the responsibility of management. Only management has the authority to take corrective action in the case of reported deficiencies.

While it is true that everyone should be responsible for the quality of his or her own work, in most organizations the overall accountability for software quality rests with one person. It is simplistic to say that the overall accountability for software quality lies with the president, chairperson, or CEO of the organization. Obviously, final accountability for everything in the organization lies with that person. The question is, to what level has the day-to-day, effective accountability been delegated? In most cases, the manager of the data processing organization (whatever title that person might have) has the delegated accountability. That is the person who can make the enforcement decisions, weighing the inputs from the various concerned areas such as software quality, development, and the user. The manager, in turn, will delegate the quality tasks and their performance to those parts of the organization that is best suited to accomplish them. Management must weigh the severity of the deficiency, business factors, resource utilization, schedule restrictions, political aspects, and other considerations surrounding the SLC and then make a decision as to the action that should be taken for each specific situation. The reports received from software quality practitioners are one form of input to this decision-making process. Certainly, software quality practitioners may offer recommendations with the reports' findings, but the enforcement actions are management's to take.

9.4.1 SQS task performance

The best qualified entity of the organization should perform the day-to-day quality system tasks.

Few activities in the purview of the SQS must be performed specifically by software quality practitioners. For that reason, it could be argued that there is no need to have a "group" called software quality at all. The basis for that argument is that since everyone is responsible for the quality of the software product a separate group is not needed for the SQS tasks. If all persons involved in the specification, design, coding, testing, and operations of the software were infallible, that might be a workable situation. Humans are not infallible, however; in spite of their best intentions and efforts, they make errors, which cause defects. The intent of the SQS is to help discover those defects and correct them as early as possible. In addition, the formation of a software quality group, or at least the identification of a single accountable person, tends to focus attention on quality and efforts to attain it. And, just as in a software development project, it is a good idea to have a champion for the SQS. If that champion is a member of senior management, so much the better.

The software quality group is responsible for making sure that the various SQS tasks are performed. That does not mean that software quality is always the proper group to actually perform those tasks. Remember, software quality is a monitoring group. If there are tasks for which the software quality group is qualified from a technical standpoint and there is no other more logical group, software quality practitioners certainly may be assigned to the task. In some organizations, the practitioner does, in fact, perform all the elements of the SQS. In most companies, however, the bulk of the tasks is handled outside the software quality group. Each function should be assigned to the organizational entity that is "in the business." Educational needs should be filled by the training and education entity, configuration management by the CM entity, and so forth. Each company must review its own needs, priorities, and capabilities and then determine the proper distribution of software quality tasks for its own situation. It may even be advisable or necessary to bring outside consultants in for specific tasks, at times.

9.4.2 Reporting level

Software quality must be independent of the group(s) that it monitors and thus should report to at least the same organizational level. Reporting at lower managerial levels can dilute, even negate, the influence of the software quality practitioner on the software development or maintenance projects.

Figure 9.4 shows the least favorable structure and the one that should not be used. In this case, software quality reports to the very person whose group software quality is monitoring. It is unlikely that much useful reporting of noncompliance with standards, defect trends, or other insufficiencies will reach the ears of the portion of management that can take the necessary corrective action. Organizational independence from the groups being monitored is the single most important consideration in the placement of software quality.

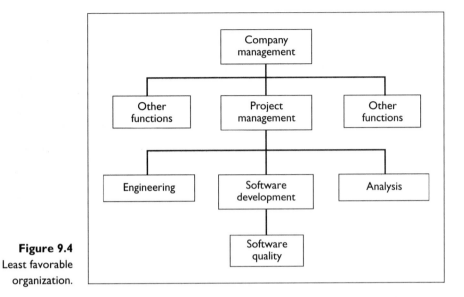

Figure 9.4
Least favorable
organization.

Figure 9.5 presents the best realistic compromise. It shows software quality reporting at the same level as each of the other groups in the data processing department. The manager of software quality is a peer with the managers whose groups are being monitored. A common higher manager is available to mediate any issues that cannot be resolved directly between the affected managers.

The advantages of this scheme are as follows:

- The software quality practitioner reviews the work of peer groups.
- A single superior is available to mediate questions or disputes.
- The software quality practitioner is independent of each of the groups to be monitored.
- The software quality practitioner is accessible to the other groups for assistance.

An important aspect of the suggested reporting level is that the software quality practitioner is specifically not a part of any of the groups that it must monitor. When a situation that may need correction is found, it is reported to the manager of the data processing organization directly, not through an intermediate level.

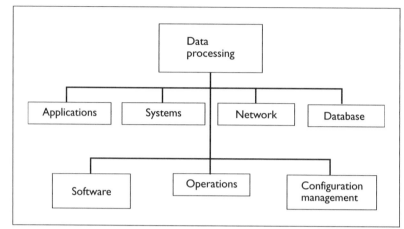

Figure 9.5
Acceptable
organization.

Another arrangement is shown in Figure 9.6. This particular reporting scheme is sometimes found in manufacturing companies that have a very strong and mature quality system. Software quality in these companies is a recognized extension of the overall quality system. In this case, the software quality practitioners report completely outside the data processing department and have a direct reporting line to top company management. A potential drawback is that, except in large organizations with experience in hardware product quality practices, this scheme may have the software quality practitioners too far removed from the development organization to be as effective on a day-to-day basis as is desirable. The success of this type of reporting structure depends on the interaction between the software quality group and data processing. If, in spite of the organizational separation, the software quality practitioner maintains a high degree of communication and rapport with the data processing groups, this can be a workable solution. It is also a candidate arrangement when there is a strong matrix organizational structure for project management.

There are probably many different reporting arrangements that can be envisioned. Most, though, if the software quality practitioner is at a lower level than the groups being reviewed, do not support a strong SQS effort. Some arrangements would place the software quality practitioner at a higher level than the other groups. That can sometimes lead to conflict because the software quality group is perceived as having inordinate power. Whatever the reporting structure chosen, software quality practitioners will be most effective when they report to at least the same organizational level as those groups whose activities they must monitor.

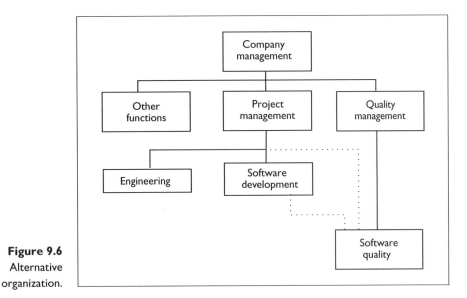

Figure 9.6
Alternative
organization.

9.5 Development organization participation

The development organizations that will be monitored by software quality practitioners must have some say in the criteria and methods to be used. Acceptance of the SQS by the rest of the organization is the critical factor in the success or failure of the SQS.

Openness by software quality practitioners in the beginning of the system will enhance openness by the developers later on. No one likes to feel that someone is constantly looking over his or her shoulder. Yet that is exactly the impression software quality practitioners can give if they have not requested and welcomed participation and involvement by the development groups in the preparation of the SQS. When the developers have been a part of the overall planning and development the system, there will be less resistance to the requests by software quality practitioners for information about progress and status, let alone data on defects being found.

Participation by the developers can also help in the creation of more meaningful measures of progress, trends, and areas in need of additional attention from the SQS. Most people know their skills and limitations. If they have the attitude that someone else is going to discover and "tattle" on their weaker capabilities, there is resistance to exposing those areas. On the other hand, if given the opportunity, most people will point out those areas in which they feel they can use assistance. If that assistance is provided, a growing trust is built, and fear and suspicion are reduced. By maintaining close contact with and participation by the developers during the planning and implementation of the SQS, the software quality group can build a feeling of SQS ownership on the part of the developers.

9.6 Implementation strategies

There are several strategies for implementation of an SQS. Probably the least effective methods are the ones that impose the SQS on the whole development organization without regard to which stage each project is at in its SDLC.

First is the all-at-once approach. In this case, the whole SQS is implemented at one time. Each project is expected to stop what it is doing and to bring the project in line with the new SQS requirements, whether or not every requirement is meaningful. The result is usually a period of confusion and a corresponding antagonism toward the SQS and the software quality group. Faced with this negative attitude, the software quality group has a very difficult time establishing itself and often fails and is disbanded.

Another poor method is the one-element-at-a-time approach. In this case, a particular element is chosen for organizationwide implementation, again without regard to the status of the various ongoing projects. Since there is varied success based on the position of each project in its SLC, the element tends to fade away due to decreasing application. When it is realized that element is ineffective, the decision is made to try one of the others. It, too, eventually fails. As each element is tried in turn, each faces the same fate. Finally the decision is made to scrap the SQS because it obviously is not effective.

Both these implementation methods can work if consideration is given to each project to which they will be applied. There must be recognition that each project will be in a different portion of its life cycle and thus will have differing abilities, or needs, to comply with a new SQS. Provisions for deviations from or waivers of specific requirements of the SQS based on the projects' needs must be allowed, which will make either method of implementation much more likely to succeed.

9.6.1 Single-project implementation

The all-at-once approach can be successful when the SQS is to be applied only to new projects.

One popular method of this type of implementation is to permit ongoing projects to complete on their own and to concentrate the software quality practitioners' efforts on new projects as they are begun. This has the drawback that some projects may be less successful since none of the system is formally applied to them. It has the advantage that no project has to change processes in the middle of its development. It is also likely that there are some portions of the SQS that will be adopted by the ongoing projects because they are seen to be of value and cause little disruption in the project's progress.

Another strong recommendation for this approach is in the data processing organization that experiences frequent project startup. Companies like defense contractors, which often have several dissimilar contracts starting and ending independently from one another, can use this method successfully. It is often favored by software vendors, as well, because, again, there is wide project-to-project separation.

9.6.2 Single-element implementation

The one-element-at-a-time implementation picks one SQS element to impose on all projects, new and ongoing, but does so with careful consideration of each project's ability and need to conform to the element. This, too, can be a successful method of implementation, but it requires careful planning.

Two primary aspects of single-element implementation must be considered: the order of implementation and the project benefit. Some SQS elements may add more value if implemented sooner, while some may actually have negative impact if implemented too soon.

Certainly, some elements are rather project-status independent. Portions of the education and security elements can be implemented irrespective of project status. Others, like documentation or CM, may require significant retrofitting of projects if implemented in the later phases of the SDLC.

An advantage of the single-element approach is that each project has the opportunity to benefit from at least a portion of the overall SQS as early as possible. In that way, development personnel are able to see benefits of the system and tend to be more supportive of elements that are introduced later. A disadvantage is that new projects may not get the full benefit from the SQS because some of its elements are not yet in place.

The most likely type of organization to use the single element approach is that in which most of the development is closely related, for example, the more traditional inhouse data processing for financial and business applications. Here, too, there is a rather steady flow of new projects, but they tend to be similar in nature. The single-element approach allows each element to take root and become a routine part of the SDLC before another element is introduced.

9.6.3 **Combined implementation**

A combination of the two methods can be the best answer in most cases. As is the case in any discussion of methods or approaches, there is no single, always correct situation.

The single-project and single-element approaches are clearly the extremes of the implementation method spectrum. The single-project approach would be successful in the information systems organization that had no ongoing development projects to consider. The single-element approach could be the best answer if there is no new project activity. Neither situation is likely to be the case in most organizations. The answer, obviously, is to fit the implementation method or combination of implementation methods to the actual experience of the particular organization and to the specific projects being affected.

For new projects, it is almost always best to implement as much of the total system as possible. Only those elements that, in a given organization, would conflict with ongoing projects should be delayed. An example might be a new form of database security system that would seriously affect an ongoing development effort. In most cases, however, new projects can be started using the full SQS with little or no impact on the rest of the development activity.

Ongoing projects can be the subject of various subsets of the full SQS, depending on their status and needs. Projects late in the SDLC probably would be unaffected by the imposition of new programmer training, but could benefit from increased user training requirements. A project early in the SDLC can be placed under more stringent configuration management procedures without much impact on completed work. Each project must be evaluated against the full SQS, and those elements that are feasible should be implemented.

As the SQS is implemented and experience is gained with it, it should be evaluated and modified as appropriate. The experiences of each project should be considered and changes, additions, and deletions made. Provisions for deviations and waivers will make the actual implementation of each element to each project as smooth as possible. A study of the waivers and deviations will show the modifications that may be needed in the overall system.

9.6.4 **Adapting the SQS**

It must be remembered that no one SQS is suited to all information systems organizations. The elements presented in this text are the building blocks, but the organization itself is the architect of its specific SQS. Each element will mean different things to different people. The various priorities, business considerations, political influences (both internal and external), and many other factors will determine the provisions of the SQS for a specific company.

In exactly the same manner, there will be adapting of the basic company SQS to meet the needs of each specific project. Contracts, visibility, official sponsorship, and other factors will affect the final contents of the project software quality plan and system.

It is desirable that each company develop a basic SQS. The SQS will present the minimum software quality requirements that must be met by all projects undertaken by the development groups. For each individual project, additional requirements may be added as the basic system is tailored to fit. The elimination of any portion or of the basic company SQS should be permitted only in the most justifiable of circumstances. All adaptation should be of an additive nature. The increase, not the reduction, of potential for quality software should be the goal.

9.7 SQS improvement

One of the goals of the SQS is to find ways in which to improve the development and maintenance processes being applied to the software. Clearly, the SQS and its implementation are also a process. As a process, the SQS, too, is open to review, assessment, and improvement. Several process investigation and evaluation avenues apply to the software quality process. Among the process evaluation approaches are:

- Assessment of the process;
- Certification of the process;
- Recognition of process quality.

The goal of assessments, certifications, and awards should go beyond the single event. The results, winning or not, should serve as starting points for intentional improvement of the quality system or practitioner. It must be remembered that each of these events provides only a single snapshot of the situation at a specific time. Their real value is serving as benchmarks from which improvement can be addressed and measured.

9.7.1 Assessment

The most widely known of the process assessment approaches is that developed by the SEI. Founded to provide software development process evaluation for the DoD, the SEI has conceived the software CMM. While the CMM is specifically intended for the assessment of the software development process, it can be applied to the software quality process. By answering a series of questions about the process, an assignment of "maturity level" is accomplished.

The quality system is an integral part of the level determination, and some of the questions are intended to assess its effectiveness. The answers to the quality system–oriented questions can give an idea of the maturity of the quality process and indicate areas for its potential improvement.

9.7.2 Certification

Two types of certifications are directed specifically at the quality system: organizational and personal.

Organizational certification can be based on the ISO 9000 series of standards (see Section 2.2.1). The standards can be used inhouse as self-evaluation or applied through assessments by third-party assessors. An inhouse assessment cannot result in a recognized certification as can a third-party assessment. The value of an inhouse assessment is that it gives a picture of the effectiveness of the quality system within the needs and resources of the organization. Third-party certification is of value when the outside world needs to be considered or when absolute independence of the assessors is desirable.

Personal certification of quality practitioners is available through the American Society for Quality Control for most hardware quality applications. The software-oriented Quality Assurance Institute administers certifications for both software quality analysts and software testers. Personal certifications do not guarantee that the SQS will succeed, but they do offer assurance that the software quality practitioners are capable of their tasks.

9.7.3 Awards

A number of awards for organizational quality system excellence are available throughout the world. Many countries now have national quality awards such as the Malcolm Baldrige Award in the United States. Additionally, several individual states also grant quality system excellence awards. One such state award is the New York Excelsior Award. There are also awards for individuals in the quality field, such as the Japanese Deming Award, that can be presented to either organizations or individuals.

9.8 Summary

The software quality activities, like hardware quality activities, are a monitoring and reporting function. The role of the SQS is to monitor the status and progress of the software development and maintenance processes. It then reports its findings to the level of management that has the authority to take any necessary corrective action.

Implementation of an SQS requires planning by the software quality group, and the involvement of the affected groups.

Early in the planning stages, a statement of what the system will accomplish is necessary. A charter will describe the expectations and the authority of the SQS and group. Without management commitment, any quality system is unlikely to succeed. The charter demonstrates management's commitment to the SQS.

Involvement of the development groups is also necessary to the success of the SQS. Encouraging the groups to be monitored to have a say in what the monitoring will comprise ensures that the system will be met with reduced resistance when it is implemented.

Many system implementation schemes exist. No one approach is likely to be useful in all cases. Likewise, no one SQS will be appropriate in every case. Each system and its implementation must be tailored to the particular company needs and the project being addressed.

It is desirable in the case of the SQS itself that a minimum set of quality assurance functions be established. Each project may add to that minimum set, but none may do less. In that way, all software projects are monitored to some degree, and the likelihood of requirements compliance is raised.

Three important points should be made. First, software quality practitioners may, but usually do not, perform the various activities that constitute the SQS. The actual performance is carried out by those sections of the overall organization best qualified to perform the tasks.

Second, the software quality practitioners are not an enforcement agency. Only decision-making management has the authority to enforce anything. Software quality practitioners only monitor and report.

Finally, software quality practitioners must be administratively and financially independent of the groups performing the functions that the practitioner is monitoring. Further, the software quality practitioner must report to at least the same organizational level as the monitored groups. That permits the software quality practitioner the freedom to report objectively to management.

9.9 The next step

For a discussion of the implementation of a software quality program, see *Software Quality Assurance: Volume 1—Practice and Implementation* by James Vincent, Albert Waters, and John Sinclair (Englewood Cliffs, NJ: Prentice-Hall, 1988).

ADDITIONAL READING

Arthur, L. J., *Improving Software Quality: An Insider's Guide to TQM*, New York: John Wiley & Sons, 1993.

Blakemore, John, *The Quality Solution*, Melbourne: Information Australia, 1989.

Bossert, James L., *Quality Function Deployment*, Milwaukee, WI: ASQC Press, 1991.

Curtis, Bill (ed.), *Human Factors in Software Development*, 2d Ed., Washington, DC: IEEE Computer Society Press, 1986.

Hromi, John D. (ed.), *The Best On Quality*, Milwaukee: ASQC Quality Press, 1995.

Schmidt, Warren H., and Jerome P. Finnigan, *TQManager: A Practical Guide for Managing a Total Quality Organization*, San Francisco: Jossey-Bass, 1993.

Thayer, R. H. (ed.), *Software Engineering Project Management*, Washington, DC: IEEE Computer Society Press, 1988.

Appendixes

THE APPENDIXES contain samples of several of the documents described and discussed in the text. They are offered as starting points for the reader who needs to create, manage, or review such documentation. Each outline or sample is attributed to the source where appropriate.

Appendix A

Sample outline of software development plan

(*Source:* IEEE Standard 1058.1-1987; used with permission.)

Title Page

Revision Chart

Preface

Table of Contents

List of Figures

List of Tables

1. Introduction
    1.1   Project Overview
    1.2   Project Deliverables
    1.3   Evolution of the SPMP
    1.4   Reference Materials
    1.5   Definitions and Acronyms

2. Project Organization
    2.1   Process Model
    2.2   Organizational Structure
    2.3   Organizational Boundaries and Interfaces
    2.4   Project Responsibilities

3. Managerial Process
    3.1   Management Objectives and Priorities
    3.2   Assumptions, Dependencies, and Constraints
    3.3   Risk Management
    3.4   Monitoring and Controlling Mechanisms
    3.5   Staffing Plan

4. Technical Process
    4.1   Methods, Tools, and Techniques
    4.2   Software Documentation
    4.3   Project Support Functions

5. Work Packages, Schedule, and Budget
    5.1   Work Packages
    5.2   Dependencies
    5.3   Resource Requirements

5.4   Budget and Resource Allocation

5.5   Schedule

Additional Components

Index

Appendices

Appendix B

Sample outline of SQS plan

(Based on IEEE Standard 730.1-1989; used with permission.)

1. Purpose

2. Reference Documents

3. Management
   3.1 Organization
   3.2 Tasks
   3.3 Responsibilities

4. Documentation
   4.1 Purpose
   4.2 Minimum Documentation
       4.2.1 Software Requirements Specification
       4.2.2 Software Design Description
       4.2.3 Software Verification and Validation Plan
       4.2.4 Software Verification and Validation Report
       4.2.5 User Documentation
       4.2.6 Configuration Management Plan
   4.3 Other Documentation

5. Standards, Practices, Conventions, and Metrics
   5.1 Purpose
   5.2 Documentation, Logic, Coding, and Commentary Standards and Conventions
   5.3 Testing Standards, Conventions, and Practices
   5.4 Metrics

6. Review and Audits
   6.1 Purpose
   6.2 Minimum Requirements
       6.2.1 Software Requirements Review
       6.2.2 Preliminary Design Review
       6.2.3 Critical Design Review
       6.2.4 Software Verification and Validation Review
       6.2.5 Functional Audit
       6.2.6 Physical Audit
       6.2.7 Inprocess Reviews
       6.2.8 Managerial Reviews
       6.2.9 Configuration Management Plan Review

6.2.10   Postmortem Review

  6.3   Other Reviews and Audits

7. Test

8. Problem Reporting and Corrective Action
   8.1   Practices and Procedures
   8.2   Organizational Responsibilities

9. Tools, Techniques, and Methodologies

10. Code Control

11. Media Control

12. Supplier Control

13. Records Collection, Maintenance, and Retention

14. Training

15. Risk Management

Appendix C

Sample outline of configuration management plan

(Based on IEEE Standard 828-1990; used with permission.)

1. Introduction

2. SCM Management

3. SCM Activities
   3.1   Configuration Identification
   3.2   Configuration Control
   3.3   Configuration Status Accepting
   3.4   Configuration Audits and Reviews
   3.5   Interface Control
   3.6   Subcontractor/Vendor Control

4. Schedules

5. Resources

6. SCM Plan Maintenance

Appendix D

Sample outline of software requirements specification

(*Source:* IEEE Standard 830-1993; used with permission.)

1. Introduction
    1.1 Purpose
    1.2 Scope
    1.3 Definitions, Acronyms, and Abbreviations
    1.4 References
    1.5 Overview

2. Overall Description
    2.1 Product Perspective
    2.2 Product Functions
    2.3 User Characteristics
    2.4 Constraints
    2.5 Assumptions and Dependencies

3. Specific Requirements
    3.1 External Interface Requirements
        3.1.1 User Interfaces
        3.1.2 Hardware Interfaces
        3.1.3 Software Interfaces
        3.1.4 Communications Interfaces
    3.2 Functional Requirements
        3.2.1 Information Flows
        3.2.2 Process Descriptions
        3.2.3 Data Construct Specifications
        3.2.4 Data Dictionary
    3.3 Performance Requirements
    3.4 Design Constraints
    3.5 Software System Attributes
    3.6 Other Requirements

Appendixes

Index

Appendix E

Sample outline of software preliminary design specification

(Adapted from IEEE Standard 1016-1987.)

1. Introduction
   1.1 Purpose
   1.2 Scope
   1.3 Definitions and Acronyms

2. References

3. Functional Decomposition Descriptions
   3.1 Function 1
       3.1.1 Functional Components
       3.1.2 Concurrent Processes
       3.1.3 Data Components

       .

       .

       .

   3.n Function n
       3.n.1 Functional Components
       3.n.2 Concurrent Processes
       3.n.3 Data Components

4. Dependency Descriptions
   4.1 Interfunction Dependencies
   4.2 Interprocess Dependencies
   4.3 Data Dependencies

5. Interface Descriptions
   5.1 Functional Interfaces
       5.1.1 User Interfaces
       5.1.2 Hardware Interfaces
       5.1.3 Software Interfaces
       5.1.4 Communications Interfaces
   5.2 Process Interfaces

Appendix F

Sample outline of software detailed design specification

(Adapted from IEEE Standard 1016-1987.)

1. Introduction
   1.1 Purpose
   1.2 Scope
   1.3 Definitions and Acronyms

2. References

3. Detailed Decomposition Descriptions
   3.1 Module Decomposition
       3.1.1 Module 1 Description

       .

       .

       .

       3.1.n Module n Description
   3.2 Concurrent Process Decomposition
       3.2.1 Process 1 Description

       .

       .

       .

       3.2.m Process m Description
   3.3 Data Decomposition
       3.3.1 Data Entity 1 Description

       .

       .

       .

       3.3.p Data Entity p Description

4. Dependency Descriptions
   4.1 Intermodule Dependencies
   4.2 Interprocess Dependencies
   4.3 Data Dependencies

5. Module Interface Descriptions
   5.1 Module 1 Interfaces
       5.1.1 User Interfaces
       5.1.2 Hardware Interfaces

5.1.3   Software Interfaces

5.1.4   Communications Interfaces

.

.

.

5.*n*   Module *n* Interfaces

6. Process Interfaces

6.1   Process 1 Interfaces

.

.

.

6.*m*   Process *m* Interfaces

7. Detailed Design

7.1   Module Detailed Design

7.1.1   Module 1 Detail

.

.

.

7.1.*n*   Module *n* Detail

7.2   Data Detailed Design

7.2.1   Data Entity 1 Detail

.

.

.

7.2.*p*   Data Entity *p* Detail

Appendix G

Sample outline of test plan (system)

(Source: IEEE Standard 829-1983; used with permission.)

1. Test Plan Identifier
2. Introduction
   - 2.1 Objectives
   - 2.2 Background
   - 2.3 Scope
   - 2.4 References
3. Test Items
   - 3.1 Program Modules
   - 3.2 Job Control Procedures
   - 3.3 User Procedures
   - 3.4 Operator Procedures
4. Features To Be Tested
5. Feature Not To Be Tested
6. Approach
   - 6.1 Conversion Testing
   - 6.2 Job Stream Testing
   - 6.3 Interface Testing
   - 6.4 Security Testing
   - 6.5 Recovery Testing
   - 6.6 Performance Testing
   - 6.7 Regression
   - 6.8 Comprehensiveness
   - 6.9 Constraints
7. Item Pass/Fail Criteria
8. Suspension Criteria and Resumption Requirements
   - 8.1 Suspension Criteria
   - 8.2 Resumption Requirements
9. Test Deliverables
10. Testing Tasks
11. Environmental Needs
    - 11.1 Hardware
    - 11.2 Software

11.3 Security

11.4 Tools

11.5 Publications

12. Responsibilities

12.1 Test Group

12.2 User Department

12.3 Development Project Group

13. Staffing and Training Needs

13.1 Staffing

13.2 Training

14. Schedule

15. Risks and Contingencies

16. Approvals

Appendix H

Sample outline of test case

(*Source:* IEEE Standard 829-1983; used with permission.)

1. Test Case Specification Identifier

2. Test Items

3. Input Specifications

4. Output Specifications

5. Environmental Needs
   5.1 Hardware
   5.2 Software
   5.3 Other

6. Special Procedural Requirements

7. Intercase Dependencies

Appendix I

Sample outline of test report

(Based on IEEE Standard 829-1983; used with permission.)

1. Test Report Identifier

2. Summary
   2.1 Tested Items
   2.2 Environment
   2.3 Documentation References

3. Variances
   3.1 Tested Item(s) Variances from Specifications
   3.2 Test Design and Procedure Variances

4. Comprehensiveness Assessment

5. Summary of Results
   5.1 Resolved Incidents
   5.2 Unresolved Incidents

6. Evaluation
   6.1 Test Item Limitations
   6.2 Test Item Pass/Fail
   6.3 Risk of Future Failure

7. Summary of Activities
   7.1 Major Activities and Events
   7.2 Resource Consumption

8. Approvals

Appendix J

Sample quality management charter

The information in this appendix was contributed in its entirety by an organization that requested anonymity.

TITLE	NUMBER
PLANNING & MIS SERVICES – INTERNAL PRACTICES	

SECTION	SUBJECT
MIS Planning and Policy	Management Information Services
Systems Assurance	System Assurance Charter

DATE	REV.# SUPERSEDES	PAGE [1 of 6]

SCOPE:

It is the policy of the Management Information Service Organization to provide a SYSTEMS ASSURANCE function as an internal means of maintaining the quality and effectiveness of applications, facilities, and services
provided by MIS.

A primary purpose of the Systems Assurance function is to assure that
adequate MIS policies, standards, and guidelines exist and are followed in
accordance with the company's strategic direction. The major emphasis is
on the measuring and monitoring of the internal development and operational process at appropriate times ensuring quality systems and reduced
business risk.

In defining the scope of Systems Assurance, the following should be
highlighted:

1.   The Systems Assurance function performs reviews from an
      internal MIS perspective primarily evaluating the installed
      systems development and methodology to assure through
      reviews that systems are being designed and implemented
      according to MIS policy, standards, and/or guidelines.

2.   Reviews of operational systems will determine the effectiveness
      of, and adherence to, policy and standards and design criteria
      related to overall controls and security features.

3.   Systems Assurance reviews will frequently be conducted on MIS
      policies, procedures, standards and/or operating guidelines
      without respect to a specific system. The internal coordination of
      these procedures and standards from one MIS group to another
      (i.e., Systems to D.P. Services) will be reviewed for effectiveness.

TITLE	NUMBER
PLANNING & MIS SERVICES – INTERNAL PRACTICES	

SECTION	SUBJECT
MIS Planning and Policy Systems Assurance	Management Information Services System Assurance Charter

DATE	REV.#	SUPERSEDES	PAGE [2 of 6]

RESPONSIBILITY:

The Systems Assurance function is responsible for the following functions:

I.   Systems Development Reviews

Conducts systems assurance phase reviews of MIS development projects to assure ADHERENCE TO established MIS policies, procedures, standards and operating guidelines.

Systems Assurance reviews examining the adherence to established procedures and standards relative to specific projects will be conducted on a scheduled basis.

Selection of which systems will undergo an evaluation process will be primarily based upon the significance of the application to business objectives, operations, or strategic plans.

Selecting from the annual planned objectives of each group within MIS, Systems Assurance reviews objectives with the appropriate MIS development group's management and confirms the systems assurance schedule. On a quarterly basis, the schedule is reviewed with MIS management and updated.

In conducting systems development reviews, a phased approach will be followed. A review will be conducted at the completion of each of the following phases: (See Sequence of Events.)

- Systems Design Alternatives (SDA)
- Systems External Specifications (SES)
- Systems Internal Specifications (SIS)
- Implementation Phase (IMPL)
- Post Implementation (PIR)

TITLE		NUMBER
PLANNING & MIS SERVICES – INTERNAL PRACTICES		

SECTION	SUBJECT
MIS Planning and Policy Systems Assurance	Management Information Services System Assurance Charter

DATE	REV.# SUPERSEDES	PAGE [3 of 6]

Each review will, when applicable, evaluate the following criteria:

- design meets business/project/economic objective
- conformance to standards/guidelines
- clarity of material
- operating efficiency
- adequacy of controls/security considerations
- presence of restart and recovery consideration
- file/data retentions
- conversion procedures
- test procedures

The Systems Assurance staff will have reasonable access to all the information, records, and personnel of the project or activities under review. Certain sensitive information may require user approval for access during the review process. Systems will determine the need for user approval prior to the start of the review.

Formal reports regarding accuracy of the findings and the achievability of recommendations will be agreed to by both Systems Assurance and the MIS area involved. (See Sequence of Events.)

Systems Assurance will follow-up to ensure that all recommendations have a planned implementation date and are completed.

II.   Standards Review

Systems Assurance develops and maintains program/plans for conducting systems assurance reviews to assure the ADEQUACY OF MIS policies, procedures, standards, and operating guidelines.

All MIS policies, procedures, standards, and operating guidelines in effect will be utilized by Systems Assurance as the base from which to conduct their reviews.

TITLE	NUMBER
PLANNING & MIS SERVICES – INTERNAL PRACTICES	

SECTION	SUBJECT
MIS Planning and Policy Systems Assurance	Management Information Services System Assurance Charter

DATE	REV.#	SUPERSEDES	PAGE [4 of 6]

As well as using this information as a base, there is an inherent responsibility by Systems Assurance to recognize and report the need for change. Recommendations will be provided to the appropriate MIS groups management for approval and implementation. The MIS groups are:

- DATA PROCESSING SERVICES
- SYSTEMS
- OFFICE INFORMATION SERVICES
- PLANNING & MIS SERVICES

Policies, procedures, standards and operating guidelines maintained and utilized by these groups are subject to review and recommendations provided by Systems Assurance.

III.   Coordination-Audit

Upon notification by Internal Audit of EDP-related audit reports and findings relative to MIS, the Systems Assurance function will review the recommendations as they relate to MIS policies, standards and guidelines.

When applicable, Systems Assurance will review proposed changes/improvements to policies and standards with MIS management. A final report will be issued and the changes/improvements will be implemented by the responsible MIS area.

IV.   Management Review

Annually, key operational systems will be selected by Systems Assurance for review to determine adherence to standards, procedures, and operating guidelines.

One measure of selection would be based on the volume and frequency of incidence requiring corrective action. Also, Data Center or Sys-

TITLE	NUMBER
PLANNING & MIS SERVICES – INTERNAL PRACTICES	

SECTION	SUBJECT
MIS Planning and Policy	Management Information Services
Systems Assurance	System Assurance Charter

DATE	REV.#	SUPERSEDES	PAGE [5 of 6]

tems management can request a review based on their perspective of the systems condition.

Included in these operational reviews will be the examination of contingency planning and file/data retention to guarantee adequate backup provisions.

Strategic planning responsibilities within MIS will necessitate inventory type operational reviews to gain an insight into the current systems environment. Identification of the need to upgrade hardware and/or software to be in line with future planning due to technology or standardization will be recommended.

Acting in a MIS consultative capacity, selective reviews will be performed to evaluate the MIS procedures, standards and guidelines being followed.

V.   Security Standards

Systems Assurance will interface with Data Services Security, Corporate Safety, and Corporate Security through periodic meetings to share in the establishment of uniform MIS safety and security standards and guidelines.

In response to MIS management requests, review of computer centers and/or systems development departments will be performed. The review will cover existing safety and security operational and maintenance elements within the facility. Recommendations will be made to enhance protection and control through new or revised procedures or additional physical protection devices.

TITLE	NUMBER
PLANNING & MIS SERVICES – INTERNAL PRACTICES	

SECTION	SUBJECT
MIS Planning and Policy Systems Assurance	Management Information Services System Assurance Charter

DATE	REV.#	SUPERSEDES	PAGE [6 of 6]

SYSTEMS ASSURANCE REVIEW—Each Review Phase:

1. Systems presents a phase review of a given project to the user attended by Systems Assurance.

2. Documentation appropriate to the development phase is reviewed and additional input is provided by Systems when requested.

3. Findings and recommendations are drafted by Systems Assurance.

4. Draft is given to Systems for review.

5. Systems Assurance meets with Systems to discuss and correct report where required. Unresolved differences are brought to the attention of progressive levels of authority within MIS for resolution.

6. The report is formally issued to MIS management.

7. Systems drafts plans for implementation of recommendations and indicates recommendations which will be deferred or are considered impractical to implement as previously agreed.

8. Draft is given to Systems Assurance for review.

9. Systems Assurance meets with Systems to resolve differences and finalize report.

10. Report is issued with signatures from both parties.

Acronyms

ANSI	American National Standards Institute
CA	configuration accounting
CC	configuration control
CCB	change control board
CDR	critical design review
CE	critical error
CI	configuration item
CID	configuration identification

CM	configuration management
CMM	Capability Maturity Model
CMP	configuration management plan
COA	cost of achieving quality
COF	cost of failure
COQ	cost of quality
DoD	Department of Defense
EIA	Electronic Industries Association
FA	functional audit
IEC	International Electrotechnical Commission
IEEE	Institute of Electrical and Electronics Engineers
ISO	International Organization for Standardization
JTC 1	Joint Technical Committee One
KLOC	thousands of LOC
LCL	lower control limit
LOC	lines of code
NIST	National Insitute of Standards and Technology
PA	physical audit
PDR	preliminary design review
PIR	postimplementation review
QA	quality assurance
QC	quality control

RTM	requirements traceability matrices
SC	standards committee
SCN	software change notice
SDLC	software development life cycle
SDP	software development plan
SEI	Software Engineering Institute
SG	standards group
SLC	software life cycle
SQS	software quality system
SQSP	software quality system plan
SRR	software requirements review
STR	software trouble report
TRR	test readiness review
UCL	upper control limit
UDF	unit development folder

About the author

JOHN W. HORCH has an undergraduate degree in experimental statistics and Master's and Ph.D. degrees in information systems. He has been active in the software field for more than 35 years, of which some 30 years have been in software quality management. Dr. Horch has been granted professional certification as a software quality analyst, software quality examiner, and systems professional.

With extensive experience in the defense arena, Dr. Horch has worked on Army, Air Force, and Navy weapon systems in development, verification and validation, and quality management assignments. He designed systems for inventory control, configuration status accounting, secure data transmission, hardware test, and emulation of a military computer. He was responsible for documentation, standards, and software quality management on the Safeguard ABM system and was manager of systems integrity for the International Systems Division of Sperry Univac. He also managed the Verification and Validation Section for Teledyne Brown Engineering.

In the commercial area, Dr. Horch has developed and implemented formal software quality programs for large organizations, implemented and tested disaster recovery programs, performed detailed physical security risk analyses, and audited software quality and development programs for commercial enterprises.

Currently, in addition to international seminar and workshop presentations, Dr. Horch is active in verification and validation of documentation and software development programs. He reviews developers' software development, documentation, and quality programs on behalf of government and commercial clients.

Dr. Horch speaks regularly at conferences, symposia, and workshops worldwide. He is one of the authors of IEEE Standards 983-1985, 1074-1995, and 1074.1-1995 and of ISO/IEC IS 12207 and Australian Standard AS 3563-1988. He publishes on software quality management topics, referees submitted papers for conferences and journals, and is a book reviewer for software-oriented technical magazines.

Active in several professional organizations, Dr. Horch is a former member of the IEEE Standards Board and its Procedures Audit and New Standards Committees. He chaired the IEEE Computer Society Software Engineering Standards Subcommittee for seven years and was the first IEEE CS representative to ISO/IEC JTC1/SC7. Dr. Horch is an ex officio member of the board of advisors and has served as director of certification activities for the Quality Assurance Institute. He was the founding chair and is the immediate past chair of the Certification Board for Information Quality Professionals. Dr. Horch is a senior member of the IEEE and the ASQC and a member of the IEEE Computer Society, the Quality Assurance Institute, and Toastmasters International.

Index

Acceptance control charts, 111–12
Acceptance testing, 70–71, 84
    defined, 70
    as dry run, 71
    performance of, 71
    See also Testing
Activities, 2
Adaptations, 161, 164–65
    defined, 161, 164
    risk, 164
    See also Maintenance
Algorithm analysis, 55
Allocated baseline, 123, 134
American National Standards Institute (ANSI), 39
American Society of Quality Control, 39
Application metrics, 96–98
    cost of quality (COS), 97–98

process-oriented, 97
product-oriented, 96–97
See also Metrics
Arithmetic defects, 2
As-built design, 179
Assessments, 203–4
Audits, 10–11
    defined, 2
    functional (FA), 11, 52–53
    inprocess, 51
    physical (PA), 11, 52–53
    of UDF, 11
    See also Reviews
Audit trails, 83
Awards, 204

Back-out and restoration tests, 73–74

Baselines, 123
    allocated, 123, 134
    change control and, 134
    defined, 133
    design, 123, 134
    functional, 123, 133–34
    operational, 123, 134
    product, 123, 134
    See also Configuration accounting (CA)
Black box testing, 69
Build-to design, 179

Cause and effect diagrams, 108–9
    defined, 108
    illustrated, 109
    See also Quality tools
Certification, 204
Change control boards (CCBs), 131–32
    defined, 131
    hardware, 132
    multiple, 132
    size of, 131
    software, 131, 132
    See also Configuration control (CC)
Change processing, 129–31
    illustrated mechanism, 130
    procedures, 13–14
    sources for, 130
    See also Configuration control (CC)
Clients, 2
Coding
    languages, 32
    standards, 32
Combined implementation, 202
Commitment
    management, 193
    organizational, 193
    true, 194
Components, 2
Configuration accounting
        (CA), 17, 119, 120, 123–26, 133–36
    accounting, 135
    baselines, 123, 133–35
    defined, 120
    instances, 124–26, 135–36
    See also Configuration management (CM)

Configuration control
        (CC), 16, 83, 119, 120, 122–23, 129–33
    change control boards (CCBs), 131–32
    change processing, 129–31
    defined, 120
    function of, 122, 123
    software libraries, 132–33
    See also Configuration management (CM)
Configuration identification
        (CID), 16, 33, 119, 121–22, 126–29
    configuration items (CIs), 126–28
    defined, 119
    documentation levels, 122
    edition, 121, 129
    release, 121, 128
    version, 121, 128–29
    See also Configuration management (CM)
Configuration items (CIs), 126–28
    defined, 126
    naming schemes, 127
Configuration management (CM), 15–17, 119–37
    activities, 16
    configuration accounting
        (CA), 17, 119, 120, 123–26, 133–36
    configuration control
        (CC), 16, 119, 120, 122–23, 129–33
    configuration identification
        (CID), 16, 33, 119, 121–22, 126–29
    defined, 15
    documentation and, 170
    elements, 119, 121–26
    maintenance and, 21
    overview, 120
    plan (CMP), 174
    plan sample outline, 217–18
    quality practitioners and, 21
    trouble report closures, 94
Consumers, 2
Contracted software, 19, 159–60
    "dog and pony shows," 159
    maintenance, 159–60
    See also Vendor management
Control defects. *See* Defects
Cost of achieving quality (COA), 97
Cost of failure (COF), 97–98
Cost of quality (COQ), 97–98

contributors, 98
defined, 97
See also Metrics
Critical design review (CDR), 52, 58, 59
Critical errors (CEs), 88–89
Customers, 2

Database design review, 59
Database security, 140–42
components of, 140
dial up protection, 141, 142
techniques, 141
See also Security
Database specifications, 180
Defect analysis, 13–15, 87–117
concepts, 88–90
data location, 90–92
defined, 13, 87
detection, 90
implementing, 112–16
measures, 88, 100–104
metrics, 89, 96–99
process, 89–90
product, 89
program design, 114–15
purpose of, 14
rules, 112–13
Defects
arithmetic, 101
classification of, 100–102
control, 2, 101
correction of, 20
detection and correction, 13–14
frequency of, 102
location of, 101
method of finding, 101–2
number of, 102
processing example, 95
record of, 14
repair costs, 102
repairing, 93–95
repair priority of, 100
reporting, 90–92
severity of, 100
source of, 101
trend analysis, 13–15

tracking system, 95
types of, 101
See also Defect analysis
Design baseline, 123, 134
Design reviews, 58–59
CDR, 59
database, 59
defined, 58
interface, 59
PDR, 58–59
See also Documentation reviews
Design specification, 175, 178–79
as-built design, 179
build so design, 179
detailed sample outline, 223–25
preliminary, 179
preliminary outline, 221–22
See also Development documents
Detailed design specification, 179
defined, 179
sample outline, 223–25
Developers
defined, 148
education, 148–49
world of, 150
Development documents, 175–80
database specifications, 180
design specifications, 175, 178–79
interface specifications, 180
list of, 175
requirements specification, 175, 176–78
See also Documentation
Development organizations, 199–200
Disaster recovery, 146–47
alternative processing site and, 146–47
tests, 147
See also Security
Documentation, 21–22, 169–88
CM and, 170
components of, 170
defined, 169
depth of, 21–22
development, 175–80
levels, 122
maintenance, 165
management, 171–74

Documentation (continued)
    purpose of, 21
    recommendations, 171
    standards, 31, 186–87
    test, 80, 180–83
    test program, 82
    training, 185–86
    user, 183–85
Documentation reviews, 54–63
    algorithm analysis, 55
    design, 58–59
    formal format, 55
    format, 55
    peer walkthrough, 54–55
    requirements, 56–58
    test, 60–61
    user, 61–62
    See also Documentation; Reviews

Editions, 129
    defined, 121
    use of, 129
    See also Configuration identification (CID)
Education, 18, 147–55
    delivery, 153–55
    developer, 148–49
    formal classes, 154
    importance of, 147
    needs, 155
    on-the-job training, 153–54
    operations training, 152–53
    quality practitioner role in, 152
    sources, 155
    support training, 149–51
    user, 151–52
Electronic Industries Association (EIA), 39
Emerging technologies, standards for, 36
Encryption, 143, 144
Enhancements, 161, 163–64
    defined, 161
    SDLC and, 163
    See also Maintenance
Entities, 2
Equivalents
    defined, 125
    illustrated, 125

    See also Configuration accounting (CA)
Event recorders, 81

Flowcharts, 107–8
    defined, 107
    illustrated, 108
    See also Quality tools
Format reviews, 55
Functional audits (FAs), 11, 52–53
Functional baseline, 123, 133–34

Glass box testing. *See* Module testing
Government agencies, 39
Graphs, 105–6
    defined, 105
    illustrated, 106
    See also Quality tools
Gray box testing. *See* Integration testing
Guidelines, 2

Histograms, 106

IEEE, 39
    software development standards, 28
    Standard 1061-1992, 112
Implementation, 23–24, 189–206
    combined, 202
    concerns, 189
    development organization participation, 199–200
    organizational considerations, 194–99
    organizational culture and, 192–94
    planning, 190
    quality charter and, 191–92, 235–41
    single-element, 201
    single-project, 200–201
    SQSP, 190
    strategies, 200–203
    See also SQS
Inhouse standards development, 40–42
    ad hoc, 40–41
    standards committees, 41–42
    standards coordinator, 42
    standards groups, 41
    See also Standards
Inprocess reviews, 49–51
    characteristics of, 50

inprocess audits, 51
inspections, 51
peer reviews, 49–50
walkthroughs, 50–51
See also Reviews
Input/output defects, 2
Inspections, 10
characteristics of, 51
defined, 3
results of, 51
teams of, 51
See also Reviews
Instances, 124–26
coordination, 135
defined, 124
equivalents, 125
multiple application, 136
tracking, 136
variants, 124–25
See also Configuration accounting (CA)
Integration testing, 69–70, 84
defined, 69
result reporting, 70
result review, 70
See also Testing
Interface design review, 59
Interface specifications, 180
International Organization of Standardization.
See ISO
International standards, 37
ISO
ISO 9000 series, 3, 37
ISO 9001, 37
ISO/IEC/JTC1, 37

Lines of code (LOC), 88
Lower control limit (LCL), 109, 111

Maintenance, 20–21, 160–66
adaptations, 161, 164–65
configuration management during, 21
cost of, 160
documentation, 165
enhancements, 161, 163–64
polishing, 162–63
process, 20

quality practitioner role in, 160
regression testing, 165–66
repairs, 160–61, 162
standards, 44, 45
types of, 160–65
user documentation, 185
Management
commitment, 193
SQS implementation and, 24
Management documents, 171–74
additional plans, 174
CM plan, 171, 174
list of, 171
software development plans (SDPs), 171, 172–73
SQS plans, 171, 173–74
See also Documentation
Management reviews, 10
Measures, 88, 100–104
characteristics of, 115
collecting, 100–104
comparative, 103
defect classification, 100–102
defect frequency, 102
defect source, 101
defect type, 101
derived, 104
nondefect, 103–4
number of defects, 102
priority repair, 100–101
severity, 100
soft, 104
time between defect detections, 103
See also Defect analysis; Defects
Metrics, 96–99
application, 96–98
available, 96
characteristics, 115–16
cost of quality (COS), 97–98
damaging to, 113
defect, 89
design, 114–15
goals and, 99
IEEE standard, 112
process-oriented, 97
productivity, 97
product-oriented, 96–97

Metrics (continued)
  selecting, 96–99
  SQS goal-oriented, 98–99
  understanding/applying, 115
  validity of, 115
  See also Defect analysis
Modules, 121
  defined, 3
  See also Subsystems; Units
Module testing, 68–69
  defect recording, 68
  defined, 68
  program, 68
  results of, 82
  review prior to, 69
  See also Testing

Naming standards, 32–34
  configuration identification, 33
  hierarchy, 33
  identifiers, 33
  See also Standards
National Institute of Standards and Technology
  (NIST), 39

Off-the-shelf software, 19, 156–58
  quality assurance steps, 156
  requirements, 157
  reverse engineering techniques, 157
  risk and, 158
  See also Vendor management
Operating procedures, 34
Operational baseline, 123, 134
Operations
  defined, 152
  instructions, 184
  training, 152–53, 154
Organization, 22–23
  alternative, 199
  commitment, 193
  culture change, 192
  development participation, 199–200
  least favorable, 197
  management commitment, 193
  placement of quality practitioners in, 22
  traditional style, 22

Pareto diagrams, 107
Path analyzers, 81–82
Peer reviews, 49–50
  characteristics of, 50
  defined, 3
  results of, 49
  See also Reviews
Peer walkthroughs, 54–55
Phase-end reviews, 52–54
  critical design review (CDR), 52, 58, 59
  illustrated, 53
  postimplementation review (PIR), 52, 54
  preliminary design review (PDR), 52, 58–59
  software requirements review (SRR), 52
  subject documents, 53
  test readiness review (TRR), 52
  See also Reviews
Phases, 3
Physical audits (PAs), 11, 52–53
Polishing, 162
Postimplementation review (PIR), 52, 54
Preliminary design review (PDR), 52, 58–59
Preliminary design specification, 179
  defined, 179
  sample outline, 221–22
Process
  analysis, 89–90
  assessment, 203–4
  behavior, 110
  defined, 3
  reviews, 10
Process control charts, 109–12
  acceptance, 111–12
  run, 109–10
  See also Quality tools
Process-oriented metrics, 97
Producers, 3
Product analysis, 89
Product baseline, 123, 134
Product-oriented metrics, 96–97
Products
  defined, 3
  mismatched, 135
Professional groups, 39
Programmer
  education, 148–49

testing, 83
Programs, 3
Protocols, standardization of, 34
Prototyping, 29–30
    defined, 29
    illustrated, 30
    See also Software development life cycle (SDLC)

Quality, 87
    defined, 3
    in organization, 23
Quality assurance, 88
    defect classification and, 100
    defined, 3
    practitioners, 96–97, 103
Quality charter, 191–92
    defined, 191
    responsibility, 237–40
    sample, 235–41
    scope, 236
    systems assurance review, 241
Quality control, 47, 88
    defect classification and, 100
    defined, 4
    insufficient, 103
Quality groups
    defined, 4
    in organization, 23
Quality management, 4
Quality practitioners, 25
    configuration management and, 21
    defined, 4
    documentation reviews and, 62
    education role, 152
    in maintenance, 160
    operations training and, 153
    in organization, 22
    reviews and, 48
    role of, 18
    standards coordinator, 44
    in testing process, 85
Quality systems. *See* SQS
Quality tools, 104–12
    cause and effect diagram, 108–9
    flowchart, 107–8
    graph, 105–6

histogram, 106
Pareto diagram, 107
process control charts, 109–12
scatter diagram, 105
tally sheet, 104–5

Recovery tests, 73
Regression tests, 72, 84
    maintenance and, 165–66
    results of, 166
Releases, 128
    defined, 121
    See also Configuration identification (CID)
Repairs, 160–61, 162
    defined, 162
    estimates, 162
    results of, 162
    See also Maintenance
Reporting
    arrangements, 198
    defect, 90–92
    level, 196–99
    test, 13, 183, 233–34
    See also Software trouble reports (STRs)
Requirement reviews, 56–58
    criteria, 56
    defined, 56
    purpose of, 57
    See also Documentation reviews
Requirements
    defined, 4
    user documentation input, 183–85
Requirements specification, 175, 176–78
    completeness, 177
    consistency, 178
    correctness, 176
    measurability, 177
    necessity, 176–77
    sample outline of, 219–20
    unambiguity, 177–78
    See also Development documents
Requirements traceability matrices (RTMs), 74–76
    defined, 74
    illustrated, 75
Reviews, 9–11, 47–64
    audits, 10–11, 51

Reviews (continued)
 critical design (CDR), 52, 58, 59
 defined, 4
 design, 58–60
 documentation, 54–63
 format, 55
 inprocess, 49–51
 inspections, 10, 51
 management, 10
 peer, 49–50
 phase-end, 52–54
 postimplementation (PIR), 52, 54
 preliminary design (PDR), 52, 58–59
 process, 10
 purpose of, 48
 quality practitioner role in, 48
 requirements, 56–58
 SDLC, 9–10
 SDP, 172
 software requirements (SRR), 52
 subjects of, 54
 test documentation, 60–61
 test program, 82
 test readiness (TRR), 52
 types of, 49–54
 user documentation, 61–62
 walkthroughs, 10, 50–51
Risk analysis, 145–46
 results of, 145
 using, 146
 See also Security
Run charts, 109–10
 illustrated, 110
 Kaizen concept, 110, 111
 lower control limit (LCL), 109
 process behavior, 110
 upper control limit (UCL), 109
 See also Quality tools

Scatter diagrams, 105
Security, 17, 140–47
 database, 140–42
 disaster recovery, 146–47
 encryption, 143, 144
 risk analysis and, 145–46
 teleprocessing, 142–44

viruses and, 144–45
SEI CMM, 4
Simulators, 79, 81
Single-element implementation, 201
Single-project implementation, 200–201
Software
 contracted, 19, 159–60
 defined, 4
 off-the-shelf, 19, 156–58
 tailored-shell, 19, 158–59
 types of, 19
Software change notice (SCN), 93
 illustrated sample, 94
 using, 93
Software development life cycle (SDLC)
 defined, 4
 phases, 29
 reviews, 9–10
 SQS and, 24
Software development methodology, 30
Software development plans (SDPs), 62, 171, 172–73
 defined, 62, 172
 reviewing, 172
 sample outline for, 209–11
 sections in, 172
Software Engineering Institute capability maturity
  model. See SEI CMM
Software Engineering Standards Committee. See IEEE
Software libraries, 132–33
Software life cycle (SLC)
 defined, 5
 divisions, 6–7
 phases, 29
 standards, 8, 29
 testing, 66, 67
Software quality system. See SQS
Software quality system plan. See SQS plan (SQSP)
Software requirements review (SRR), 52
Software systems, 5
Software trouble reports (STRs), 89
 closure of, 93–94
 counts, 102, 103
 data, 91
 form, 91
 illustrated sample, 92
 incorrect, 103

open and resolved, 102
See also Reporting
SQS
  adapting, 202–3
  charter, 191–92, 235–41
  configuration management, 15–17, 119–37
  defect analysis, 13–15, 87–117
  documentation, 21–22
  education, 18, 147–55
  elements, 1–26
    connecting, 190
    list of, 6
  goals, 6, 25
  implementation, 23–24, 189–206
  improvement, 203–4
  life cycle periods, 7
  maintenance, 20–21, 160–66
  management and, 24
  organization and, 22–23
  reviews, 9–11, 47–64
  SDLC and, 24
  security, 17, 140–47
  standards, 7–9, 27–46
  successful, 23
  task performance, 195–96
  testing, 11–13, 65–86
  total, 5
  vendor management, 18–19, 155–60
SQS plan (SQSP), 62, 173–74
  defined, 173
  sample outline of, 213–15
Standards, 7–9, 27–46
  ad hoc, 40–41
  areas for, 28–36
  coding, 32
  committees (SC), 41–42
  compliance, 44–45
  coordinator, 42, 44
  cost of maintaining, 44
  defined, 5
  degree of, 27
  documentation, 31
  emerging technology, 36
  enforcement, 44–45
  external developers, 37–39
  groups (SG), 41

  importance of, 28
  inhouse development of, 40–42
  international, 37
  maintaining, 44, 45
  manual, 43
  naming, 32–33
  noncompliance to, 44–45
  online, 44
  operation procedure, 34
  promulgation of, 43–45
  protocol, 34
  purchased, 39–40
  reasons for, 9
  selection of, 42–43
  SLC, 8, 29
  sources of, 8, 8–9, 28, 36–42
  user development, 34–35
Standards Australia, AS 3563, 37
Stress tests, 72–73
Subsystems, 121
  defined, 5
  See also Modules; Units
Support training, 149–51

Tailored-shell software, 19, 158–59
  after-purchase maintenance, 158
  testing, 158–59
  vendor reputation and, 158
  See also Vendor management
Tally sheets, 104–5
  defined, 104
  illustrated, 105
  See also Quality tools
Teleprocessing security, 142–44
  encryption, 143, 144
  interruption, 143
  prevention, 144
  See also Security
Test analysis, 80–81
Test cases, 76–78, 182
  comparison of, 77
  example, 77–78
  review of, 78
  sample outline, 231–32
Test data, 182
  generators, 81

Test data (continued)
    scope of, 182
Test design, 11
Test documentation, 180–83
    test cases, 182
    test data, 182
    test plan, 181–82
    test procedures, 182
    test reports, 182
    See also Documentation
Test documentation reviews, 60–61
    acceptance, 61
    walkthroughs, 60
    See also Documentation reviews
Testing, 11–13, 65–86
    acceptance, 70
    activities, 11
    back-out and restoration, 73–74
    data input, 78–79
    development, 181
    documentation, 80
    execution of, 12–13
    flow illustration, 76
    goals of, 65
    illustrated process, 12
    integration, 69–70
    module, 68–69
    programmer, 83
    recovery, 73
    regression, 72, 165–66
    results expectation, 80
    SLC, 66, 67
    stress, 72–73
    tailored shells, 158–59
    types of, 66, 67–74
    unit, 67–68
    user, 70–71
    who performs, 83–85
Test plans, 11, 74–76, 74–82
    growth of, 182
    reviewing, 70
    sample outline of, 227–29
Test procedures, 78, 182
Test program, 66
    documentation, 82
    reviewing, 82

Test readiness review (TRR), 52
Test reports, 13, 183
    defined, 183
    sample outline, 233–34
    See also Reporting
Test tools, 81–82
    availability, 82
    event recorders, 81
    path analyzers, 81–82
    simulators, 81
    test data generators, 81
Total quality, 5
Total quality systems
    defined, 5
    implementation of, 23–24
Training documentation, 185–86
    defined, 185
    preparation of, 186
    See also Documentation
Trend analysis, 97

Unit development folders
    audits of, 11
    defined, 5
Units, 121
    defined, 5
    See also Modules; Subsystems
Unit testing, 67–68
    defined, 67
    expense of, 68
    results of, 82
    See also Testing
Upper control limit (UCL), 109, 111
User development
    benefits of, 35
    growing capability of, 35
    standards, 34–35
User documentation, 183–85
    input requirements, 183–84
    maintenance, 185
    operation instructions, 184
    output description, 184
    See also Documentation
User documentation reviews, 61–62
    defined, 61
    trial use, 61

See also Documentation reviews
User education, 151–52
  areas of, 151
  in house seminars, 154
  system limits and, 152
  See also Education
User groups, 39
Users, 5
User testing, 70–71
  defined, 70
  review/execution of, 71
  See also Testing

Variants, 124–25
  defined, 124
  illustrated, 125
  See also Configuration accounting (CA)
Vendor management, 18–19
  contracts, 159–60
  off-the-shelf software, 156–58
  tailored shells, 158–59

Versions, 128–29
  concept of, 128
  defined, 121
  See also Configuration identification (CID)
Viruses, 144–45
  defense against, 145
  introduction of, 144
  timed, 144–45
  See also Security

Walkthroughs, 10, 50–51
  characteristics of, 50
  defined, 5
  peer, 55–56
  results of, 51
  test review, 60
  See also Reviews
White box testing. *See* Module testing